The Cinema of Paula Markovitch

Visionaries
Series Editors: Lucy Bolton and Richard Rushton

Titles in the series include:

The Cinema of Marguerite Duras: Multisensoriality and Female Subjectivity
Michelle Royer

Ana Kokkinos: An Oeuvre of Outsiders
Kelly McWilliam

Gillian Armstrong: Popular, Sensual & Ethical Cinema
Julia Erhart

Kathleen Collins: The Black Essai Film
Geetha Ramanathan

The Cinema of Mia Hansen-Løve: Candour and Vulnerability
Kate Ince

Céline Sciamma: Portraits
Emma Wilson

Shirley Clarke: Thinking Through Movement
Karen Pearlman

Habiba Djahnine: Memory Bearer
Sheila Petty

Marleen Gorris: Practices of Resistance
Sue Thornham

Nahid Persson Sarvestani: Towards A Liquid Authorship
Boel Ulfsdotter

The Cinema of Paula Markovitch: Contested Marginality
Inela Selimović

The Cinema of Paula Markovitch

Contested Marginality

Inela Selimović

EDINBURGH
University Press

Edinburgh University Press is one of the leading university presses in the UK. Publishing new research in the arts and humanities, EUP connects people and ideas to inspire creative thinking, open new perspectives and shape the world we live in. For more information, visit www.edinburghuniversitypress.com.

We are committed to making research available to a wide audience and are pleased to be publishing Platinum Open Access ebook editions of titles in this series.

© Inela Selimović, 2025, under a Creative Commons Attribution-NonCommercial-NoDerivatives 4.0 International licence

Grateful acknowledgement is made to the sources listed in the List of Illustrations for permission to reproduce material previously published elsewhere. Every effort has been made to trace the copyright holders, but if any have been inadvertently overlooked, the publisher will be pleased to make the necessary arrangements at the first opportunity.

Edinburgh University Press Ltd
13 Infirmary Street, Edinburgh EH1 1LT

Typeset in 12/14 Arno and Myriad by
IDSUK (DataConnection) Ltd

A CIP record for this book is available from the British Library

ISBN 978 1 3995 4918 9 (hardback)
ISBN 978 1 3995 4919 6 (paperback)
ISBN 978 1 3995 4920 2 (webready PDF)
ISBN 978 1 3995 4921 9 (epub)

The right of Inela Selimović to be identified as the author of this work has been asserted in accordance with the Copyright, Designs, and Patents Act 1988, and the Copyright and Related Rights Regulations 2003 (SI No. 2498).

EU Authorised Representative:
Easy Access System Europe
Mustamäe tee 50, 10621 Tallinn, Estonia
gpsr.requests@easproject.com

Contents

List of Figures vi
Acknowledgements viii

Introduction 1

1. Intersensory Bonds in *Perriférico* (1999) 33
2. *Marilina* (2001) and *Música de ambulancia* (2009): Incongruous Surprises 47
3. *El premio* (2011): Affect and Political Resocialization 65
4. *Armando y Genoveva* (2013): Vociferous Canvases 83
5. Unpretentious Specters in *Cuadros en la oscuridad* (2017) 102
6. *El actor principal* (2019): Emotional Gestures 121
7. *Ángeles* (2025): Between Play and Suicide 146
Conclusion 164

Filmography 169
Bibliography 171
Index 192

Figures

Figure 1.1   The protagonist's homeless encampment. Margarita Sanz (the main character) in *Perriférico*. Reproduced by kind permission of Paula Markovitch.   40

Figure 2.1   Javier Swedzky (Lucas) happens upon his former lover in *Marilina*. Reproduced by kind permission of Paula Markovitch.   54

Figure 2.2   The characters [Flor Gurrola (Cecilia) and Martha Aura (mother)] exhibit their fragile attempts at levity in *Música de ambulancia*. Reproduced by kind permission of Paula Markovitch.   62

Figure 3.1   Paula G. Hertzog (Ceci) and Sharon Herrera (Silvia) play outside of class in *El premio*. Reproduced by kind permission of Paula Markovitch.   75

Figure 4.1   Markovitch haptically engages with an unnamed portrait in *Armando y Genoveva*. Reproduced by kind permission of Paula Markovitch.   92

Figure 5.1   Alvin Astorga (Marcos) tries to engage with Maico Pradal (Luis) about art multiple times in *Cuadros en la oscuridad*. Reproduced by kind permission of Paula Markovitch.   109

Figure 6.1   Marcelo Cerón (Luis) on the streets of Mexico
City in *El actor principal*. Reproduced by kind
permission of Paula Markovitch.   124
Figure 7.1   Isabel Ramírez (Isa) and Ángeles Pradal
(Ángeles) at Córdoba's *villa* in *Ángeles*.
Reproduced by kind permission of Paula
Markovitch.   149

Acknowledgements

To my parents

I am deeply thankful to Paula Markovitch for her bigheartedness regarding my research-related queries during the past seven years. Wellesley College generously supported this project through several research grants and stipends (2020–22, 2023–24 and 2025). The Huntington Fund at the Spanish and Portuguese Department and the Albright Institute have been essential in assisting with different research phases of the book. A big thank you to my departmental colleagues and my research assistants, namely Anna Blake Patrick and Leah Thorburn. I am grateful to our LTS team and numerous staff members at Wellesley College, especially Mac Stewart, Pam Pfeiffer, Kimberley A. Shaw, Kayla Valdivieso, and Jael Matos. I am also thankful to the anonymous readers for their thoughtful and generous comments. Parts of Chapter 3 have appeared in *The Feeling Child: Affect and Politics in Latin American Literature and Film* (2018). Sections of Chapter 4 have appeared in *Mistral: Journal of Latin American Women's Intellectual & Cultural History*. Parts of Chapter 6 have appeared in the *Journal of Latin American Cultural Studies* (https://doi.org/10.1080/13569325.2023.2239171) and in *Encuentros fortuitos. Agencialidad en conflicto y poder en movimiento en el cine hispano* (2023). I express my gratitude to Pamela Haag for her useful comments on the initial manuscript draft. I extend my sincere thanks to Gillian Leslie, Kelly O'Brien, Grace Balfour-Harle, Jenna Dowds, James Helling, Lucy Bolton, and Richard Rushton at Edinburgh University Press.

Introduction

Filmmaker Paula Markovitch (b. 1968) has been celebrated at film festivals and through international and national awards since 2011. She won several awards across Latin America and internationally for *El premio* (2011), including the Silver Bear for Outstanding Artistic Achievement awarded at the 61st edition of the Berlin International Film Festival.[1] Following *El premio*, she also wrote and directed another four films: *Armando y Genoveva* (2013a/b), *Cuadros en la oscuridad* (2017), *El actor principal* (2019b), and *Ángeles* (2025). More recently, *El actor principal* won the best screenplay award at the 2023 Festival Internacional de Cinema da Fronteira in Brazil. She has additionally written for television: a series titled *La periodista* (2024), which is in post-production at the time of this writing, and a pilot chapter for *Al borde* (1998).[2] Before *El premio*, Markovitch wrote and directed three short films: *Perriférico* (1999), *Marilina* (2001), and *Música de ambulancia* (2009).[3] For Markovitch, moreover, filmmaking and fiction writing are inextricably entwined processes; to write creatively means to commence filming.[4] In addition to her short story collection *El monstruo* (2014), the filmmaker has recently completed her notebook, *Cacerías imaginarias* (2022), in which she discusses her artistic inspirations, hindrances, and processes. As discussed in the ensuing chapters, the aesthetic connections between filmmaking and fiction writing have significantly inspired the director's overall professional maturation and trajectory. Since the late 1990s, Markovitch's productivity and growing international recognition have contributed to

'Latin American cinemas [that] have undergone something of a renaissance – an increase in output, popular appeal and critical acclaim' (Martin: 2019:1). Although Markovitch's contributions to this rebirth have inspired critics to engage with some of her films, *The Cinema of Paula Markovitch* is the first comprehensive and interdisciplinary exploration of the award-winning director's work in its entirety.

Markovitch grew up in a family of Jewish descendants – political dissidents and prolific artists – in Buenos Aires, Córdoba, and San Clemente del Tuyú. As Markovitch said in a 2020 interview, an existentially precarious life was not foreign to the Markovitch family.[5] In addition to her poverty-stricken childhood, her youth was crippled by fears of political repercussions, for 'I lived during the dictatorship in San Clemente del Tuyú. [...] My parents were semi-clandestine, in the sense that I consider the whole country to have been a bit clandestine. My parents were very leftist but they were not militant activists in any organization. We were in hiding, however, and I have relatives among the disappeared' ('yo viví durante la dictadura en San Clemente del Tuyú. [...] Mis padres estaban semi clandestinos, en el sentido de que considero que todo el país estaba un poco clandestino. Mis padres eran muy de izquierda pero no estaban militando activamente en ninguna organización. Pero estábamos escondidos y tengo familiares desaparecidos') (Ranzani 2020: n. pag.).[6] In *Cacerías imaginarias*, the filmmaker remembers her parents' quiet resistance through art, games, and simple pastimes in the face of various hardships. 'My parents painted in the afternoons[,]' ('Mis padres pintaban en las tardes[,]'), Markovitch reveals and continues, 'in the evenings we played chess by candle or lamplight. I was bored or played with animals: there were cats, dogs, carrier pigeons and even a penguin that had gone astray, swept away by cold ocean currents' ('en las noches jugaban al ajedrez a la luz de velas o lámparas. Yo me aburría o jugaba con los animales: había gatos, perros, palomas mensajeras y hasta un pingüino que se había extraviado, arrastrado por las corrientes marinas frías' (16). Her parents – Armando Markovitch (1936–95) and Genoveva Edelstein (1929–01) – spent most of their lives as prolific painters, leaving behind over 3,000 artworks, including drawings, oil paintings, engravings, and watercolors. Their home was a humble sanctuary for those with artistic proclivities; they painted in their home but also opened it up to the nearby communities' underprivileged children through regular art workshops.[7]

At the age of twenty-two, Markovitch left this artistically lively home for Mexico City and began her career as a screenwriter. The initial years in exile coincided with Argentina's early days of Carlos Menem's neoliberal policies in the 1990s.[8] Alfredo Raúl Pucciarelli states in *Los años de Menem: la construcción del orden neoliberal* (2011) that Menem's neoliberal policies, above all, generated the 'ideological, political and operational emptiness' ('vaciamiento ideológico, político y operativo') (31). More specifically, extreme forms of socioeconomic struggles (riots and protests) erupted across the nation as 'the confiscation of bank deposits in a last-ditch attempt to defend parity between the national currency and the US dollar, [...] [led] to the downfall of the *Alianza* government' (Andermann 2013: 158). In *New Argentine and Brazilian Cinema: Reality Effects* (2013), Jens Andermann notes that the 2001 economic crisis manifestly brought 'to the fore the true realities of exclusion, poverty, and hunger; the open secret of neoliberal globalization' (158). Ana Amado likewise articulates these socioeconomic and existential struggles in *La imagen justa: cine argentino y política (1980–2007)* (2009) as the direct aftermath of 'the politics of social neglect, extreme inequality, misery, and exclusion in the years of Menem's democratic regime' ('las políticas de abandono social, desigualdad extrema, miseria y exclusión en los años del gobierno democrático de Menem') (Amado 2009: 149). Markovitch's memories of said period similarly stem from an expressly intimate vantage point, 'I [r]emember the nineties. The feeling of apparent democracy... Repression was still everywhere. I had the impression that the dead had become disproportionately present in memory, while the living seemed infected with absence, sick with emptiness' ('[r]ecuerdo los noventa. La sensación de una democracia aparente [...] La represión aún estaba en todas partes. Tenía la impresión de que los muertos se habían vuelto desmesuradamente presentes en la memoria, mientras que los vivos parecíamos contagiados de ausencia, enfermos de vacío') (2022: 45).[9] Markovitch had left these circumstances behind but nonetheless maintained consistent attachments to her home, not only owning to the familial ties but also because of her interest in exploring cinematographically sociopolitical and cultural realities of Argentina.[10]

The Cinema of Paula Markovitch pays close attention to the director's work and its dynamic contributions to aesthetic trends in Argentinian as well as world cinema at the beginning of the twenty-first century. In so doing, the book makes a cross-disciplinary contribution to evolving debates on the challenges and possibilities of strengthening Latin American women's filmmaking 'without ghettoizing women and their work' (Martin and Shaw 2017: 2).[11] Markovitch's cinema continues, remarkably, to be underexamined overall, but critics have studied some of her films extensively; in particular, *El premio*. Her feature debut focuses on the child protagonist, Ceci, and her mother, who are in hiding away from Buenos Aires during Argentina's military dictatorship (1976–83). This film emerged as she drew on different childhood memories about the repressive military regime, multiple family displacements across the country, and the family's overall economic hardship.[12] Her interest in exploring Argentina's political turmoil in *El premio*, especially from a familial vantage point, aligns her with other post-dictatorship filmmakers, whose pasts and creative interests are tied to intergenerational tensions and historical memory, including Benjamín Ávila, Marcelo Piñeyro, and Daniel Bustamante, to mention but a few (Garibotto 2015; Maguire 2017; Selimović 2018; Rocco 2021; Severiche 2023; and Hogan 2023). *El premio*'s debut positioned Markovitch on an international cinema map and has continued to generate interest among critics in Latin America and abroad (Chapter 3).

Several of her subsequent films have also stimulated scholarly analyses. Inspired by the filmmaker's father, *Cuadros en la oscuridad*

(Chapter 5) centers on the existential delights and angsts of a socially marginalized yet prolific painter in Córdoba's shantytown. Lonely yet passionate about his artistic undertakings, the painter strikes up an unusual friendship with a local, Indigenous boy named Luis. This relationship returns indirectly to the country's political past of the 1970s. According to Alessandro Rocco, 'together with the film, titled *El premio* (2011), [*Cuadros en la oscuridad*] engenders a cinematographic cycle, dedicated to the recreation of the author's personal and familial past and the remembrance of her parents, especially regarding the impact of the repressive violence of the Argentine dictatorship (1976–83) on their lives' ('[j]unto con el filme, titulado *El premio* (2011), [*Cuadros en la oscuridad*] conforma un ciclo cinematográfico dedicado a la recreación del pasado personal y familiar de la autora y la rememoración de las figuras de sus padres, especialmente por lo que concierne el impacto que tuvo la violencia represiva de la dictadura argentina (1976–83) sobre sus vidas') (2023: 135). As discussed in Chapter 5, the film also interlaces the protagonist's artwork with his marginalization as a political dissident. This deftly exposes but also challenges his ghostly existence. Ironically, his art ends up posthumously in the hands of an unlikely audience, the neighborhood children, with their curiosity, play, and mischief. Markovitch's documentary, *Armando y Genoveva*, likewise returns to her parents' lives largely through the materiality of the family home in Córdoba. Markovitch mediates this return by plainly *being in* the film as well as providing a voice-over narration, reminiscent of Jean-Louis Comolli's remarks in *Ver y poder* (2007) in the sense that 'the director's filmed body imposes further proof of the film's documentary essence, capable of producing an effect of truth that would no longer need to be discussed' ('cuerpo filmado del cineasta impone una prueba más de la esencia documental del filme, capaz de producir un efecto de verdad que ya no habría que discutir') (560) (Chapter 4). Primarily, the film documents the surviving member of the Markovitch's immediate family, the filmmaker herself, as she assumes the responsibility – tangibly (she collects the inherited artwork) and emotionally (she reflects on and begins to process the loss) – of the parents' bequest after their deaths. Gonzalo Aguilar, moreover, refers to said presence as 'the inscription of the first person in the image' ('la inscripción de la primera persona en la imagen') (Aguilar 2015: 78). Markovitch's 'inscripción' throughout the family home in Córdoba not only engages the viewer with the found artwork but also with the deeper layers of the parents' social and emotional everydayness while she resided abroad. More specifically, her use of voice-over straightforwardly allows us to deepen our understanding of the parents' personal qualms and professional trajectories. Pablo Piedras' postulations in *El cine documental en primera persona* (2014) are also relevant for *Armando y Genoveva*, especially the idea that 'autobiographical documentaries tend to use the voice-over of directors to narrate aspects of their experiences, to delineate the questions at the story's core as well as to refer retrospectively to personal history' ('los documentales autobiográficos suelen recurrir a la voz en off de los directores para narrar aspectos de sus vivencias, para trazar los interrogantes que se hallan en el núcleo del relato así como para remitirse en forma retrospectiva a la historia personal') (83). The film achieves this with the director's subtle returns to the parents' past, which ultimately reveals *Armando y Genoveva* as 'a unique artefact of intermedial mourning' (Selimović 2023: 101). Indeed, Markovitch's self-exile keeps her engaged with Argentina thematically without curbing her interests in other cultural contexts, for some of her films take place in other Latin American and European settings. *El actor principal*, her fourth film, illustrates this (Chapter 6). The film distances itself from the filmmaker's homeland and its devastatingly complex impact on her family, opting instead for a bicultural setting that oscillates between marginal sites of Mexico City (Iztapalapa) and peripheral sites of the 2017 Berlinale in Germany. *El actor principal* centers on an unplanned encounter between a Kosovar refugee and a Mexican non-professional actor in emotionally complex ways. Their inability to speak well a common language facilitates their togetherness, for it 'mobilises the protagonists' mutual openness in order to reveal the paradoxical side of their exclusion' (Selimović 2023: 491).

The rest of her films have yet to be explored significantly, and the present study seeks to fill in parts of that lacunae. Markovitch's aesthetic approaches, themes, and techniques have complexly addressed gendered experiences, thus contributing to what Mirna Vohnsen and Daniel Mourenza have reiterated in *Contemporary Argentine Women Filmmakers* (2023) as 'the ways Argentine women filmmakers have redressed the under-representation of women and girls onscreen and the perpetuation of stereotypes, arguing that contemporary women directors in Argentina have reworked cinematic practices by questioning, challenging, and debunking hegemonic patriarchal systems of representation' (3). In *Latin American Cinema: A Comparative History* (2016), Paul S. Rodríguez has simply called this phenomenon 'the rise of the woman director' (265). This rise has led Deborah Shaw to highlight the significance of broader scholarly engagements with women directors' cinema across disciplines (Shaw 2018: 14). *The Cinema of Paula Markovitch* builds on and responds to these critics' scholarly contributions and insights by focusing on thematic and aesthetic singularities that engage the senses with an equally broad spectrum of political, economic, and cultural forms of marginality.

At the Margins – Anew

Argentine cinema has been consistently and keenly interested in marginalized subjectivities as has cinema elsewhere in Latin America and worldwide.[13] In Argentina, the topics of marginality have infiltrated the 'seventh art' almost from its inception. One of the first – and arguably least neglected – Argentine women filmmakers, Josefina Emilia Saleny (1894–1978), interlaces destitution with altruism in *El pañuelo de Clarita* (1919).[14] In this case, unemployment and poverty are foregrounded and embodied straightforwardly through the child's generosity and her subsequent defenselessness. According to Moira Fradinger, the 'most striking feature is the point of view of the girl Clarita. She finds a beggar on a park bench and gives him her handkerchief and a coin' (2014: n. pag.). Unemployment, destitution, and crime shape Saleny's film in intertwining ways. Street vulnerabilities were also fortified cinematographically as the Second World War (1939–45) inflicted deep wounds globally. In film, these reverberations led to Italian neorealism (1943–54). Italian neorealism films also responded to the political, social, and economic consequences of Benito Mussolini's fascist regime (1922–43). The poor and the working class are at the thematic heart of this movement, and its filmmakers took to the streets to reflect on the most disadvantaged 'in the face of the immediate post-war reality' ('frente a la realidad de la inmediata posguerra') (Soria 2014: 39). Italian neorealism filmmakers relied predominantly on nonprofessional actors and filmed on location. Aesthetically, furthermore, as Deleuze reflects in *Cinema 2: The Time-Image* (1986) on André Bazin's theories, 'neo-realism aimed at an always ambiguous, to be deciphered, real' (1). Known as the Golden Age of cinema, the movement produced Roberto Rossellini's *Rome, Open City* (1945), Luchino Visconti's *La Terra Trema* (1948), Vittorio De Sica's *Bicycle Thieves* (1948), to mention just a few.

These filmmakers' aesthetic tendencies reverberated across Latin America as well (Burns 1975; Burton 1986; King 1987; Rich 1997). They also led to what is known as the New Latin American Cinema, which sought to reject 'the long-dominant Hollywood style' before it unfolded into almost 'a unilateral model' across several Latin American countries, including Argentina, Brazil, Colombia, Cuba, and Mexico (Rich 1997: 274 and 277).[15] According to Rich, 'the early years of the New Latin American Cinema were characterized by a neo-realist style adapted to meet Latin American needs and realities' (277). Such artistic approaches to the region's 'realities' signaled intimate ties between aesthetics and politics (Rich 1997: 278).[16] Marginalized subjectivities continued to suffuse the cinematic classics from the 1950s, 1960s and 1970s, including Fernando Birri's *Tire Dié* (1960) and *Los inundados* (1962); Matilde Landeta's *La negra Angustias* (1950), Sara Gómez's *De cierta manera* (1974), and from Brazil, Nelson Pereira dos Santos' *Vidas secas* (1963) and Glauber Rocha's *Cancer* (1972), to mention some of the most renowned examples.

In a recent collection of essays, Constanza Burucúa and Carolina Sitnisky (2018) invoke the 'precariat' as the shared concern among filmmakers from the 1960s onward. Burucúa and Sitnisky specify that 'the New Latin American Cinema filmmakers gathered around the concern to develop a medium true to what they saw as the common denominators of the region, namely poverty and underdevelopment' (2018: 2). In Brazilian contexts, Ivana Bentes has argued that '[f]rontier territories and social fractures, mythical lands laden with symbolism and signs, the *sertão* (arid backlands) and the *favelas* (slums) have always been the "other side" of modern and positivist Brazil' (2003: 121). In the 1980s, the films of the New Latin American Cinema, above all, were 'concerned [...] [with] the interior world of persons [...] and reflect the political circumstances of the continent' (Rich 1997: 281–2). At the same time, differently pursued democratic tendencies started to take place in several Latin American countries, including Argentina.[17] Such political changes have affected these countries' respective industries by highlighting new cinematic voices, including more women filmmakers – in addition to those who had directed since the 1960s – such as, Marie Louise Alemann and Narcisa Hirsch – but also Suzana Amaral's *A hora da estrela* (1985), María Luisa Bemberg's *Camila* (1985), and Busi Cortés' *El secreto de Romelia* (1988). Each of these films explores gendered forms of marginality, ranging from Amaral's adaptation of Clarice Lispector's eponymous novella about an impoverished young girl, Macabea, and her inability to learn the city codes to survive; Cortés' focus on virginity and gender; and Bemberg's aesthetic return to the execution of Camila O'Gorman (1825–48) in the context of the Manuel de Rosas' dictatorship (1829–52).[18]

Markovitch's films challenge and rebut tired representations of the margins. Although the protagonists' multifaceted marginality is constantly foregrounded in Markovitch's films, the protagonists are hardly ever reduced to simplified victimizations or persistent inertia.[19] Such an approach to the marginalized aligns with María Lugones' conceptualization of 'active subjectivity' in *Pilgrimages/ Peregrinajes: Theorizing Coalition Against Multiple Oppressions* (2003). For Lugones, the notion of 'active subjectivity' is

> a sense of intentionality that we can reinforce and sense as lively in paying attention to people and to the enormously variegated ways of connection among people without privileging the word or a monological understanding of sense. We can reinforce and influence the direction of intention in small ways by sensing/ understanding the movement of desires, beliefs, and signs among people. (Lugones 2003: 6)

As this quote indicates, Lugones' conceptualization of 'active subjectivity' also includes sense-based considerations with the intention of strengthening 'resistant subjectivity' which 'often expresses itself infra-politically, rather than in a politics of the public' (Lugones 2010: 746). Lugones' conceptualization of resistance is based on 'decolonial feminism,' which she envisions 'as the possibility of overcoming the coloniality of gender' and 'where liminality of the border is a ground, a space, borderline' (747 and 753). At their core, Lugones' theoretical postulations dissect the dehumanization of the colonized cross-disciplinarily, to demonstrate how it leaves 'little room for adjustments that preserve their own senses of self in community and in the world' (748). Building on Aníbal Quijano's discussions of colonial domination and Walter Mignolo's 'border thinking,' Lugones furthermore teases out the possibility for subtle forms of agency from within 'the relational subjective/intersubjective spring of liberation, as both adaptive and creatively oppositional' (746).[20] Such subtle forms of agency spell out resistance as 'the tension between subjectification (the forming/informing of the subject) and active subjectivity, that minimal sense of agency required for the oppressing -> <- [sic] resisting relation being an active one, without appeal to the maximal sense of agency of the modern subject' (746). Returning to the films under consideration, then, the differently marginalized ways of being – due to the intersectionality of gender, sexuality, race, class, and nationality – through barely anticipated intersubjectivities, the minutest experiences, and cross-cultural interactions reveal their 'minimal sense of agency,' above all, through sense-based attentiveness.

Such an approach distances Markovitch's aesthetic explorations from canonic depictions of the marginalized in 'political documentaries and social filmmaking' in the 1960s, such as those by Fernando Birri, Octavio Getino, and Fernando Solana (Rocha 2017: 5).[21] Christian León, in fact, suggests that the marginalized in film in the 1960s and 1970s were often essentialized. In *El cine de la marginalidad: Realismo sucio y violencia urbana* (2005), León details that such cinematic representations tend to

> inaugurate an essentialist and localized vision of marginality that is incapable of giving a response to the problems of cultural diversity in which Latin America is debated. One in service of change, the other in service of revolution, they condemned the marginal subject to ignorance. In doing so, they ended up affirming the matrix of colonialist thought that they intended to challenge. (León 2005: 11)[22]

> (inauguran una visión esencialista y localizada de la marginalidad que es incapaz de dar respuesta a la problemática de la diversidad cultural en la que se debate Latinoamérica. La una en función del cambio, la otra en función de la revolución, confinaron al sujeto marginal a la ignorancia. Al hacerlo, terminaron por afirmar la matriz de pensamiento colonialista que pretendieron contestar.)

León's analysis reaffirms Lugones' rejection of the colonial difference implicitly and clearly echoes Gayatri Spivak's concerns as expressed in her seminal *A Critique of Postcolonial Reason: Toward a History of the Vanishing Present* (1999). Spivak's seminal postcolonial postulations highlight 'the possibility that the intellectual is complicit in the persistent constitution of the Other as the Self's shadow' (266). While Spivak's postcolonial writing insists on spotlighting the marginalized, she also writes against romanticizing such groups and their positionalities. Returning to the 1960s and film in Latin America, Serge Daney explains in *Cine, arte del presente* (2004) that the insistence on the marginalized self's desperation held such cinematic representations together. More specifically,

> [i]n the sixties, the marginalized character was a good theme for a screenplay. A victim of society, a reanimator of utopias, or a revealer of contradictions, the marginal character had something of the antihero, sympathetically positive. In order to consider society obliquely, it was enough to follow him; his fall, like that of a falling star, would illuminate it. ([2004: 258] quoted in Aguilar 2008a: 23)

Gonzalo Aguilar revives Daney's discussion by highlighting the reemergence of marginality in New Argentine Cinema (NAC) in the 1990s.[23] In *New Argentine Cinema: Other Worlds* (2008a), Aguilar writes that 'the characters of many of the films from the 1990s are marginal [...]' yet that 'marginality carries no sense of change or heroism [...] but simply the condition of exclusion and absolute disposability' (23). For Aguilar, most of NAC films offered 'an attempt to think with films about what had happened in Argentina in the 1990s' ('un intento de pensar con las películas lo que había pasado en la Argentina en los noventa') (2008b: 5). 'New Argentine Cinema,' Joanna Page elaborates in *Crisis and Capitalism in Contemporary Argentine Cinema* (2009), 'borrows from neorealism its rawness and newness in order to present contemporary Argentina as a territory in need of charting, dissecting and recording and to present film as a tool ideally suited to the construction of social knowledge' (36). On the topic of economic marginality (extreme poverty in particular) after the 2001 economic crisis in Argentina, Aguilar underscores the intensification of cinematic interests particularly in 'the shantytowns [that] transformed into protagonists of a large number of films' ('las villas miseria [que] se transformaron en protagonistas de un gran número de películas') (Aguilar 2015: 196). Referring to Rodrigo Parra's *Las migraciones internas* (1972), Paula Morguen concurs with Aguilar and adds that 'marginality supposes structural poverty, in which the subject is expelled from the production system without occupying any economic role inside of it' ('la marginalidad supone la pobreza estructural, en la que el sujeto se encuentra expulsado del sistema de producción, sin ocupar ningún rol económico dentro de él') (Morguen 2014: 70). Morguen identifies such forms of marginality across several NAC-related films as well, including *Mala época* (1998) by Nicolás Saad, Mariano De Rosa, Salvador Roselli and Rodrigo Moreno, Pablo Trapero's *Mundo grúa* (1999) and *El bonaerense* (2002), Gustavo Corrado's *El armario* (2001), and Adrián Caetano's *Bolivia* (2002) and *Un oso rojo* (2002) (2014: 72). These films share elements particular to marginality, that is, 'the world in which they develop embodies the notion of otherness; it is about small *homogenous groups* which belong to the same sector and do not establish relations with *social others*' ('el mundo en el que se desenvuelven encarna la noción de otredad, se trata de pequeños *grupos homogéneos* que pertenecen a un mismo sector y que no establecen relaciones con *otros sociales*') (Morguen 2014: 73, original emphasis).[24]

While Markovitch's thematic and aesthetic interests in marginality have endured since the late 1990s, she does not seek to revive what might be called pure forms of 'the construction of Italian neorealism's *mise en scènes*' ('la construcción de puestas del neorrealismo italiano') (Morguen 2014: 72).[25] Markovitch's focus on seeing the marginalized cinematographically in novel ways aligns with core concepts in *The Precarious in the Cinemas of the Americas* (2018), which reconceptualizes 'the precarious' in Latin American cinema, thus 'shifting the accepted interpretations that focus on periphery in a negative manner (non-Hollywood, non-European, low budget, etc.) to showcase the cinemas of the Americas in a new, creative, and multifaceted light' (6). Indeed, Markovitch's oeuvre both features and complicates certain forms of marginality by evoking her protagonists as playfully or unexpectedly transgressive, often at the subtlest intersubjective level. Such protagonists, who are often unambiguously afflicted by political dissent, displacement, poverty, illness, and immigration, also emanate powerful glimpses of complex emotional lives, sophisticated desires, and agency. Alva Noë writes in *Action in Perception* (2004) that 'experience is a dynamic process of navigating the pathways of [different] possibilities' (2004: 217). In this light, Markovitch emphasizes the complexities of marginalization in her protagonists' lives and presents experiences of marginalization for empowering ends, whether due to political violence (*El premio*), terminal illness (*Música de ambulancia*), political dissent (*Armando y Genoveva* and *Cuadros en la oscuridad*), poverty (*Ángeles*), family fragmentation (*Marilina*), ethnicity and cross-cultural background (*El actor principal*). The crux of Markovitch's cinema therefore is her multidimensional challenge to reductionist depictions of the marginalized. This is achieved through engagement with the senses.

The sensescapes of agency and vulnerability

Aesthetic engagements with the sensory dimension have been pivotal among contemporary Argentine women filmmakers and continue to gain attention among critics.[26] In *Contemporary Argentine Women Filmmakers* (2023), Vohnsen and Mourenza reiterate that 'an increasing number of women filmmakers in Argentina ... employ senses such as touch, hearing, and proprioception to define their aesthetics' (2). The differently imagined sensoria-based dynamics in the films of Lucrecia Martel, Albertina Carri, Anahí Berneri, Celina Murga, Lucía Puenzo, María Victoria Menis, Melisa Liebenthal, Milagros Mumenthaler, Sol Berruezo Pichon-Rivière, but also Paraguayan Paz Encina, among others, have innovatively questioned 'the hegemony of the visual' (Martin 2016: 21). Focusing particularly on the cinema of Martel, Martin has elaborated theoretically on Julia Solomonoff's term '*planeta ciénaga*' to highlight the use of 'tactile and immersive film languages and experimentation with sound to destabilise the cultural hegemony of the visual, the masculine, and the adult' (2017: 242). Similarly, Paulina Bettendorff and Agustina Pérez

Rial have identified the notion of 'synaesthetic realism' ('realismo sinestético') in several NAC women filmmakers' works, including those by Martel, Carri, Berneri, and Murga (2014: 6). For Bettendorff and Pérez Rial, *realismo sinestético* multisensorially unsettles normative expectations of quotidian home-bound life, achieving to 'broaden the visual through its sensory expansion' ('ampliar el visible fílmico a través de su expansión sensorial') (2014: 19). It could be said that Markovitch instantiates this notion in her films by relying on her characters' stimulated sensoria to problematize simple assumptions about their marginalized subjectivities. Engaging critically with such films might reveal how the 'sentient body is a placeholder for a larger discussion of the effects of state practices on its people' but also '[...] traces the ways in which the population resists or transforms social life' (Masiello 2018: 3). If, as David Howes claims, the senses are 'our means of perception,' then the minutest sensorial interactions on the margins in Markovitch's films connote possibilities of transgression, autonomy, and agency (2022: 11).

The differently marginalized and their sensescapes are a vital force of Markovitch's oeuvre. More elementally, the characterization of 'marginalized dwellers' in this book coincides with what the *Oxford Dictionary* defines as the corollary of a 'process of social exclusion in which individuals or groups are relegated to the fringes of a society, being denied economic, political, and/or symbolic power and pushed towards being "outsiders"' (n. pag.). This definition straightforwardly indicates different aspects of social stratifications (political, economic, and cultural) and topographic demarcations (places). In *For Space* (2005), Doreen Massey states that 'space can never be that completed simultaneity in which all interconnections have been established, and in which everywhere is already linked with everywhere else. A space, then, is neither a container for always-already constituted identities, nor a completed closure of holism' (12). Yi-Fu Tuan's *Space and Place: The Perspective of Experience* [1977] (2014) interprets space as the antithesis of place, 'if we think of space as that which allows movement, then place is a pause; each pause in movement makes it possible for location to be transformed into place' (6). Markovitch's choice of places (sites of homelessness, hospice-like places, dilapidated communities, uninhabitable localities, and shantytowns) underscore social marginality as the most constant common denominator in her films.

Yet Markovitch also turns her camera toward their dynamic manifestations of *socioemotional complexities* in spaces the marginalized create and the places they occupy, above all, sensorially. If we consider that 'the senses are,' as Howes suggests in *Empire of the Senses: The Sensual Culture Reader* (2005a), 'the media through which we experience and make sense of gender, colonialism, and material culture' (4), then studying the sensorial dynamics of said socioemotional complexities illuminates an array of concerns related to political threats and interpersonal defiance (*El premio* and *Marilina*); class and ethnicity (*El actor principal*); mental afflictions and economic vulnerabilities (*Música de ambulancia* and *Ángeles*); and artistic creativity and (un)belonging (*Perriférico*, *Armando y Genoveva*, and *Cuadros en la oscuridad*). In other words, Howes' notion of the senses as 'cultural systems' highlights that 'individual ways of sensing are always elaborated within the context of communal sensory orders' (2005a: 5). In her recent book, *The Senses of Democracy: Perception, Politics, and Culture in Latin America* (2018), Francine Masiello concurs with Howes and views the senses as dynamic instruments for the exploration of broader cultural issues. For Masiello, whose discussions also draw on Marx's *Economic and Philosophic Manuscripts of 1844*, 'the senses are powerful agents to tell us about cultural progress. They illustrate how human perceptions protect us from danger; they announce the power of individual bodies against the authority of state; and they allow us to narrate stories of pleasure, pain, and resistance' (Masiello 2018: 3).[27] Such narratives infuse Markovitch's films, especially if we believe that 'sensory critique is the beginning of social critique' (Howes 2022: 13). Markovitch's explorations of marginality through sensoria are consequently endowed with vigorous imprints of universal relevance and are often concerned with abandonment, mental illness, betrayal, and addiction – all of which cannot be divorced from love, altruism, regret, and curious friendships.

By inviting the viewer to explore the socioemotional layers of homeless sites, hospice-like spaces, assisted-suicide intersubjectivities, and political displacements, Markovitch revitalizes the complexity of the margins in novel and expansive ways. Her socioemotional and sensory engagements at and with the margins are conceptualized as *contested marginality*. This concept refers to the complexly interpersonal and ostensibly unanticipated manifestations of agentic potential through sensory experiences in peripheric sites and circumstances. The concept also aims to illuminate the rejection of facile and predictable forms of representing marginalized groups. One could argue that Markovitch imagines her characters based on what Gilles Deleuze calls an individual in *Spinoza: Practical Philosophy* (1970). For Deleuze, 'an individual is first of all a singular essence, which is to say, *a degree of power*' (1970: 27, emphasis added). While the director seeks to illuminate her marginalized characters' multifarious navigations of emotional, social, and cultural circumstances in Latin American contexts and beyond, as forms of affirmation and resistance, she seems equally interested in exploring how such navigations take centerstage sensorially. 'The human sensorium,' writes Howes, '[...] never exists in a natural state. Humans are social beings, and just as human nature itself is a product of culture, so is the human sensorium' (2005a: 3). The notion of contested marginality at the most minute levels therefore allows us to discern the protagonists (and other characters) as *unpredictably intricate* in sensorial ways. This unpredictability becomes discernable, particularly when we subscribe to the notion that 'each sense is in fact a nodal cluster, a clump, confection or bouquet of all other senses, a mingling of the modalities of mingling' (Connor 2005: 323). One might argue that this 'mingling,' in fact, intensifies 'the relationship between inner and outer landscapes' (Porteous 1990: 9). According to Douglas Porteous' discussions in *Landscapes of the Mind* (1990), such an interplay springs from 'the internal aspects of human consciousness, the sensations and perceptions that contribute to experience and by which a person makes sense of his [their] environment' (9). Paul Rodaway's *Sensuous Geographies: Body, Sense, and Place* (1994) further unpacks both overt and subtle layers of perception, given that each sense could be considered to be simultaneously the medium as well as the message, in accordance with Maxwell McLuhan's seminal theory (1962), stating that 'what might first appear to be visual perception may on closer inspection be seen to include important auditory, olfactory, and tactile components' (Rodaway 1994: 26). In this respect, 'sensuous experience' is best understood as 'a complex of senses working together offering a range of 'clues' about the environment through which the body is passing' (Rodaway 1994: 25).[28] The act of animated senses, in Steven Connor's words on Michel Serres' *Les cinq sens* (1985), further crystalizes what contributes to the notion of sensescapes in the present study '[w]here the other senses give us the mingled body, vision appears on the side of detachment, separation. Vision is a kind of dead zone, as the petrifying sense, the non-sense, which it is the role of the other senses to make good or redeem' (2005: 328). In film, Laura Marks studies such sensorial surges in *The Skin of the Film* (2000) with the intention of dissecting 'a bodily relationship between the viewer and the image' (2000: 3). For Jennifer Barker in *The Tactile Eye: Touch and the Cinematic Experience* (2009), 'cinema's tactility' has many dimensions of meaning and 'opens up the possibility of cinema as an intimate experience and of our relationship with cinema as a close connection' (2009: 2). In Markovitch's films, the human sensorium relies most potently on 'the mingled body' that 'can open our mind to myriad other ways of sensing and making sense of the world,' thus highlighting the subtle potential for contested marginality (Howes 2022: 12).[29]

Contested marginality

Although Markovitch's protagonists are relegated to the peripheries of their communities or society to varying degrees, they also frequently exhibit an intricate combination of vulnerabilities, aptitudes, and strengths, and thus defy easy categorizations according to class, gender, ethnicity, sexuality, or race. In other words, the filmmaker features the protagonists who challenge, circumvent, and question their marginalization through complex individualities and multisensorial interfaces. From the outset of her filmmaking career, including most evidently in her first short film, *Perriférico*, Markovitch engages marginality in singular ways (Chapter 1). While the other two shorts – *Marilina* and *Música de ambulancia* – focus on motherhood characterized by commonplace struggles as well as unforeseen and singular vitality, *Perriférico* isolates a particular kind of care and friendship, even mothering, across species. Set in Mexico City, *Perriférico* brings the viewer into the life of a homeless woman as a stray dog stumbles upon her belongings. As the viewer engages with the initial sequences of the film, the short asserts straightforwardly that a 'sense of displacement,' to borrow Howes' words, 'is often the plight of the socially marginal' (2005a: 7). The lead character, moreover, initially appears to be the dog himself, whose determination to cross one of the busiest bypasses in the capital usurps but also broadens the homeless woman's everyday life through their intersensoriality. Markovitch's camera slices through this urban space like a laser, revealing some of the most intimate and detail-oriented moments and qualities of the homeless character, and equally unique traits of her new companion. We see the homeless woman sunbathe, apply makeup, examine her skin in a mirror, and appropriate lost objects along the highway with humor and zest. The sudden and unexpected cohabitation with the dog ultimately generates a singular bond in *Perriférico*, uplifts intersensorial soundscapes and cross-species conviviality but also reveals the admixture of spontaneity, protection, and affliction of the marginal. *Marilina* and *Música de ambulancia* (Chapter 2) also insist on complex manifestations of marginal subjectivities. While the protagonists' difficulties (an incurable disease of the middle-aged mother in *Música de ambulancia* and tension-filled single motherhood in *Marilina*) are foregrounded in each film, these difficulties are also defied in paradoxical ways. Emotionally incongruous conduct saturates these shorts and renders their protagonists' marginalized state more complex. Laughter is coupled with terminal illness in *Música de ambulancia*. The paternity revelations in *Marilina* border on parody precisely because of their nonchalance. In both cases, the mother–daughter relationship is centralized but hardly ever romanticized; these relationships do not exhibit perfection but rather its complex lack thereof. The politics of odor (*Música de ambulancia*) and sound (*Marilina*) furthermore demonstrate how such senses (olfactory and hearing) are employed to reinforce subtle forms of social intimacy and conflict.

In her fifth film, *Ángeles*, the director focuses on the struggles and ploys of street children, who slip in and out of Córdoba's *villas* (Chapter 7). As we follow the two minors and peddlers (Ángeles and Isa), their urban surroundings disclose a world weighted down by drug addiction, alcoholism, and apathy. Simultaneously, this world is coupled by the children-protagonists' efforts to survive and their audacity to play. The protagonists' often transgressive play in *Ángeles* differs from Ceci's in *El premio* as well as from the children's attempts at play in Luis Buñuel's classic *Los olvidados* (1950). Ángeles and Isa appear to be orphans, and much of their existence depends on their peddling skills and knowledge of certain survival-oriented codes in the city. *Ángeles'* focus on numerous sensorial collisions between the manipulative adults and street children illuminates the economic precarity of Córdoba's poor during what in the film appears to be the COVID-19 pandemic, which also prefaces a shambolic national runup to the 2023 victory of the right-wing contender Javier Milei.[30]

The filmmaker occasionally couches subtly defiant interpersonal connections at the margins in foreign places by means of unpredictable agentic intersubjectivities. Such intersubjectivities indicate different forms of sociopolitical dispossession without reducing characters to stereotypes. The ostensibly facile emotional connection between the protagonists (Azra and Luis) in *El actor principal* exposes unique layers of their personhood through their ludic haptics and carnivalesque interactions (Chapter 6). The protagonists' emotional bonding links us to their past, specifically Azra's endurance throughout the political violence in Kosovo (1998–1999) and Luis' tenacious navigation of informal labor sectors in Mexico.

This complexity in Markovitch's diegetic worlds, which often implies subtle forms of resistance, emerges out of seemingly incidental instances that mirror and probe into certain social ills, including poverty, unemployment, political ostracism, and homelessness. 'The senses stand', insists Masiello, 'as the basis of a particular experience in a particular time and place. They are relevant to how we see ourselves on the cusp of disorder or civil war, in the movement between tradition and modernity, in the tension between national and cosmopolitan yearnings, or even at the dawn of an age when technological innovation threatens the integrity of what we identify as human' (2018: 3). Keeping Masiello's observations in mind, some of the most discernable sociopolitical and cultural implications in Markovitch's cinema indeed stem from the ubiquity of sensorial interactions. The filmmaker reveals the emblematic power of the characters' smallest forms of contention sensorially: children's play, frivolous escapades, laughter, artistic undertakings, and erotic impulses, to mention a few. The conceptualization of the marginalized in Markovitch's films cannot be separated from all of the complex socioemotional proclivities that the protagonists embody, seek to exhibit, or straightforwardly practice through their sensoria.

Such contestations might be further appreciated and crystallized if approached through what Gilles Deleuze and Félix Guattari call 'the nomadic assemblages' in *A Thousand Plateaus* (1987 [2005]) (415). The essence and unlimited potential of the roaming subjectivity – 'the nomad' – derives from incessant forms of movement, organic interchanges, and intricate forms of belonging. In accordance with Deleuze and Guattari, for the nomad, literally and figuratively, 'every point is a relay and exists only as a relay. A path is always between two points, but the in-between has taken on all the consistency and enjoys both an autonomy and a direction of its own' (Deleuze and Guattari 2005: 380). The 'in-between,' which appears to be both somewhat confined and continuously in flux in nomadic assemblages, has a particular rebelliousness, containing bold possibilities. If the senses 'mediate the relationship between idea and object, mind and body, self and society, culture and environment,' then their presence is naturally ubiquitous (Howes 2022: 13). In other words, the nomad metaphorically or literally gets associated with different degrees of vulnerabilities, self-assurance, and a surprising sensorial mélange. 'The life of the nomad,' clarify Deleuze and Guattari, 'is the intermezzo. Even the elements of his dwelling are conceived in terms of the trajectory that is forever mobilizing them' (Deleuze and Guattari 2005: 402). In addition to belonging, this mobility can also reveal othering despite (or because of) the acquisition of new forms of knowing. Given that 'othering by means of the senses (i.e., sensory discrimination) is at the core of process of social inclusion and exclusion,' then the notion of nomadic assemblages in this book is interdependent with sensory epistemologies (Howes 2022: 17).

The notion of contested marginality becomes elucidated through a multidimensional theoretical framework in the book. While the director's stylistic and thematic leitmotifs have characterized her cinema as primarily infused with paradox, they have also inspired a rich sensescape-oriented 'assemblage' of inquiry through affect, spectrality, intermediality, emotional gestures, surprise, prehension, and intersensoriality. A brief delineation is in order for now, since each chapter details its theoretical anchor subsequently. Howes' notion of intersensoriality theoretically supports the analysis of *Perriférico* in Chapter 1. In *The Sensory Studies Manifesto: Tracking the Sensorial Revolution in the Arts and Human Sciences* (2022), Howes states that to sense means to grasp, which inevitably leads to 'the interaction and integration of the senses in perceptual processes' (11). *Perriférico*'s aesthetic dealings with the protagonist's heightened sensorial attunement to the immediate urban sites' soundscape and her friendship with a stray dog become crystallized through a synesthesia-oriented framework of touch, hearing, and sound. In Chapter 2, *Marilina* and *Música de ambulancia* share certain characteristics around the notion of surprise in a carnivalesque mode. Anchored analytically in what is known as incongruity theory, each film seeks to depict certain forms of defenselessness as well as vigor among the impoverished, terminally ill, or single mothers in contemporary contexts of Mexico. The notion of surprise in *Marilina* and *Música de ambulancia* is carried out differently in each film to reveal the depth of the protagonists' sensorial interactions. In Chapter 3, Brian Massumi's discussion of affect informs the analysis of *El premio* to underscore the political tensions in the child's immediate family and new community. As the film unfolds, we watch the protagonist, Ceci, learn how to dull her responses and control her emotional reactions in public spaces during the military regime in Argentina (1976–83). While her mother's coaching on how to be and feel publicly is emotionally taxing for the seven-year-old, it also functions symbolically in the film to reveal deeper layers of political belonging. In Chapter 4, Ágnes Pethő's theoretical postulations on 'in-betweenness,' as a form of intermediality in *Armando y Genoveva*, helps us unpack the parents' political inclinations as key reasons for their life-long social exclusion but also to commemorate the parents' commitment to artistic expression despite such circumstances. *Cuadros en la oscuridad* (2017) is examined at the theoretical crux of spectrality and disgust in Chapter 5. The analysis first problematizes the filmmaker's notebook entries on the film from her written and digital notebooks and subsequently examines how the notion of disgust anchors the film's explorations of publicly unrecognized artistic productivity. Although the chapter takes William Miller's *The Anatomy of Disgust* (1997) as its point of departure to examine metaphorical manifestations of social invisibility through disgust, it ultimately exposes the protagonist's ghostly existence as a critical reflection on Argentina's recent and politically turbulent past. Situated theoretically at the intersection of Laura Marks' *The Skin of the Film* (2000) and Joyce Davidson, Liz Bondi, and Mick Smith's *Emotional Geographies* (2005), the discussion of *El actor principal* focuses on the protagonists' emotional gestures to highlight the playful melding of their ethnic and class marginality and rebellion in Chapter 6. The main characters' perilous livelihoods and delicate forms of agency become revealed through the intersection of their basic emotions, bold gestures, and insolently occupied sites. In Chapter 7, *Ángeles* is examined in conversation with Erin Manning's discussion on 'prehensions' or 'events of perception' in *Relationscapes* (2009). For Manning, prehensions 'pull what becomes actual occasions from the extensive continuum of experience [...] with its unfolding into an event comes the expression of life in the making' (76). Parting from these theoretical postulations, this analysis explores the street children's attempts to navigate and circumvent their daily homelessness as peddlers in the early 2020s.

Although Markovitch's protagonists are not all literal practitioners of nomadism, the notion of nomadic assemblages allows us to tease out an array of sociopolitical circumstances and conditions around different forms of marginality in her films. This is particularly relevant when thinking about what Deleuze and Guattari situate at the heart of the nomadic assemblage, particularly 'autonomy and a direction of its own' (380). Regardless of their marginality, Markovitch's protagonists seek as well as exhibit fierce need and inclination toward autonomous, even if fleeting, conduct to different degrees. Indeed, the notion of nomadic assemblages allows us to contemplate Markovitch's explorations of the margins as a multidimensional phenomenon and, more importantly, uncovers the minutest forms of socioemotional and interpersonal defiance. Considering that 'all assemblages are assemblages of desire,' then nomadic assemblages additionally heighten different forms of resistance in small, ephemeral moments on the fringes among the poor, the sick, the homeless, the displaced, the persecuted, and the foreign (Deleuze and Guattari 1987: 399).

The convergence of marginality and politics through the senses holds the filmmaker's stories together. This is particularly clear when we think broadly of Deleuze's and Guattari's discussion of politics; namely, 'everything is political, but every politics is simultaneously a macropolitics and a micropolitics' (213). Markovitch's films insist on vividly composite stories and characters from culturally specific localities without diminishing their universal relevance. According to the filmmaker's *Cacerías imaginarias*, which is rendered as a creative writing and a contemplative lab on filmmaking,

> the stories that use small-scale events are those which have received the name 'minimalists.' In this aesthetic search, in which I dabbled for many years, there has been much confusion. In stories with subtle events, the conflicts should be even more powerful and clear. In those cases, it does not matter 'what happens;' instead, the importance lies in *what is happening*. (Markovitch 2022: 74, original emphasis)

> ([l]as historias que se valen de eventos de pequeña dimensión, son las que han recibido en la actualidad el nombre de 'minimalistas.' En esta búsqueda estética, en la que yo misma incursioné durante muchos años, han existido muchas confusiones. En las historias con eventos sutiles, los conflictos deberían ser aún más poderosos y claros. No importa en esos casos, 'lo que pasa'; en cambio es fundamental lo que *está pasando*.)

The director's layered focus on those barely perceptible moments 'in progress' is manifested in her films as both multifaceted and plentiful, particularly during her characters' sensorial interactions that reveal the 'the nonfixity of boundaries' (Braidotti 1994: 36). As discussed in each chapter, this 'nonfixity' leads to the most palpable transgressions at the margins in Markovitch's films from deeply sensescape-focused and intersubjective moments. Underscoring analytically those barely perceptible yet ongoing moments in Markovitch's diegetic worlds evokes Deleuze's notion of sensation, particularly given the cinema's ability to engender a 'shock to thought, communicating vibrations to the cortex, touching the nervous and cerebral system directly' (Deleuze 1989: 151). Although marginal experiences in Markovitch's films nearly always intimate sources of the 'interiorizing [of] an inspecting gaze,' they also appear grounded in Lugones' notion of 'infra-politics,' thus inviting us to reflect on different modes of hegemonic control – totalitarian governments, neoliberal regimes, and patriarchal domination (Lugones 2010: 746).[31] The margins in Markovitch's films ultimately reveal certain moments when sensorial interactions manage to circumvent, subvert, or ridicule the hegemon, even if only temporarily, or are at least fully aware of such possibilities.

The Cinema of Paula Markovitch anchors itself in a multipart nomadic assemblage of sensescapes that simultaneously frames and contests marginalized sites of enunciation most potently from the littlest intersubjective spaces in the director's films. Such infinitesimal happenings between her characters overwhelmingly admix paradoxical, ludic, or carnivalesque components, which, in turn, symbolically crystallize intrepid takes on marginality. The book's theoretical framework diverges in multimodal ways and unfolds singularly in each chapter to explore the contested marginality of sensorial being, including through affect (*El premio*); intermediality (*Armando y Genoveva*); emotional geographies (*El actor principal*); spectrality (*Cuadros en la oscuridad*), prehensions (*Ángeles*), surprise (*Marilina* and *Música de ambulancia*), and intersensoriality (*Perriférico*). The status of marginalization in Markovitch's films repeatedly intersects with differently unpredictable possibilities for agentic expression, which further intensifies the relations between politics and sensescapes. The filmmaker's aesthetic explorations of the infinitesimal and multisensorial happenings at the margins bring to light the notion of contested marginality, thus identifying fecund modes for sociocultural critiques in Markovitch's films.

Notes

1 See more details on the accolades regarding Markovitch's first film here: https://mubi.com/en/us/films/the-prize-2011. Accessed 23 January 2024.

2 Interview with Markovitch 30 January 2024 (see Filmography).
3 Markovitch's three-minute short, which is not analyzed in this book, is, in essence, a brief phone conversation recording with her aunt. The short, *Anita*, is part of a larger collection of short films entitled *Ayotzinapa 26* (2016). The collection was sponsored by Amnesty International as a human rights-oriented response to the violent kidnappings and disappearance of 43 Mexican college students in Iguala, Guerrero. *Anita* captures the director and her aunt remembering the disappearance of the aunt's daughter, Zulema Bendersky. Bendersky disappeared on 10 June 1976 in Córdoba, Argentina. Inspired by Bendersky's story, Markovitch is currently mapping out the initial stage of her sixth film, which is tentatively entitled *Paisajes*.
4 Markovitch's screenwriting has been the cornerstone for other directors' works (see Filmography).
5 Interview with the filmmaker on 30 March 2020.
6 All translations are mine. I thank my research and translation assistant Leah Thorburn for her attention to detail.
7 Interview with the filmmaker on 30 March 2020.
8 See Antonius Robben, *Political Violence and Trauma in Argentina* (Philadelphia: University of Pennsylvania Press, 2005); Ana Ros, *The Post-Dictatorship Generation in Argentina, Chile, and Uruguay: Collective Memory and Cultural Production* (London: Palgrave Macmillan, 2012); Geoffrey Maguire, *The Politics of Postmemory: Violence and Victimhood in Contemporary Argentine Culture* (London: Palgrave Macmillan, 2017b); and Jordana Blejmar, *Playful Memories: The Autofictional Turn in Post-Dictatorship Argentina* (London: Palgrave Macmillan, 2017), to mention but a few.
9 Markovitch has written about her displacement as an experience that bewildered her identity in *Cacerías imaginarias* (2022: 28). These subtle identitarian anxieties align with Francine Masiello's statement in *The Senses of Democracy* (2018) that 'the exiled author bends the mirror of representation in order to announce her discomfort' (12).
10 Like Lucrecia Martel, whose films seek to cut deeper into the sociopolitical and cultural fabric of Salta, Markovitch has frequently situated her films beyond Buenos Aires in places that are culturally meaningful and intimately familiar to her – namely, Córdoba, San Clemente del Tuyú but also Mexico City, thus 'displacing the perpetual epicenter, which is Buenos Aires, in the majority of Argentine film production' ('desplazando el eje del perpetuo centro que es Buenos Aires en la mayor parte de la producción fílmica argentina') (Paladino 2014: 67).
11 In addition, see Gustavo Noriega, *Estudio crítico sobre* Los rubios (2009); Parvati Nair and Julián Daniel Gutiérrez-Albilla, eds., *Hispanic and*

Lusophone Women Filmmakers: Theory, Practice, and Difference (2013); Deborah Martin, *The Cinema of Lucrecia Martel* (2016); Deborah Martin and Deborah Shaw, eds., *Latin American Women Filmmakers: Production, Politics, Poetics* (2017); Traci Roberts-Camps, *Latin American Women Filmmakers: Social and Cultural Perspectives* (2017); Inela Selimović, *Affective Moments in the Films by Martel, Carri, and Puenzo* (2018); Ana Forcinito, *Óyeme con los ojos. Cine, mujeres, visiones y voces* (2018); Gerd Gemünden, *Lucrecia Martel* (2019); Matt Losada, *Before Bemberg: Women Filmmakers in Argentina* (2020); Natalia Christofoletti Berrenha, Julia Kratje, and Paul R. Merchant, eds., *The Films of Lucrecia Martel* (2022), Daniel Mourenza and Mirna Vohnsen, eds., *Contemporary Argentine Women Filmmakers* (2023), and María Helena Rueda and Vania Barraza, eds., *Female Agency in Films Made by Latin American Women* (2024), to mention a few.

12 Regardless of different sociocultural happenings that differently sustain or simply inform Markovitch's stories, the consequences of the military dictatorship (1976–83) permeate several of her films in direct ways, most notably *El premio*, *Armando y Genoveva*, and *Cuadros en la oscuridad*. In *Cacerías imaginarias*, Markovitch offers bits and pieces of her childhood vividly when she writes, 'In the town there was only one café with a black-and-white television. We lived on the beach, in a wooden hut that functioned as a bathhouse in the summer. We spent several years without electric light and, even when the electricity worked, the cables were knocked down by the wind' ('En el pueblo había solo un café con un televisor en blanco y negro. Nosotros vivíamos en la playa, en una casilla de madera que en verano funcionaba como balneario. Pasamos varios años sin luz eléctrica y, aun cuando la electricidad funcionaba, los cables eran derribados por el viento') (2020: 16).

13 Several recent studies from different cultural studies perspectives are relevant, such as Erika Almenara, *The Language of the In-Between* (2022); José O. Fernandez, *Against Marginality: Convergences in Black & Latinx Studies* (2022); Niall H. D. Geraghty and Adriana L. Massidda, eds., *Creative Spaces: Urban Culture and Marginality in Latin America* (2019). In addition, Maristella Svampa has commented on the historical embeddedness of marginality across Latin America in *Entre la ruta y el barrio* (2003: 12). Matt Losada's *The Projected Nation: Argentine Cinema and the Social Margins* (2018) moreover traces the ways in which the process of Argentine modern state construction depended on the marginality of certain sociocultural groups of people, which in 'the all-encompassing terms of Argentina's foundational binary [...] could only be *barbarie*' (xiii). Losada furthermore examines how the past 'erasures' link to those in contemporary contexts of Argentina, stating that 'while the objects of erasure vary over time – from *indios* to gauchos to, with the shift to

a modern discourse network, immigrants, hunger, and social unrest – the act of erasure that opened a chasm between representation and reality remained constant' (2018: xiv). In addition, Cynthia Tompkins' *Affectual Erasure: Representations of Indigenous Peoples in Argentine Cinema*, discusses 'the cultural genocide of Indigenous peoples' and their revitalized presence in cultural production of today in Latin America and beyond (2018: xxiii).

14 Other pioneer Argentine women filmmakers include Angélica García de García Mansilla, María B. de Celestini, and Renée Oro, to mention the most documented ones.

15 Rich's eloquent reflection in 'An/Other View of New Latin American Cinema' on the aesthetic and thematic rebellion against Hollywood is worth citing at length: 'Freeing the camera from its confinement and isolation, the eye of this political movement roamed the streets. Instead of the customary replication of the Hollywood studio system, nonprofessional actors replaced the stars. The preoccupations of a leisure class, and the presentation of a sanitized history, were replaced by the here-and-now, historical reclamations, the lives of a class that had not seen itself reflected in the cinema. It was oppositional cinema at every level, self-consciously searching out new forms for the new sentiments of a Latin American reality just being recovered. It was a cinema dedicated to decolonialization, at every level including, frequently, that of cinematic language. A cinema of necessity, it was different things in different countries: in Cuba, an "imperfect cinema"; in Brazil, an "aesthetics of hunger" in Argentina, a "third cinema"' (1997: 277).

16 Different literary voices of the same period also explore distinct class-based apprehensions. Relevant to the present study is Laura Podalsky's *Specular City: Transforming Culture, Consumption, and Space in Buenos Aires, 1955–1973* (2004) in general and her analysis of Julio Cortázar's work in particular. Podalsky focuses on the class-based shift that Juan Peron's presidency causes in Argentina through her analysis of Cortázar's short stories from *Bestiario* (1951). Offering an insight on a different kind of marginality in Argentina's context, Podalsky suggests that 'Casa tomada' and 'Omnibus' 'map out the social anxieties of Buenos Aires' middle- and upper-class sectors who felt themselves marginalized by the nine-year Peronist administration (1946–55)' (2004: 3).

17 See Chapter 4, endnote 7.

18 In addition, see Laura Podalsky's study on relatively contemporary Latin American films on non-adults' estrangement which 'depart from the older models by privileging the perspective of working-class and lower-middle-class subjects and, in doing so, harshly indict societies riddled by mundane acts of violence, exploitation, and emotional brutality' (2007: 109).

19 According to Markovitch, 'I think that many films propose marginal beings as anemic, defeated, defined by their circumstances. If being poor were the

only problem of the poor, misery would be very relaxed ... but marginal characters and people ... they are people!!!! [sic] who are, mysterious, contradictory, eager, cruel or inexplicable depending on the day' ('[c]reo que muchas películas plantean a los seres marginales como anémicos, vencidos, definidos por sus circunstancias. Si ser pobre fuera el único problema de los pobres la miseria sería muy relajada ... pero los personajes y las personas marginales ... ¡¡¡son personas!!!! es decir, misteriosas, contradictoras, anhelantes, crueles o inexplicables según el día') (Selimović 2023: 121).

20 In *Local Histories/Global Designs: Coloniality, Subaltern Knowledges and Border Thinking* (2000), Mignolo conceptualizes 'border thinking' as 'a logical consequence of the colonial difference' (x).

21 Drawing on the scholarly work of several critics, including Burton, 1986; King, 1990; Falicov, 2007; Lusnich and Piedras 2011, and Stites Mor, 2012, Rocha observes in *Argentine Cinema and National Identity 1966–1976* (2017) that socially committed filmmakers in Argentina in the 1960s 'saw film as a powerful medium to enlighten the illiterate rural masses as well as the students and working class who could develop class-based solidarity to fight for radical social change' (2017: 5).

22 Markovitch's focus on the margins might be moderately aligned with what León calls 'El Cine de la Marginalidad,' especially if we think of the core such cinema conserves, that is, cinema that 'makes the orphans, the forgotten, the helpless, and the criminals its main characters' ('hace de los huérfanos, de los olvidados, de los desamparados, de los delincuentes sus personajes principales') (León 2005: 13). León explores a particular kind of marginality that unsettles the binary fixities of sociopolitical and cultural life. The represented margins, affirms León, '[...] appear as a symptom of that which is imperceptible to social institutions. [...] Hence, marginality maintains an ambivalent position regarding social institutions: it is external to them and, at the same time, their shameful interior' ('[...] aparece[n] como un síntoma de aquello que es imperceptible para las instituciones sociales. [...] De allí que la marginalidad mantenga una posición ambivalente respecto a las instituciones sociales: es exterior a ellas y al mismo tiempo su interior inconfesable') (2015: 14). León further conceptualizes the term by explaining that 'marginality is a non-place that designates a condition of the multiplicity of subaltern subjects. It alludes to that significance which operates from the depths of modern cultural institutions in a constant relocation which mocks the inner and outer categories. This ambivalent location is shown clearly in the marginal practices that permanently violate discursive polarities: the private and the public, the home and the street, the family and the gang, the citizen and the criminal, the moral and the immoral, the sameness and the otherness, the included and the excluded' ('[l]a marginalidad es un no lugar que

designa una condición de la multiplicidad de sujetos subalternos. Alude a aquella significación que opera desde las entrañas de las instituciones culturales modernas a partir de una deslocalización constante que burla las categorías del adentro y del afuera. Esta ubicación ambivalente se muestra con claridad en las prácticas marginales que violan permanentemente las polaridades discursivas: lo privado y lo público, el hogar y la calle, la familia y la pandilla, el ciudadano y el delincuente, lo moral y lo inmoral, la mismidad y la otredad, lo incluido y lo excluido') (2005: 12–13).

23 The history of New Argentine Cinema has been extensively studied. See in particular Gonzalo Aguilar's seminal *Otros mundos: un ensayo sobre el nuevo cine argentino* (2006) and its translation *New Argentine Film: Other Worlds* (2008a), as well as Jens Andermann's *New Argentine Cinema* (2012).

24 According to Emilio Bernini, NAC films often zoom in on 'contemporary realism, those alien but appropriate worlds, which appear reduced to a sphere, a group, or a class, always homogeneous, limited in their horizon' ('el realismo contemporáneo, esos mundos ajenos, pero apropiados, aparecen reducidos a un ámbito, un grupo, o una clase, siempre homogéneos, limitados en su horizonte') (2003: 90). This context has also led to a transgressively boisterous (re)inscription of the marginalized from within most overtly in Federico León and Marcos Martínez's renown *Estrellas* (2007) in which all those involved generate 'an aesthetic proposal. Or rather, a counterproposal: to escape from the clichés of the hegemonic representation of the shantytown' ('una propuesta estética. O más bien una contrapropuesta: escapar de los clichés de la representación hegemónica de la villa') (Bordigoni and Guzmán 2011: 602).

25 That said, Markovitch's usage of non-professional actors, filming on location, and her focus on sparce dialogue in several of her films may be suggestive of the previous generations' influences but even more importantly of her own aesthetic preferences and budgetary limitations. Markovitch has also commented on her preference to work with children, 'I love to work with child actors. I think they have a unique savagery and mystery. Also, the child character is often conceived of as exhibiting naive traits and I hope to move away from these classifications. I try to move closer to child characters and young actors, utterly receiving their strength and lucidity. Of children, I also love that they appear to have recently landed on the planet and still have a slightly extraterrestrial point of view' ('[m]e encanta filmar con niños actores. Creo que ellos tienen un salvajismo y un misterio único. También el personaje niño muchas veces es concebido con rasgos de ingenuidad y yo espero alejarme de esas tipificaciones. Trato de acercarme a los personajes niños y a los jóvenes actores, recibiendo toda su fuerza y su lucidez. De los niños también me encanta que son recién llegados al planeta así que aún tienen un punto de vista levemente extra-terrestre') (Selimović 2023: 121).

26 Bettendorff and Pérez Real 2014; Russell 2008; Ríos 2008; Molloy 2017; Martin 2017; Martin and Shaw 2017; Forcinito 2018; Selimović 2018 and 2023; Severiche 2023; Gemünden 2019; Losada 2020; Kratje and Visconti 2020; Mafud 2021; Christofoletti Barrenha, Kratje, and Merchant 2024, to mention the most relevant ones.

27 In this treatise, Marx states that 'man is affirmed in the objective world not only in the act of thinking, but with all his senses' (cf. Masiello 2018: 2–3 [1964: 140]). Masiello's discussion (2018) on literary explorations of the senses from the nineteenth century to present in Argentine and Chilean contexts is equally relevant in terms of gender, politics, and creativity. For Masiello, '[w]hile sensory responses among nineteenth-century Argentine thinkers were evoked to prove political acumen or to express the civilization-versus-barbarism trope in its full corporeal dimensions, women writers switched this model around and enunciated a particular sense work to show the weakness of authoritarian regimes' (2018: 13).

28 In Martine Beugnet's *Cinema and Sensations* (2007), the notion of 'the cinema of sensations' leads to amorphousness. Beugnet explains that '[w]hen cinema becomes a cinema of the senses it starts to generate worlds of mutating sounds and images that often ebb and flow between the figurative and the abstract, and where the human form, at least as a unified entity, easily loses its function as the main point of reference. One way or another, the cinema of sensation is always drawn towards the formless (*l'informe*): where background and foreground merge and the subjective body appears to melt into matter' (65).

29 Serres offers a stirring conceptualization of the mingling body and writes the 'body goes out from the body in all senses (*dans tous les sens*), the sensible knots up this knot, the sensible in which the body never persists in the same plane or content but plunges and lives in a perpetual exchange, turbulence, whirlwind, circumstance. The body exceeds the body, the I surpasses the I, identity delivers itself from belonging at every instant, I sense therefore I pass' (cf. Connor 2005: 329).

30 See https://apnews.com/article/argentina-election-president-milei-massa-a4811c5229d35551f8dbf7056d87aae6. Accessed 20 Nov 2023. The most recent victory of Javier Milei (in December 2023) unleashed almost instantly numerous protests across the capital, reminding us of the similarly conducted protests during the last economic crisis (1998–2002).

31 In his classic, *Power/Knowledge* (1972), Foucault outlines the ways in which ongoing external surveillance can and often does trigger self-surveillance (155). More specifically, in his essay, 'The Eye of Power,' '[a]n inspecting gaze, a gaze which each individual under its weight will end by interiorizing to the point that he is his own overseer, each individual thus exercising his surveillance over, and against, himself. A superb formula: power exercised continuously and for what turns out to be a minimal cost' (155).

1
Intersensory Bonds in *Perriférico* (1999)

In *Animals in Film* (2002), Johnathan Burt notes that animals 'appear, with greater or lesser significance, in all genres of moving film throughout its history: from wildlife films to Hollywood blockbusters, from scientific films to animation, as well as occurring in surrealist, avant-garde and experimental films, all of which use a multitude of different formats and technologies' (19). Latin American films have also featured animals complexly across different eras and genres. Luis Buñuel's surrealist repertoire of animals comes to mind immediately: ants inhabiting and eating away the living flesh, rotting, dead donkeys, and a solitary death's-head moth in *Un chien andalou* (1929). Alejandro Iñárritu's *Amores perros* (2000) features graphic imagery of cruelty with and toward animals – in particular, dogfighting as another practice riddled with the afflictions of human errors, sadism, and death. Albertina Carri's *La rabia* (2008) is another example of violent acts toward animals (sheep, weasels, and pigs) as straightforward transpositions of human interactions around them. Lucrecia Martel's sequences of trapped animals, including the cow swallowed in mud and the dog-rat's (*perro rata*) vociferous barking in *La ciénaga* (2001), lead to the film's tragic culmination. The instinctively rebellious llamas and horses zigzag around the antagonist's dream-like, forsaken, and dead-end journeys in *Zama* (2017).[1] In Markovitch's *El actor principal*, a black kitten appears briefly in Azra's hands, within her hidden site at the hotel's basement – the kitten is the sole witness of Azra's and Luis' multilingual and incomplete exchanges on trauma, survival, and intimacy (Chapter 6). In her most recent film, *Ángeles* (2025), another stray black kitten is fleetingly cared for by one of the street children (Chapter 7). In contrast to most of these films, Markovitch's *Perriférico* (1999) predominantly focuses on a stray dog's vitality and determination.

Perriférico is Markovitch's first short film.[2] The short was part of the programming of 123 international films at the 26th International Short Film Festival in Berlin in 2010. Markovitch builds the short around an impromptu encounter between an adrift dog and a homeless woman and their hustle to survive during one full day. Almost nineteen minutes long, the short unfolds entirely in a bustling urban area of Mexico City. At first, the stray dog, might be part of, in Rob Nixon's words, 'abject picaros' *[sic]* (451). For Nixon, the animal 'joins a long line of picaros: canny, scheming, social outliers governed my unruly appetites, scatalogically obsessed, who, drawn from polite society's vast impoverished margins, survive by parasitism and by their wits' (451). *Perriférico*'s opening scene privileges a wheat-colored, medium-sized dog walking decisively through an unnamed city street only to arrive at the epicenter of the film's plot: the massive and notoriously traffic-plagued bypass of Mexico City – the Anillo Periférico. This site also alludes to the film's title – as a play on words of sorts (marginal dog/underdog, as it were) – at the Periférico and its traffic upwellings. As the camera pans around the site, the viewer sees and hears the dense, slowly moving city traffic, gets a glimpse of several nearby skyscrapers, and notices a towering billboard that pierces the sky. Markovitch's camera slices through the protagonist's transient camp like a laser, seeking to establish that 'the counterpart of emplacement is displacement, the feeling that one is homeless, disconnected from one's physical and social environment' (Howes 2005a: 7). From the outset, we are invited into the traffic's roaring soundscape of the actual bypass: cars, trucks, radio broadcasts, and conversations but also silence within the moving vehicles. The traffic not only stops the dog from crossing the road. It also surrounds the dog's awareness of another main character in the short – a homeless woman – whose encampment borders the bypass. The dog's presence indeed calls attention to the woman's homelessness in a unique, swift, and episodic way, while the urban soundscape signals their vulnerabilities but also their agency-oriented dispositions. This chapter explores the protagonist's paradoxical forms of self-rule and socioemotional attunement, despite her homelessness, by focusing on the soundscape that unsettles the cross-species frontier and her marginality.[3]

Sounds and soundscapes are essential for the bond between the main characters. This bond in *Perriférico* reminds us that sound guides our perception of images. Filmmakers expectedly manipulate different components of sound to direct this perception (Porteous 1990; Nancy 2007; Classen 2014; Howes 2022; Bordwell 2024).[4] The soundscape has been conceptualized differently across disciplines. In 1967, Michael F. Southworth coined the concept as 'the quality and type of sounds and their arrangements in space and time' (2). More recently, Pijanowski et al. (2011) have extensively discussed its etymology and have offered their working definition of soundscape as 'the collection of biological, geophysical, and anthropogenic sounds that emanate from a landscape and which vary over space and time reflecting important ecosystem processes and human activities' (1214). In *Perriférico*, the protagonist's encounter with a stray dog in an urban setting of Mexico's capital generates a singular 'collection' of both 'geophysical and anthropogenic sounds,' and the cacophony exposes gender and homelessness from a uniquely intersensory angle.

Privileging soundscapes and intersensoriality in *Perriférico* analytically permits an equally nuanced approach to the main characters' rebellious union at the margins. The short's soundscape, for instance, immediately inspires several related questions: How do sounds produced in nature, including biophony (sounds generated by animals) evoke certain emotions in this film? How might certain sources of soundscape (geophony, for example – sounds related to earth) help neutralize or accentuate the tone in specific scenes? While these questions animate much of the ensuing discussion, intersensoriality suggests another element regarding the featured encounter in the short, or what David Howes calls 'the geography of the senses' (23). In *The Sensory Studies Manifesto: Tracking the Sensorial Revolution in the Arts and Human Sciences* (2022), Howes explains that 'the geography of the senses' fundamentally assists in understanding how 'the differing ways in which the senses are constructed and lived generate distinct sensory worlds' (23). During this construction of new 'sensory worlds,' clarifies Howes, 'the senses mediate the apprehension of space and in so doing contribute to our sense of place' (Howes 2022: 26). The use of the characters' senses (sight, smell, hearing, and touch) to negotiate their initial interactions reveal deeper and more complex attributes of the woman's emplacement as homeless. More specifically, the woman's gaze, words for, and touches of the dog facilitate a '*sense-based* inquiry' and thus begin to shape their cross-species familiarization (Classen, 1993b, qtd in Howes, 1997: 4, original emphasis).[5] The geophony in *Perriférico* first highlights the difference between visual space (the bypass and its immediate surroundings) and auditory space (nearly anything that the homeless woman is able to hear in and beyond her immediate surroundings). This distinction subsequently allows us to contemplate the multifaceted power of the nonverbal – yet sound-infused and touch-based – attributes in the protagonist's relationship with the stray dog.

In *Sensing the City* (2005b), David Howes remarks on the notion of 'sensing the city' in and 'through multiple sensory modalities' (323). In *Senses and the City* (2011), Mădălina Diaconu concurs and specifies that to 'experience the *atmosphere* of an urban site presupposes that we open our senses. The visual as well as touch, sound, and smell are called upon here' (2011: 40, emphasis added). Both critics insist on the multisensory potential of nearly any place, especially across urban settings of simultaneous movement and intricate soundscapes. Both critics also seem to suggest that individuals' activated senses contribute to and are drawn from the sites they interact with in performative ways. This is particularly compelling if we refer to Friedlind Riedel's discussion of the notion of atmosphere in *Affective Societies* (2019). For Riedel, atmosphere 'refers to a feeling, mood, or *Stimmung* that fundamentally exceeds an individual body and instead pertains primarily to the overall situation in which bodies are entrenched' (2019: 85). The concept of multisensory performativity is especially palpable in cities with their enhanced dynamism. According to Lewis Mumford, the city largely entails 'a consciously dramatic setting for the more significant actions and the more sublimated urges of a human culture. The city fosters art and is art; the city creates the theatre and is the theatre. It is in the city, the city as theatre, [...] [where] more purposive activities are formulated and worked out, through conflicting and cooperating personalities, events, groups, into more significant culminations' (1970: 480, quoted in Diaconu, 2011: 41). The notion of the city as 'theatre' is also manifested through the intersensory attunements of the two main characters in *Periférico*, whose marginality does not prevent them from becoming the focal point of the film.

In the multisensorial theater of this urban site, the two main characters engage in a sensory intersubjectivity that playfully and frivolously interrupts the immediacy of purposeful activities at the bypass. This occurs between the two of them with the protagonist's soliloquies and the dog's patient stay. The homeless woman acts out her enthusiasm for the dog by petting him, offering him her possessions, and advising him on safer sites to cross. In gesturing to the dog to avoid crossing the traffic-jammed bypass, we hear her engage with the dog, 'Where are you going?,' and proceed to reason with the dog by telling him, 'No, this road cannot be crossed. It is called Periférico' ('¿Adónde vas? No, esta calle no se puede cruzar. Se llama Periférico.') Yet the scent of recently tossed food from the passing car lures the dog to cross. His olfactory determination leads him to retrieve the sandwich abruptly, which stops the traffic and nearly kills him. He fails in getting the sandwich on his first attempt, yet this brief sequence reaffirms while it also challenges his marginalized state. Through this straightforward incident, Markovitch features and centers frequently unnoticed city dwellers. She represents them as active 'theatrical' participants of the urban site, even though they are normatively sidelined and barely visible. The collision between the dog and a massive truck alerts the protagonist multi-sensorially, for she first hears and then sees an accident. She becomes mobilized to stop the traffic and ultimately rescues the wounded animal. This moment also underscores how urban settings defy the notion of 'ocular-centricity' – the presumption of the visual as the dominant sense (Adams and Guy 2007: 133). Urban sites that brim with multisensoriality – particularly sounds and smells – accommodate different kinds of attunements as well as random expressions of agency. The same moment reaffirms the protagonist's subversive engagement: she interrupts the traffic flow and makes herself seen, heard, and regarded. Markovitch's focus on the seemingly inconsequential accident highlights these characters as unquestionably vulnerable but also indisputably resourceful.

In *Consumidores y ciudadanos* (1995), Néstor García Canclini compares the existent and standard bypass traffic that we see in Markovitch's short to classical music by evoking German Baroque composer Georg Philipp Telemann and the changing dynamism of his *Trumpet Concertos*. According to Canclini, the city's soundscapes animate our imaginative perceptions of real spaces through, above all, the vertiginousness of our senses (1995: 101). Recalling this passage as we screen *Perriférico*, the bypass almost becomes an orchestra of differently potentiated and audible instruments (oboes, trumpets, and horns, among others). When the protagonist stops the urban 'concierto/concert,' as it were, by walking into the moving traffic with her drifter cart solely to rescue the dog, we see her as an activated subjectivity that runs on decisiveness, determination, and agency (Canclini 1995: 101). Through this multisensorial engagement the protagonist's urban presence is recalibrated. Such a recalibration contrasts with her initial positionality as a seemingly passive onlooker.

As the woman begins to engage verbally with the dog, however, the site begins to present itself as both limited *and* expansive. The limited aspects include the site's plain and confining physical dimensions – a small area that the main characters occupy for twenty-four hours at the highway's edge. The expansiveness of the otherwise marginalized site, in contrast, manifests through the characters' intersensory connection but also its symbolic implications. When screened in 2024, the protagonist's reality in *Perriférico* might convey symbolically retrospective social and political undertones regarding poverty in Mexico at the outset of the new millennium. In 1999, Mexico's population was 98 million inhabitants – 61 million of whom lived in poverty, and homelessness was a key concern.[6] The director's focus on homelessness additionally might be signaling toward the notorious 1999 destruction across Mexico caused by a severe storm. Gerardo Nebbia reported on this catastrophic event that at least '253,000 have been left homeless in 9 out of 31 Mexican states' (1999: 1). According to Nebbia, the Mexican government and its president Ernesto Zedillo responded sluggishly to communities that were 'considered supporters of another opposition party, the Party of the Democratic Revolution (PRD)' (1999: 2). Underserved communities were lastingly affected, especially after the obliteration and damage of mudslides. Indeed, homelessness was one of the most injurious outcomes of this catastrophic event (Nebbia 1999: 2).[7] Returning to the intersensory interaction in the short, the city soundscape constantly prods the characters beyond the confined homeless site, just as they are governed by the traffic. Since sound and hearing are 'sometimes thought of as the most libertine and promiscuously sociable of the senses,' the soundscape of the encampment in Markovitch's short opens new spaces of subtle engagement that shatter the protagonist's visible marginalization (Connor 2005: 323). As the camera zooms in on her placidity and focus, the protagonist and the viewer begin to hear the chatter from the passing cars and their radio music. This kind of hearing encapsulates what Steven Connor calls, 'hearing that constitutes the social contract: the blaring bedlam of the exchange of noise and signals, signals and noise' (2005: 325). While Markovitch builds the capital's multidimensional energy – its 'bedlam' – through her jump cuts from one car to another and

Figure 1.1 The protagonist's homeless encampment. © Paula Markovitch

simultaneous urban occurrences, the protagonist increasingly manifests as a sensorially alert vagabond (Fig. 1.1). As the jump cuts intensify from one angle of the homeless encampment to different cars, Canclini's notion of the city as a videoclip reemerges as well. In *Consumidores y ciudadanos*, Canclini writes '[n]ow the city is like a video clip: an effervescent montage of discontinuous images' ('[a]hora la ciudad es como un videoclip: montaje efervescente de imágenes discontinuas') (1995: 36). The jump cuts in *Perriférico* revitalize Canclini's notion of the city as a flow and intensify the mélange of intersensoriality and soundscape, thus calling attention to the characters' homelessness, survival, and fragile forms of autonomy.

Hearing and the auditory realm are mobilized in *Perriférico* to articulate the protagonist's ambiguously expanded agency in the city. In *Eskimo Realities* (1973), Edmund Snow Carpenter highlights the power of sound that generates and is of itself limitless. According to Carpenter,

> Auditory space has no favoured [sic] focus. It is a *sphere without fixed boundaries*, space made by the thing itself,

not space containing the thing. It is not pictorial space, boxed-in, but dynamic, always in flux, creating its own dimensions moment by moment. It has no fixed boundaries; it is indifferent to background. The eye focuses, pinpoints, abstracts, locating each object in physical space, against a background; the ear, however, favours [sic] a sound from any direction. (Carpenter 1973: 36 quoted in Porteous 1999: 50, emphasis added)

As the protagonist intensifies her focus on the passing traffic to protect the dog, her aural space begins to expand. In Jean-Luc Nancy's terms this moment is also about listening, particularly since 'to be listening is to be *at the same time* inside and outside, to be open *from* without and *from* within, hence from one to the other and form one in the other (Nancy 2007: 14, original emphasis). The camera begins to oscillate between several conversations in cars, seeking to show how 'sound offers a fundamentally different knowledge of the world than vision' (Smith 2004: 390–1). The soundscape that the protagonist gains from the passing cars indeed leads to a uniquely 'different knowledge,' which might at first seem inconsequential. The knowledge generated by the audio bits and pieces produced – from conversations, arguments, tranquility and the distraction of the drivers and other car passengers – is incomplete and patchy but also constant. From her site of social and physical marginalization, she aurally moves through the passing cars' silence, conversation, gossip, and arguments. Such soundscapes, which are perceived through the homeless woman's patchy eavesdropping, shatter her isolation. While her sight might restrict her to only a few nearby areas of the bypass and objects (the things in her encampment and the surrounding billboards), her *tuning into* the site's shifting soundscape of the passing cars broadens her involvement.

These multisensorial attunements reaffirm her visibility in new ways. Markovitch does so without romanticizing the protagonist's precariousness in *Periférico* through two different modes of sensing. Both kinds appear to anchor the encounter between the dog and the homeless woman and imaginatively challenge their invisibility. This anchoring happens through a particular kind of sensing, which Douglas Porteous discusses in his seminal essay 'Intimate Sensing' (1986). Porteous distinguishes between two kinds of sensing – namely, '[r]emote sensing is clean, cold, detached, easy. [. . .] [While] [i]ntimate sensing [. . .] is complex, difficult, and often filthy. [. . .] But intimate sensing is rich, warm, involved. People appear as individuals with characters and idiosyncracies' (1986: 251). The difference between these two types of sensing sustains the characters' interactions from the outset, especially through the woman's engagement with the immediate surroundings and her impromptu care for the dog. Her connection to the dog is based above all on intimate sensing. When the camera zooms in on her hand-held mirror at the beginning of the short, we see the protagonist catching the seated dog's gaze. This segment reminds us of Bill Viola's comments on his film *I Do Not Know What It Is I Am Like* (1986). According to Viola, when we look into the eye of the animal, we confront the 'irreconcilable otherness of an intelligence ordered around a world we can share in body but not in mind' (1995: 143). When the camera zooms in on the protagonist's hand-held mirror, we notice the protagonist's and the dog's shared reflection in it. This moment reiterates their otherness in accordance but also beyond Viola's observation. Both are cast as 'strays' – on the margins of the (social) spaces they roam – yet they are hardly ever passively complacent.

Tracing the importance of animals around and for humankind in his seminal *About Looking* (1980) through the works of Homer, Aristotle, Lévi-Strauss, Rousseau and Descartes, John Berger echoes that the animal's 'lack of common language, its silence, guarantees its distance, its distinctness, its exclusion from and of [people]' (4). The dog's arrival ignites and enables her visibility in deeper ways and creates a platform for the protagonist's voice, a fleeting 'companionship which is different from any offered by human exchange. Different because it is a companionship offered to the loneliness of a man [or humankind] as a species' (4).[8] While the notion of 'loneliness' in Berger's 'Why Look at Animals?' encompasses broader and deeper layers of humankind's solitude, to which the animals' company has served as a literal and figurative antidote, the dog's presence in the short broadens the viewers' knowledge about the woman's subjectivity. The short does that first aurally, for the protagonist begins to narrate several detailed moments from her life before the dog. 'I have to tell you something' ('Tengo que decirte una cosa'), she tells the dog as soon as she notices him. She then follows up with another question: 'In fact, do you know who I am?' ('¿Sabes quién soy yo, en realidad?'). The dog's quietude is perceived as a curious nod to continue as she points to a nearby billboard and says 'I am her' ('Esa'). The camera shifts, as if to follow the dog's gaze, and the spectator finds herself before an image of a department store ad. On it, we see an image of younger woman on the left side of the billboard that simply reads 'MARSEL.'[9] The simplicity of the billboard ad and physical resemblance between the protagonist and the ad image reawaken the viewer's curiosity, even prompting us to ask: How reliable are her voice and narrative? Are these memories or mere daydreams? Is she being playful, imaginative, or hallucinatory? 'Seriously,' she continues to tell him, 'that's how I was before,' referring to her past before she survived a car accident. Touching her torso, she concludes: 'Look how it left me' ('En serio, así era yo antes. Mira como me dejó.'). These utterances also signal a form of cross-species solidarity, in which the protagonist's stories of misfortune run parallel to her caresses of the dog.

As she extends her legs to deepen her silent, haptic comfort next to the dog, the camera frames their backs in a momentary and levelling unification. This togetherness illustrates, as Howes writes, that the 'geography of the senses is concerned with mapping sensory diversity in space,' that is to say, 'how different environments shape perception, and how space becomes place through sensory interaction with differing surroundings, both natural and built' (2022: 23). Sitting before the passing traffic (in togetherness and in different forms of otherness), the homeless woman and the stray dog begin to generate a novel meaning of the place that teems with sounds, uncertainty but also possibilities. The site's changing and changeable soundscape connotes their fragility, as well as glimmers of transgressive potential.

The soundscape of the city and the sensescape between the two characters are featured to highlight these marginalized urbanites' refusal to resign. Their tenacity manifests through both their intersensory togetherness but also through their active attunement to the soundscapes surrounding them. Despite the visual anchoring of the story in *Perriférico*, it is the dog's and the woman's interpersonal sensescape – several of their mutually activated senses (most prominently sight and touch for her and smell for the dog) – that deepen the site's meaning. For the dog, the site is also a place that sates his hunger and tides him over to the next meal of litter. For the protagonist, their encounter broadens her modes of subtle social engagements. Before the short ends, the dog engages again and this time successfully reaches the sandwich, causing an accident in the process for a lonely motorcyclist who happens upon that section of the bypass in the middle of the night.

As in most of her films, Markovitch builds in *Perriférico* another playful contradiction wherein the protagonist's intricate urban habitus evokes Yi-Fu Tuan's analysis of the complex transformations of spaces into places. For Tuan, '[w]hat begins as undifferentiated space becomes place as we get to know it better [through our senses] and endow it with value' (Tuan 1977: 6). Markovitch focuses on the multisensorial interaction between these two characters to highlight the site as an 'undifferentiated space' – namely, just another bypass shoulder that transiently houses the homeless. By the end of the short, the same space has grown into a place 'endowed with value' regarding certain particularities on gendered homelessness, poverty, and cross-species' intersensoriality. The short ends with an undisclosed answer to the posed question that unites the protagonist sonically with those passing cars and other sites across the city; we hear only, 'The name of the first woman to reach the moon was...' ('El nombre de la primera mujer que llegó a la luna fue...'). The playfulness of this incomplete statement hovers as we encounter the protagonist the next morning at her usual site. As at the beginning of the short, she amuses herself at its end with humor and levity: having appropriated the dead motorcyclist's sunglasses, she whistles while holding a dismantled motorbike radio. The broken radio naturally emits nothing. Instead, the homeless woman's whistle fills up the screen – her voice, playfulness, and good humor close the short.

Notes

1 Other relatively contemporary films that centerstage different forms of sociopolitical and cultural implications of animals are Lucía Puenzo's *XXY* (2007), Julia Solomonoff's *El último día de la boyita* (2009), Paz Encina's *EAMI* (2022), to mention a few.
2 Markovitch has written about the bypass in *Cacerías imaginarias* (2022) from a phenomenological perspective, explaining that 'when I arrived in Mexico, at twenty-two years old, I knew nothing of this. I settled in an apartment in the Torres de Mixcoac, located next to the Periférico. Through my apartment window, I watched thousands of cars pass by, slowly cutting through the smoggy cloud. The landscape seemed extraordinarily sad to me, almost as much as the melancholic afternoons of San Clemente del Tuyú' ('[c]uando llegué a México, a los veintidós años, no sabía nada de esto. Me instalé en un departamento de las Torres de Mixcoac, situadas al costado del Periférico. Veía pasar miles de autos por la ventana de mi casa, desfilando en una nube cenicienta. El paisaje me parecía extraordinariamente triste, casi tanto como las melancólicas tardes de San Clemente del Tuyú') (2022: 28).
3 An early version of this idea calcified in my essay on *El actor principal* entitled 'La marginación empoderada en *El actor principal* (2019) de Paula Markovitch' in *La Jornada Zacatecas*. 5 September 2021. https://ljz.mx/05/09/2022/las-paradojas-exquisitas-de-paula-markovitch/.
4 See in particular, Douglas J. Porteous, *Landscapes of the Mind: Worlds of Sense and Metaphor* (1990); Jean-Luc Nancy, *Listening* (2007); Constance Classen et al., *Ways of Sensing: Understanding the Senses in Society* (2014); David Howes, *The Sensory Studies Manifesto* (2022); and David Bordwell et al., *Film Art: An Introduction* (2024).
5 According to Classen, the notion of 'sense' 'encompasses both sensation *and* signification, feeling *and* meaning (as in the sense of a word) in

its spectrum of referents. *Sensation-signification* is seen as forming a continuum, which is modulated by the sensory order' (quoted in Howes 2022: 4, original emphasis).
6 World Bank's Report, 'Poverty in Mexico: An Assessment of Condition, Trends, and Government Strategies,' https://documents1.worldbank.org/curated/en/539241468752996263/pdf/286120ME.pdf Accessed 30 March 2024.
7 See the current data on homelessness in Mexico via the World Population Review's report https://worldpopulationreview.com/country-rankings/homelessness-by-country. Accessed 4 August 2024.
8 Berger further clarifies that '[w]hat distinguished man from animals was the human capacity for symbolic thought, the capacity which was inseparable from the development of language in which words were not mere signals, but signifiers of something other than themselves. Yet the first symbols were animals. What distinguished men from animals was born of their relationship with them' (1980: 7).
9 MARSEL was founded in 1973 and is a Mexican department store for women. See www.marsel.com.mx. Accessed 1 August 2023.

2

Marilina (2001) and *Música de ambulancia* (2009): Incongruous Surprises

As in most of Markovitch's films, paradox is a vital element in *Marilina* (2001) and *Música de ambulancia* (2009), both thematically and aesthetically.[1] The paradoxical elements in these shorts emerge out of emotional incongruity – namely, laughter and terminal illness in *Música de ambulancia* and silence and revelations around paternity in *Marilina*. In both cases, the mother–daughter relationship is centralized, not because of its flawlessness, but precisely because of its complex imperfection. Although both short films belong to the director's earlier filmmaking career and might appear aesthetically less intricate than later works, their appeal to the senses brims with originality.

Surprise in both shorts, moreover, unsettles certain normative expectations. The thematic and aesthetic build-up to these surprises (an incurable disease in *Música de ambulancia* and a single motherhood in *Marilina*) is treated sensorially, and the surprises themselves are confronted in unexpectedly defiant ways. Kenneth Lash reminds us that 'it is not the surprise of the spontaneous that makes us laugh, but rather its incongruous relationship with the more or less static pattern it interrupts' (1948: 116). In more recent debates, John Morreall (2011) concurs with Lash and elaborates on the concept of incongruity. Morreall notes that incongruity emerges when 'some thing or event we perceive or think about *violates* our normal mental patterns and normal expectations' (2011: 405, emphasis added). This 'violation' or interruption of our anticipations occurs throughout both shorts to explore and uniquely question marginality due to ailment (*Música de ambulancia*) and miscommunication (*Marilina*). *Música de ambulancia* focuses on an adult daughter's imminent loss of her mother; *Marilina* on a daughter's unexpected discovery of her biological father. In both shorts, the figure of the father is either completely absent (*Música de ambulancia*) or only tentatively re-engaged (*Marilina*). This chapter analyzes how *Marilina* and *Música de ambulancia* simultaneously emphasize defenselessness and vigor among the terminally ill or single mothers to shed light on the gendered complexities of elderly care and responsible paternity across Latin American contexts.

Marilina

Marilina's main plot is deceptively simple. A mother and her young daughter arrive at an urban bus station coincident with another passenger named Lucas. Both adults react instantly when they recognize each other – they are former lovers. As Lucas inquires about the little girl, the mother first retorts in a surprised manner. As she seeks to reawaken Lucas' memory about their shared past and a written note she had left for him about her pregnancy, she finally says 'she is yours' ('es tuya') (Fig. 2.1). Both are abruptly enmeshed in a multilayered surprise: the mother had left a note in what she thought was Lucas' apartment about her condition, and Lucas apparently never received it. As the short unfolds, the viewer learns that the apartment they frequented together was not his. From the outset, the encounter is muddled socioemotionally, since both characters have been operating under false premises about their past together. As the bus arrives, Marilina and her mother rapidly leave but not without inviting Lucas to reengage soon, which he does.

The father's absence (*Música de ambulancia*) or loose presence (*Marilina*) could be read as an indirect reference to the phenomenon of 'responsible paternity' that has reemerged to varying degrees across Latin America. According to Nara Milanich, responsible paternity 'describes a slew of policies to track down biological fathers and hold them responsible for their children born outside of marriage' (2017: 9). While Costa Rica was the first to pass a law on responsible paternity, other Latin American countries have passed similar laws since 2001 (Panama, Guatemala, and Honduras) (Milanich 2017). Other countries, such as Mexico, Brazil, and the Dominican Republic, have carried out 'public outreach campaigns' to send out 'civil officials and DNA kits to remote communities' (Milanich 2017: 9). Markovitch's shorts were filmed in Mexico and debuted during the first decade of the 2000s, when the policymakers across Latin America pursued 'a historic refutation of discrimination against unmarried mothers, illegitimate children and informal families as part of an attempt to reduce poverty and inequality and modernize society' (Milanich 2017: 11). While *Música de ambulancia* entirely sidelines the figure of the father without explicit explanation, as it focuses on the gendered care of the elderly, *Marilina* tackles the phenomenon of responsible paternity in a unique way, namely, without a heavy-handed emphasis on the mother's victimization.

Lucas' quiet and bewildered presence allows Markovitch to explore certain idiosyncrasies implied by new paternity reforms, especially 'responsibility, commitment, and emotional intimacy' (Milanich 2017: 12).[2] Lucas' re-engagement with his biological daughter unfolds in the short before his departure for an international performance as a puppeteer. On several occasions in the short, Lucas engages his puppet at social gatherings and during one of his early conversations with Marilina. The puppet's presence naturally communicates through a distinct mélange of silence and movement. We watch Lucas make room for his puppet by being simultaneously present (the puppet depends on his skills) and absent (the puppet inevitably claims her own territory visually and sensorially). These brief moments of puppet theater in the manner of *marionnette portée* uniquely accentuate the interpersonal strangeness in the short.[3] This atmosphere of strangeness is established in the initial bus station encounter among the three family members, and the short maintains the strange mood primarily through, at least, three connected elements. First, the mother's absence beyond the opening scene could be read as a subtle way to signal her independence and indifference toward Lucas. Milanich has argued that those 'in position of power tend to assume that households need fathers and that biological progenitors are always the most appropriate partners and caretakers. But women do not always agree. In the decade after Costa Rica passed its paternity law, only a third of single mothers took advantage of the legislation to pursue paternal recognition' (2017: 13). Unlike Lucrecia Martel's protagonist in *Rey muerto* (1995), who needs to wound the father of her children to leave him, the mother's notable absence in *Marilina* accentuates her forceful autonomy.[4] Marilina, on the other hand, becomes emotionally animated and energized. She is eager to share her excitement (her friends' birthdays), abilities (her progress in English), and concerns (parent–teacher conferences at school). Finally, the loquacious child in the second part of the short becomes a metaphorical sensorium between the parents. This recalls David Howes' discussions in *The Sensory Studies Manifesto* (2022) regarding the link between knowing and the senses (11–12). The act of knowing regarding the out-of-wedlock child consists of nonchalance (the mother), shock (father), and exhilaration (Marilina). Marilina straightforwardly associates knowing with hearing as she articulates her choppy soliloquy. Lucas listens yet apparently hears only bits and pieces, which fortifies the father's bewilderment and disconnect from the social unit constituted by Marilina and her mother.

Despite the different responses to the new situation and knowledge, the main characters are affected in shared and lasting ways. Indeed, Thomas Fuchs delineates how an atmosphere settles in interpersonally. According to Fuchs, '[t]he mutual bodily resonance in social encounters, mediated by posture, facial, gestural, and vocal expression, engenders our attunement to others and functions as a carrier of basic interpersonal atmospheres such as warmth, ease, familiarity, and belonging, or in the negative case, coldness, tensions, unease or unfamiliarity' (Fuchs 2013: 222). In addition to a nod to phenomenological approaches to embodiment (Merleau-Ponty 1945 [2012]), Fuchs anchors the notion of atmosphere in social relations affectively. Markovitch achieves an affectively tense atmosphere in the first minute of the short through a fortuitous encounter, which both establishes an interpersonal asymmetry in knowledge and suggests the short's culmination right at the start.

The tension is furthermore carried out in two antithetical modes of communication: nearly complete silence (Lucas) and loquaciousness (Marilina). Lucas' learned professional silence with puppeteering translates into his time with Marilina, for his attunement unfolds mostly in silence. Marilina, on the other hand, speaks, laughs, and asks questions as they hold hands and move through different city sites. The interpersonal asymmetry (the father seeks to make sense of this new role and identity; the daughter seeks to share abundantly as if in a quest to catch up for the lost years) resides in a particular kind of tension. This kind of tension evokes Jennifer Barker's *The Tactile Eye* (2009) regarding Andrey Tarkovsky's *Mirror* (1975), as an atmosphere-based tension, which, in this case, is also 'inextricably bound up with motion and materiality' (2009: 1). We are pulsed into the newfound father–daughter tactility (the father holds Marilina's hand to protect her), thus also generating an effulgent instance of 'cinema's tactility' (Barker 2009: 2). Barker arrives theoretically at this notion through her reconceptualization of touch – namely, 'from surface to depth, from haptic touch to total immersion' (2009: 2). Barker's concept underscores a multidirectional experience for 'film and viewers so that we *share* things with it: texture, spatial orientation, comportment, rhythm, and vitality' (Barker 2009: 2, original emphasis). The father–daughter interactions are tactile but hardly ever at a 'monosensory level' (Howes 2022: 147). Barker's notion of 'total immersion' in *Marilina* manifests as they stroll the city streets that bustle with passersby, activities, and social engagements. As the urban sites team with life and unpredictability, each space and place the characters pass through further deepens their (and our) immersion and multisensory attunement. As strangers to each other amid the bustling site of Mexico City, the father and his newly discovered daughter cohabit multisensorially – the father observes her mostly in awe and confusion, listens to her stories and descriptions, holds her hand, and makes smoke-induced bubbles with his cigarettes for her amusement.

In *Marilina*, Markovitch relies on the senses to establish a bridge between the father's and the daughter's recent discovery of each other and unshared pasts. *Marilina*'s most significant surprises unfold outdoors – at bus stops, parks, and city streets. Markovitch privileges the contrast between the city movement and the main characters' intersubjective bafflement. The city's bustling streets are a contrastive backdrop for the father's slowness in comprehending the newest layer of his identity. Yet Markovitch's camera does not linger and privileges a surface approach. This surface approach to the immediate surroundings parallels the absence of any in-depth development of the short's main characters. Just as th mother and Marilina stumble upon the father at an urban bus station at the beginning, the viewer vertiginously follows Lucas from one interpersonal situation to the next, with or without his daughter. This seemingly inconsequential presentation of the characters in fact reaffirms the short's theme – namely, the main characters' emotional bafflement in the encounter.

Markovitch employs bits and pieces of puppet theater to further accentuate, above all, that while 'our senses are our means of perception [...] [,] sensations do not always correspond; oftentimes they clash and conflict' (Howes 2022: 11, 19). Puppet theater primarily depends on the visual while subtly evoking or awakening other senses. Roman Paska has written on the (emotional) dynamics among puppets, puppeteers, and audiences, underscoring that seeing a puppet come to life on stage must be approached as it were a text. According to Paska,

> The Puppet Theater is written, above all, to be shown. And puppet plays always have something to show (even when they have nothing to say), because the text in puppet theater is always dictated and circumscribed by visual composition and visual activity. It's a script of movements, gestures. Colors and forms. A script in space . . . a script that cannot be isolated from the performance. (Paska trans. Swedzky [1995] 2015: 1)

(El Teatro de títeres se escribe por sobre todo para ser mostrado. Y las obras de títeres siempre tienen algo para mostrar (incluso cuando ellas no tienen nada que decir), porque el texto en el teatro de títeres está siempre dictado y circunscrito por la composición visual y la actividad visual. Es una escritura de movimientos, gestos. Colores y formas. Una escritura en el espacio ... una escritura que no puede ser aislada de la actuación.)

Yet engaging with puppet theater requires subtle forms of multisensorial and synesthetic attention. As Swedzky furthermore says 'an animated figure takes charge of the scenic discourse', ('una figura animada toma a cargo el discurso escénico'), which in puppet theater not only animates movements and gestures but also overpowers words (Swedzky 2018: 51). Silence, according to Swedzky, is a multidimensional component of puppet theater because it incites the viewers to think and sense multidimensionally. The dynamic between the puppeteer and its puppet often demands a particular kind of silent negotiation which is anchored in the link between the puppeteer's absence and the puppet's presence. In his piece, 'El silencio', Swedzky names this negotiation as el *teatro de los ausentes* to highlight the importance of silence between the two entities (the puppeteer and her puppet) to synchronize their communication, accentuate the puppet's visibility, and ensure a more forceful communication with the audience. 'Silence', clarifies Swedzky, 'generates an unexpected space for creation and fiction. It directly transfers the non-existent discourse to the viewer's mind and generates a spatial dynamic between the stage and the audience. [Such an approach] thus breaks any type of wall and provokes a constant circulation of senses, much like in Eisenstein's montage' ('El silencio genera un espacio inesperado de creación y de ficción, traslada directamente la concreción del discurso inexistente a la cabeza del espectador y genera una dinámica espacial entre la escena y el público, rompiendo así cualquier tipo de muro y provocando una circulación constante de sentidos, como las ideas del montaje de Eisenstein') (Swedzky 2014: 1). This 'flow of the senses' is also relevant for what transpires intersubjectively between the characters beyond the puppet's performative interjections. As such, the puppet scenes in the short are an emblematic microcosm for certain familial tensions.

Markovitch establishes such a flow narratively (the father's silence) and interpersonally (the father's quiet ways of processing his fatherhood). Unlike the dynamics of puppet theater, where silence is essential for unobstructed modes of communication, silence in the short is based on Shakespearean misunderstanding – it reinforces the surprising incongruity with the expected (Lash 1948: 116). When Marilina's mother left a written note in her lover's apartment when she learned about her pregnancy many years ago, she was unaware that the apartment was not his. As noted, Lucas consequently never receives the note, and the apartment owner commits suicide soon thereafter, which further complicates the matter. Given that she does not hear from Lucas, she carries on with her pregnancy, motherhood, and professional duties in physiotherapy. The accidental silence between them consequently erects

Figure 2.1 Lucas happens upon his former lover. © Paula Markovitch

something of an existential wall and generates an asymmetrical power dynamic after her pregnancy. The initially perceived rejection by Lucas is now revealed to have been groundless. As a result, the single motherhood reaffirms the mother's agency, decisiveness, and choice; it is not a result of a deliberate rejection or Lucas' involvement. The father's departure and the mother's physical absence beyond the opening scene in the short film subvert what might be seen as a recalibration toward the traditional family. Markovitch does not 'repair' the familial rupture by permanently supplementing Marilina's and her mother's social unit with the father.

Música de ambulancia

Música de ambulancia tells the story of a terminally ill mother and her adult daughter (Cecilia) during the mother's final days. Confined largely to a small apartment, the characters face the imminent outcome through a combination of care, frustration, fatigue, and affection. Pablo, however, interrupts their wait. As an in-home nurse, he visits to administer an intravenous drug for the mother. Yet the medical visit takes an unexpected turn. Pablo fails to provide the required medication, discloses himself as an illegitimate nurse, and engages in a sexual encounter with Cecilia in the apartment's kitchen. It could be said that the short culminates with this encounter – close to three minutes before the short ends – given that the mother's death is imminent from the beginning.

The surprise in *Música de ambulancia* is steeped in the absurdity of existence. Markovitch's focus on absurdity arguably engages with the notion that 'revolt gives life its value' (Camus 1955: 40). The short is moreover sustained by several antithetical experiences: the dying mother ends up being an accidental voyeur of an erotic act but also as a lively participant in subsequent fits of laughter about it. This positionality both affirms and challenges the normative take on the dying as 'removed from common experience and thus arriving at the limit of scientific power and beyond familiar practices, death is an elsewhere' (de Certeau 1980: 192). These interpersonal experiences propel the characters' emotional swings between lighthearted merriment and heavy-handed death. The perceptual engagement of Cecilia and her mother insinuates different psychological and physiological undertones. Laura Marks has identified these multisensory perceptions from a phenomenological vantage point in *The Skin of the Film* (2000) as the 'haptic visuality' of film, which generates 'an appeal to the nonvisual knowledge, embodied knowledge, and experiences of the senses, such as touch, smell, and taste' (Marks 2000: 2). *Música de ambulancia*'s haptic images not only 'respond to the image in an intimate, embodied way, and thus facilitate the experience of other sensory impressions as well', but also show the protagonists' sensorial alertness as a form of interpersonal communication (Marks 2002: 2). At their core, their acuities reinforce two connected manifestations: Cecilia's sensorial alertness mediates the mother's inevitable decay, and the mother's overall medical condition intensifies the daughter's incontestable grief.[5]

The opening scene's shallow focus spotlights Cecilia, who appears to be playing a videogame (Tetris) while wearing headphones, away from the mother's bed. Although sharing the same place, Cecilia momentarily occupies a different space through her videogame. The gadget generates what appears to be a much-needed, if intermittent, respite for the caregiver. As Cecilia remains engrossed in the game, while smoking, the shallow focus prevents us from perceiving her background sharply. This aesthetic choice highlights Cecilia's emotional state: she looks distraught and devoid of excitement, despite the videogame escapades. Yet the background, which is occupied by her ailing mother, is an equally active space. The sounds of the mother struggling to finish vomiting eventually pervade sensorially the entire scene and pull Cecilia back into her physical surroundings. In essence, the act of vomiting dominates the initial seconds of the short because it is the only sound the viewer hears. In *Aroma: The Cultural History of Smell* (1994), Constance Classen states that smells relentlessly transgress nearly all hindrances. Smells, writes Classen, 'cross boundaries, linking disparate categories and confusing boundary lines' (1994: 205). As the vomit is expelled and hits one of the books near the mother's bed, Cecilia reacts as well. Given that 'smell resists containment in discreet units', one wonders if the vomit odor – not the sound that the mother produces – reengages Cecilia with her immediate surroundings (Howes 2022: 9). One could argue that the short's odoriferous dimension disrupts the opening scene's shallow focus and sets the tone for these characters' particular togetherness. As the camera zooms in on the daughter cleaning the vomit from the book above the kitchen sink, the viewer detects the vomitus color and texture and might further consider its odor. Classen sustains that an odor renders as a multilayered sense across different cultures and contexts. An odor, elucidates Classen, 'may signify sanctity or sin, political power or social exclusion' (1997: 402). *Música de ambulancia* implies visually, emotionally – and perhaps odorously – that its *mise-en-scène* of a vividly sensorial texture signals a search for an authentic representation of affliction that supersedes or transcends words.

In *The Body in Pain: The Making and Unmaking of the World* (1985), Elaine Scarry has written about physical pain and its inexpressibility. For Scarry, '[p]hysical pain does not simply resist language but actively destroys it' (4). Scarry attends to the fact that physical pain reduces one to 'the sounds and cries', thus effectively breaking language-based articulations (1985: 4). When the ability of speech is nonexistent, suggests Scarry, 'the language for pain' is expressed by others (6). Scarry's observations are worthy citing at length:

> Because the person in pain is ordinarily so bereft of the resources of speech, it is not surprising that the language for pain should sometimes be brought into being by those who are not themselves in pain but who speak *on behalf of* those who are. Though there are very great impediments to expressing another's sentient distress, so are there also very great reasons why one might want to do so, and thus there come to be avenues

by which this most radically private of experiences begins to enter the realm of public discourse. (Scarry 1984: 6, original emphasis)

The notion of speaking in aid and on behalf of those who are unable to utter their pain is rendered sensorially in Markovitch's short. Indeed, Markovitch zooms in on certain senses of the two characters to supplement the visible but also to emphasize inarticulable anguish. The gravitas of the mother's overall circumstances is indisputably made clear through her routine: we rarely see her beyond her bed except for one debilitated and slow walk to the bathroom. The daughter's incessant alertness via her touch, sight, and perception of the mother's sounds highlights the breakage of language and the simultaneous strengthening of their sensescape.

As mentioned, the solemnity of the mother's final days is intensified most potently through smell. Diane Ackerman enumerates writers – such as Proust, Woolf, Joyce, Dostoevsky, Flaubert, Thoreau, Baudelaire, Whitman, and Miłosz, among others – who are 'attuned to smells' to awaken their readers' olfactory sensations textually (Ackerman 2011: 15). In contrast, Markovitch uses a layered olfactory imagery. Without dwelling in language, which might lead to what Scarry calls 'impediments to expressing another's sentient distress', different olfactory sources (cigarette smoke, piles of dirty dishes, human vomit) merge in the short to indicate as well as interrogate each characters' emotional state and shed light on the ceaseless pain (1985: 6). Odor, highlights David Howes, 'being by nature personal and local, enables olfactory values to be used to reinforce social intimacy and distancing' (2002: 9). Cecilia smokes frantically, her mother vomits limply, and Pablo's visit adds an unexpected odor of sweat and desire. All these actions visually insinuate forceful odors and amplify unprecedented and minutest instantiations of social closeness (Cecilia and her mother) as well as emotional detachment (Cecilia and Pablo never reunite). 'Smell', explains Ackerman in *A Natural History of the Senses* (1990), 'is the mute sense, the one without words. Lacking a vocabulary, we are left tongue-tied, groping for words in a sea of inarticulate pleasure and exaltation' (6). The main characters' odorous participation generates what Jim Drobnick, in a different context, calls 'polyodorous' dimension to frame the inescapable lightness of dying in *Música de ambulancia* (Drobnick 2005: 277).

The mother's steady path toward death through immobility and inertia remains abundantly multisensorial without any direct cultural contextualization. This scene could be happening anywhere. It is only when Cecilia heads to the nearby pharmacy – in a futile search for more morphine to alleviate the mother's anguish – that the cultural setting reveals itself to be in the capital of Mexico. As the pharmacist refuses to issue another medicine without a prescription, socioeconomic and existential questions emerge: Is the lack of a prescription symptomatic of a class difference? What is the relationship between dignity and the mother's stay at home during her last days? Is her hospice-like setting at home part of the mother's conscious wish? How do these women's agentic capacities factor in when basic painkillers are unattainable for the terminally ill? How do we think about dignified ways of dying? These (and other) questions animate the short until its end, even though Cecilia nervously explains to the visiting nurse that 'we don't like being in the hospital because the floors smell bad, right?' ('[no] nos gusta estar en el hospital porque huelen mal los pisos, ¿verdad?'). Although inspired by the loss of her own mother, Markovitch's treatment of the bedbound mother character appeals to the universal conception of human powerlessness before the imminent death. More broadly, furthermore, their makeshift hospice setting also draws attention to the role of gender in caregiving when sociocultural and economic options are scant.[6]

Several other memorable bed-ridden characters in Latin American films have embodied a rich repertoire of implications and symbolism, ranging from Perichona's entombment in the attic in María Luisa Bemberg's *Camila* (1985); the Guatemalan genocide (1982–83) perpetrator's guilt-prompted, phantasmagorical, and besieged bed-ridden existence in Jayro Bustamante's

La llorona (2019); an Indigenous marriage breakup in Alvaro Delgado Aparicio's *Retablo* (2017); and Mecha's bed-bound alcoholic existence in Lucrecia Martel's *La ciénaga* (2001). Although we could draw analytical parallels between *Música de ambulancia* and all these films to some extent, the bedbound existence in *La ciénaga* is particularly relevant. While the social relations around the mother in Markovitch's *Música de ambulancia* differ radically from those around Mecha's alcohol-debilitated life in *La ciénaga*, both characters are trapped in illness and consequently restricted those around them to a different degree. Indeed, David Oubiña has said that *La ciénaga* underscores Martel's exploration of 'the clashes between bodies, [which] are always violent, but it is not possible to discern how much of [those clashes] is attack and how much is attraction' ('[l]os choques entre los cuerpos son siempre violentos, pero no es posible discernir cuánto hay de ataque y cuánto de atracción') (Oubiña 2007: 38). Departing from Oubiña's and Ana Amado's discussions of Martel's feature debut, Jens Andermann in *New Argentine Cinema* (2012) reads the film's meticulous focus on both bedbound and mobile bodies as a mechanism that 'determines narrative progression or stagnation' (79). Similarly, Deborah Martin crafts a Freudian reading of Mecha's restriction to her bed, explaining that 'the compulsion to repeat, alongside a primary masochism or primitive urge to return to an originary state is a feature of the death drive, evoked in the film in particular by Mecha's seemingly inevitable retreat to her bed' (2017: 40). Mecha's drinking-induced immobility keeps the family ensnared as well. Most of them are at the mercy of her fiery whims and are witnesses to or victims of her discrimination through racist remarks aimed at her domestic help in general and Isabel in particular.[7]

Unlike the vociferous surroundings of Mecha's bed through Martel's singular work with sound (Oubiña 2007; Martin 2017; Forcinito 2018; and Gemünden 2019), the setting in *Música de ambulancia* remains excruciatingly quiet but sensorially thunderous. Surrounded by books and paintings on the apartment walls, the bedbound mother's presence is equally forceful despite her silence. The mother's moans of illness, inability to speak, and unfocused gaze only serve to intensify a touch-based connection with her daughter. Several scenes are likewise sequenced to instantiate the daughter's care and love through hapticity: Cecilia caresses the mother's almost lifeless toes late into the night, hugs her while watching TV in bed, and falls asleep, fatigued, either next to or over the mother's ill body. As they share the same bed, their touch-based interaction facilitates their communication but also reinforces their closeness, frustration, confusion, and grief.

That said, Markovitch approaches the act of dying in somewhat unexpected ways. She does so in contrast to what de Certeau discusses in his seminal *The Practice of Everyday Life* (1980) when he explains that it 'is *necessary* that the dying man remain *calm* and *rest*. Beyond the care and the sedatives required by the sick man, this order appeals to the staff's inability to *bear* the uttering of anguish, despair, or pain: it must not be *said*' (de Certeau 1980: 190, original emphasis). By highlighting all five senses, the short often relies on a non-verbal interface between the mother and daughter as a glimpse into their complex emotional states. Reflecting on Michel Serres' observation about the dying, namely 'intolerance of the exteriority represented by death and degradation', Steven Connor comments that 'there is nothing anyone can do with it, this slow going, this ungraspable, unknowable, unignorable squandering of energy that in the end is what we will have amounted to. There is nothing we can do with it, though it has everything to do with us' (Connor 2005: 333). Markovitch's *Música de ambulancia* puts a twist on this existential powerlessness. While the short concentrates on the dying character's daily suffering, the 'unignorable' outcome becomes unexpectedly lighthearted and frivolous as well. Just as the mother's worsening condition becomes palpable through her increasingly heavy breathing and lifeless body, Cecilia's impromptu erotic encounter with Pablo produces its own blustery gasps. This incongruous juxtaposition, in the tight space of the apartment, of the relief of a sexual encounter and the tension of pending death, is a unique paradox and surprise.

The subsequent scene, however, takes the astonishment to the next level when the mother awakens and bursts into laughter with Cecilia about the erotic encounter. 'You made him feel nervous' ('Lo pusiste nervioso'), utters the mother, while referring to Pablo's seemingly quick departure after their erotic encounter. Their laughter, as an attempt at lightheartedness amid this existential impasse, takes over the gravitas of their everyday life and even reverses their roles, albeit fleetingly (Fig. 2.2). As Cecilia lands on the mother's bed in spasms of laughter, we watch the mother hold Cecilia as if she were a newborn. This moment seems to challenge what de Certeau discusses as an antithesis of life. 'The dying are outcasts', writes de Certeau, 'because they are deviants in an institution organized by and for the conservation of life. An "anticipated mourning," a phenomenon of institutional rejection, puts them away in advance in "the dead man's room;" it surrounds them with silence or, worse yet, with lies that protect the living against the voice that would break out of this enclosure to cry' (1980: 190). The haptic and emotional warmth of the short's sequences – the women hug as they convulse in

Figure 2.2 The characters exhibit their fragile attempts at levity. © Paula Markovitch

joyfulness – reinscribes death. The mother and her daughter are together in affection and anguish; in physical pain and emotional foreboding; in quiet infirmity and frantic attempts at levity.

While illness harnesses the relationship between an adult daughter and her dying mother in sensorially multidimensional ways in *Música de ambulancia*, vitality does the same and bonds the mother and her young daughter in *Marilina*. Yet caregiving and sensorial interdependency are at the heart of both shorts. While the whereabouts and role of the father are never explained in *Música de ambulancia*, the father's role is crystallized surprisingly and unexpectedly in *Marilina*. The existential weight of the mother–daughter relationship in *Música de ambulancia* also highlights the politics of smell, that is, 'how olfaction is mobilized in the interest of social inclusion and exclusion' (Howes 2022: 9). Markovitch intensifies subjectivities that are normatively perceived as socially othered (the dying) or socio-culturally vulnerable (single mothers) to refuse reducing them to their most obvious and unquestionably burdensome attributes.

Notes

1 *Marilina* was filmed in 2001 and continues to be unreleased.
2 Milanich unpacks certain unintended consequences and states that '[p]utting fathers at the center of public policies concerning family is a welcome departure from the usual focus on mothers, but it has paradoxical effects. Responsible paternity policies often assert that children without legal fathers lack a true identity. Together with this distinctly patrilineal understanding of self, the policies also reinforce a narrow, biogenetic definition of paternity. Promoting the centrality of the father also tends to assume that a two-parent, heteronormative household is the ideal. This conception is at odds with contemporary society: In [sic] Latin America today, there is growing recognition of same sex union and rising divorce rates. More important, this vision does not reflect the lives of poor and working-class Latin Americans, whose families are often non-biological, non-nuclear, and female-headed' (2017: 12).
3 Inspired by French puppeteer Philippe Genty and his *marionnette portée*, Lucas' puppet (Fabiola de Aragón) belongs to Argentine puppeteer Javier Swedzky. Swedzky is cast as Lucas in the short. I am thankful to Swedsky

for his interview about Fabiola de Aragón and puppet theater in general on 26 July 2024.
4 See Inela Selimović, 'Sensorial Youths: Gender, Eroticism and Agency in Lucrecia Martel's *Rey muerto* (1995),' In *New Visions of Adolescence in Contemporary Latin American Cinema*, eds., Geoffrey Maguire and Rachel Randall, 81–98. Cham: Palgrave Macmillan, 2018.
5 See Mark Smith (2007: 4).
6 See the United Nations' 'Ageing in Latin America and the Caribbean: Inclusion and Rights of Older Persons.' ECLAC Santiago, 13–15 December 2022. https://repositorio.cepal.org/server/api/core/bitstreams/703b8179-ba9d-4838-8ec1-61405dbcbd18/content. Accessed 4 May 2024.
7 These and other critics have linked such social entombment in and around Mecha's bed to the country's postdictatorial tensions (Forcinito 2018), patriarchal dominion (Martin 2017); affective presence and retributions (Selimović 2018a) but also as an interrogation of the 'foundational fiction of contemporary Argentine national identity' (Gemünden 2019: 44).

3

El premio (2011): Affect and Political Resocialization

El premio (2011), which was nominated for over 30 awards, focuses on displaced childhood as a potent medium of the unspeakable. The unspeakable, as a sociopolitical subtext, is easily detectable in the film as it reveals unambiguously what Tavid Mulder calls 'the indelible, harrowing mark left by the *Proceso de Reorganización Nacional*' (2014: 183). Critics have also studied such a 'mark' regarding the figure of the child in aesthetically conventional or innovative Argentine films, including Gastón Biraben's *Cautiva* (2005), Daniel Bustamante's *Andrés no quiere dormir la siesta* (2009), Sabrina Farji's *Eva y Lola* (2010), Benjamin Ávila's *Infancia clandestina* (2011), as well as Markovitch's *El premio*.[1] Unlike most of these films, *El premio*, set in 1977, marginalizes the violent acts of the historical period in question, thus allowing an invisible and psychosocial presence of such acts to pervade the main characters' lives in affectively persistent ways.

Markovitch makes this presence palpable by focusing on the child's need to resocialize. The protagonist's resocialization – that is, an ad hoc crafted and falsified 'presentation' of herself 'to others' but also of her parents' livelihood in public – is conducted under her mother's careful guidance and serves to mask the family's origin, professions, and political persuasions (Goffman 1959: xi). This kind of resocialization demands that the seven-year-old child enters intersubjective exchanges alert, cautious, and self-censoring. Such conduct, in turn, invades the diegetic territory of *El premio* with a tense, apprehensive, and persistent discomfort within nearly every social encounter. The initial stages of her resocialization stay emotionally taxing, evoking the tension that imbues the notion of 'structures of feeling' (Williams 1977: 132). Raymond Williams argues that 'feeling' stems from the misalliance of 'meanings and values as they are actively lived and felt, and the relations between these and formal or systematic beliefs' (1977: 132). According to Williams, the notion of 'structures of feeling' reveals 'characteristic elements of impulse, restraint, and tone; specifically affective elements of consciousness and relationships: not feeling against thought but thought as felt and feeling as thought: practical consciousness of a present kind, in a living and interrelating continuity' (1977: 132). The child's 'felt' emotional discomfort is manifested affectively because of her constantly coached ways of feeling regarding social settings away from home.

At its most basic level, affect, explain Melissa Gregg and Gregory Seigworth in *The Affect Theory Reader* (2010), presents as a multidirectional matrix of unfixed intensities. For these critics, affect '*accumulates* across both relatedness and interruptions in relatedness, becoming a palimpsest of force-encounters traversing the ebbs and swells of intensities that pass between "bodies"' (Gregg and Seigworth 2010: 2, original emphasis). In *El premio*, affect swells up through the child's tense intersubjectivities while hardly ever failing to capture what Roland Barthes calls 'the microscopic fragment of emotion' (Barthes quoted in Gregg and Seigworth 2010: 10). The film, therefore, engages affect, emotion, and feeling in distinct ways through what Brian Massumi describes as asymmetrical links. As a theoretical nod to Baruch Spinoza's postulations on affect through bodies' capacity to affect and be affected, Massumi clarifies that affect and emotion are not indistinguishable, since affect 'is this passing of a threshold, seen from the point of view of the change in capacity' (2015: 4). For Massumi, moreover, 'the affect and the feeling of the transition are not two different things. They are two sides of the same coin, just like affecting and being affected' (2015: 4). In this symbiotic relationship between affect and feeling, emotion manifests as 'a very partial expression of affect' (2015: 5). Seeking to distinguish among these three conceptual categories despite their interconnectedness, Jan Slaby and Rainer Mühlhoff conceptualize affect as '*relational dynamics* between evolving bodies in a setting, thus contrasting with approaches to affect as inner states, feelings, or emotions' (2019: 27, original emphasis). The protagonist's navigations of newly established social ways are, above all, infinitesimally affective, revealing simultaneously certain emotional states that the child feels hesitantly.

This chapter studies the child protagonist's resocialization as an affective process which ultimately reinstates the merging of the child's vulnerabilities with latent, overt, or unintentional dissent, both privately and in public. In calling attention to the child's resocialization, Markovitch's film adds to contemporary debates on socio-individual memory toward the political violence in Argentina (1976–83). *El premio*'s central theme positions itself alongside those of the centrality of the *hijo* and his/her/their 're-signification ... [of] the attributes embedded in his/her parents' militancy' ('resignificación ... [de] las características de la militancia de sus padres') (Borda 2013: 1–2). Markovitch's film sidelines the absent and militant figure of the father by privileging the child's displacement and, above all, her coached feelings. The muddling of the child's familial belonging, through her subsequent resocialization, also might echo what is seemingly absent in the film's familial story, but it arguably might be one of its implicit references to the illegally appropriated childhoods during the Argentine state terror. The film indirectly reminds us that the reappropriations of political dissidents' children, now adults, seem to have recently engendered their own disruptive affect within and around the ongoing constructions of socio-individual memories. With each publicized reappropriation, a new process of mnemonic reconstruction naturally commences on the individual and collective levels. Yet certain mnemonic reconstructions of the reappropriated individuals' lives have recently challenged the core expectations that key human rights organizations have held in Argentina since at least 1983, especially the Abuelas de Plaza de Mayo/Grandmothers of Plaza de Mayo. Infrequent – yet present – responses by some reappropriated children, in the form of suicide, simply disturb and disable (and subtly affect) certain kinds of expectations that are set by the important work of the Abuelas de Plaza de Mayo and other human rights-focused associations in Argentina. The protagonist's compulsory resocializations in *El premio* might function as unlikely but fertile aesthetic territory for reaffirming certain reappropriated adults' resocialization intricacies. *El premio*'s focus on compulsory resocializations reminds viewers and critics alike of the fluidity and precariousness that socio-individual memories inevitably entail regarding the illegally appropriated childhoods – childhoods that were imbued with affective debasement at birth or soon thereafter.

El premio tells the story of the difficult adjustments made during the self-imposed displacement of a second grader, Ceci, and her mother. When the film opens, the spectator meets these characters in a remote, cold, and menacing Argentine beach setting. An abandoned beach hut – a cold and leaky space, with broken windows, doors, and tired furniture – host primarily Ceci's attempt to understand her mother's new ways of living, filled as they are with paranoia, lies, and social precariousness. Ceci's questions and remarks about missing her father – who is absent, seems to have stayed behind in Buenos Aires, and is most likely a disappeared or an active political dissident – are met with fear, concern, and discomfort on her mother's part. Publicly caring for the absent father is a complex and latent feeling; his absence at home is pervasive and persistent. The emotional dialectic that the mother and her child experience toward the husband's/father's absence frames the film's story from the outset in several affective ways, encompassing the characters' relationship to a new and inadequate home setting, their struggles to keep play emotionally spontaneous, and the child's diffident resocializations in public. Being emotionally at odds over the missing father is made manifest privately as genuine emotional care and publicly as emotional inattention.

Constrained play, in essence, opens the film when the camera zooms in on Ceci's peculiar roller-blading efforts through the beach sand. Sinking deep into the wet shore with each stride, the child moves with difficulty alongside the roaring sea. Her movement is encumbered by the ocean waves, its strong winds, and an unsuitable playground, forcing her to drag the rollerblades along the beach, not with her feet, but with her ankles. Before this prolonged first sequence transitions into another – one of the disintegrating beach hut as Ceci's final destination – it offers glimpses into an instance of play that is utterly unsatisfying, frustrating, and affectively morose. Ceci complains upon entering the hut – 'It is impossible to skate here' ('No se puede patinar aquí') – and encountering her mother's struggles to keep the menacing wind gusts from invading their temporary shelter. Ceci's visible sadness is unquestionable. The child sounds defeated, she is half-crying, and she is ignored by her mother. The hostile weather and inadequate domestic arrangements distract the mother's attention from the child's seemingly unimportant needs, thus hinting at the mother's focus on their bare survival now and after the family's political choices in Buenos Aires. The sequence grows increasingly overpowered by the mother's efforts to combat the nature-triggered 'visible forces that are not themselves visible' – that is, the cold air and repetitive slamming of the hut's semi-hinged windows and broken door. Markovitch uses such details of setting to underscore the child's helpless position and the difficulty of the adjustments she must make. Ceci, utterly ignored, stands puzzled and observes. Yet her desire to play persists. She immediately picks up a broken piece of window glass, puts it against her right eye, as if to emulate a spyglass, and mischievously smiles at her mother. The child's desire to engage in spontaneous play remains insistent, generating complex sensations of despair, playfulness, and uncertainty between the two characters from the film's outset.

The cold-ridden, abandoned, and rundown beach hut, consistently plagued by strong ocean winds, dusty storms, and rustiness, further exposes the main characters' existential insecurities. Such insecurities, initially communicated through the characters' silent co-presence, significantly complicate their interpersonal communication, turning it frequently entropic. This interpersonal chaos emerges due to the mother's dependence on her child's abilities to resocialize swiftly and persuasively, thus inverting what typically might be considered the child's social dependence on her parents' care, protection, and support. Such an inversion of social dependence between the two central characters immediately points to Ceci's peculiar emotional state of incomplete belonging, whether at home or in public. She whiningly demands, 'I want to go home' ('Quiero ir a casa'), often confronting her mother's phlegmatic stare at the precarious hut. Suggestively saturated with gray and brown tones, their unsafe diegetic setting mirrors the characters' displacement – they both sleep in the same squeaking cot, the cold obliges them to sleep fully dressed, their radio does not work, and the plastic on the broken windows mutters distressingly against the wind.

Their immediate surroundings affect them just as they both seek to affect rudimentarily their new refuge, attempting to turn it into a habitable space. Echoing Spinoza's writing on affect and body, Massumi reiterates that

> every affect is a doubling. The experience of a change, an affecting-being affected, is redoubled by an experience of the experience. This gives the body's movements a kind of depth that stays with it across all its transitions—accumulating in memory, in habit, in reflex, in desire, in tendency. Emotion is the way the depth of that ongoing experience registers personally at a given moment. (2015: 4)

If these opening scenes straightforwardly capture the characters' sense of despair, they also underscore a new form of being 'redoubled' that embodies a degree of '*in-between-ness* and resides as accumulative *beside-ness*' (Gregg and Seigworth 2010: 2, original emphasis). Physically cut off from Buenos Aires, even by means of their radio, the mother and Ceci reluctantly begin to reside 'more intensely' for the sake of (or due to) their bare survival (Massumi 2015: 3). Their now deeply affective cohabitation requires emotional stamina at home and in the public arena. Such modes of cohabitation generate complex emotional responses of sadness, anger, contentment, fear, but also joy in Ceci's young self. By underscoring these resocialization processes as being at odds with the child's emotional needs, most social encounters remain bound to self-censorship. If affect can echo 'not what something is, but how it is,' then *El premio* frames the child's compulsory resocialization around intractably disruptive affect (Shaviro quoted in Gregg and Seigworth 2010: 14).

Disruption intricately signifies 'the action of rending or bursting asunder; violent dissolution of continuity; forcible severance' (Oxford Dictionary 453). Such qualities are relevant to the kind of childhood with which Markovitch endows Ceci by placing her in a setting invisibly plagued by the political violence of the 1970s. The filmmaker indeed focuses on the ways in which disruption becomes a ubiquitous element of the protagonist's young self, echoing the ways in which, during Argentine state terror, 'violence and trauma percolated through the various levels of society. Crowds were traumatized, and so were the military, the guerrillas, the captives, and the families. Even the lives of people who remained far from the political turbulence were affected' (Robben 2005: 345). To go home, as Ceci frequently demands, would mean literally walking into a place closer to 'the political turbulence,' in Antonius Robben's terms. At the same time, staying displaced offers inadequate protection from adults' politically uncertain and embattled worlds. The resulting tension finds expression in Ceci's attempts to play. 'Children,' explains Walter Benjamin, 'produce their own small world of things within the greater one' (2004: 449–50). When the film begins, 'the greater world' – Ceci's life in Buenos Aires, her intact family, and her home – collapses, which also abruptly dismantles much of Ceci's then-'small world.' And the displacement quite plainly complicates Ceci's play. 'It is impossible to skate here,' Ceci's first phrase in the film, evokes an action she performed elsewhere with ease. The film, in fact, features Ceci's displacement as a key barrier to her reimagining of play. 'The essence of the play,' continues Benjamin, 'is not to "act as if" but an "always do it again," transforming the most moving experience in habit' (Benjamin 2004: 102). For Benjamin, sustaining play for children rests on the firming up of their 'small world' – repetition transforms a single action into a continuously organic pattern.

Yet the most 'moving experiences in habit' in *El premio* are assaulted by imposed self-censorship. Such self-censorship-imbued experiences remain emotionally strenuous. Given the circumstances the child faces with her mother in displacement, the foundation for 'the small world' remains unsettled, confusing, and averse to genuine play. Even so, Ceci is starved for play, and she seeks it, above all, at home. Being affected by these new circumstances also instigates the child's both unintentional and deliberate affect. Ceci's instances of play are effectively affective, as noted earlier, so long as one reads them in accordance with Spinoza's conceptualizations of affect. For Spinoza, put simply and as paraphrased by Massumi, affect and the body connect in mutually reaffirming ways – bodies can be affected and produce affect (Massumi 2015: 3). The mother's behavior in fact, positions the child affectively in a complex oscillation between two vastly different social and emotional roles. Ceci constantly fluctuates between, on the one hand, being a seven-year-old rightfully dependent upon adults in her life for food, cleanliness, home, and parental protection, and, on the other hand, being an accomplice to subversive adult undertakings (i.e., book burial, adopting the false narrative regarding her father's whereabouts, changing her school essay at the expense of the lived truth). Such oscillations both affirm and unsettle the girl's marginalized ways of being and engender certain innocent subversions on her part. Two instances of such transgressions come to mind immediately: Ceci's frequent mischief to undermine her mother's authority at home and Ceci's efforts to affect the consequences of nature's invasion of their hut through play.

The first such instance is related to a quick trip Ceci makes with her mother to bury several books in the nearby dunes. When they both arrive at a secluded cave-like opening on the beach, the mother begins to dig in the wet and heavy sand. Ceci, in a diligent way, wraps the books in plastic as if she were wrapping up gifts and hands them to her distressed mother. In this sequence, as previously noted, Ceci fluctuates between being a playful kid and being a serious adult-like dissident. Ceci's playfulness comes forth when she asks her mother if she could bury one of her books as well, referring to a book for children with little political threat. 'Play,' according to Sharon Stephens, 'requires some measure of physical safety or at least the possibility of dangers selectively and voluntarily undertake. The imagined boundaries of play worlds should not be subject to sudden violent disruptions from adult society' (1995: 33). When Ceci's mother responds in a short-tempered way – 'Stop messing around!' ('¡Déjate de joder!') – the spectator witnesses an example of aborted play and the harsh displacing of the child from her playful state into what is a much more serious and, more importantly, dangerous act. Upon hearing the mother's answer, Ceci slips into her assigned role again and begins to hand over the books that demand secrecy and clandestine undertakings in silence.

The second example is related to nature's rapid invasion of their hut. When the winter surf brings the ocean to the doors of the hut, the mother is forced to fight back rather primitively with a big broom. The framing gains ominousness as the mother fights the water, sending it over the threshold just as quickly as the water advances. The quick, almost incessant moves with the broom communicate a subject wracked with pain, desperation, and helplessness. Standing and jumping on a squeaky bed, Ceci observes her mother's efforts and ultimately makes her way to the closed window. Positioned at the threshold that stands between the stormy outdoors and equally threatening indoor environment, the little girl engages with the peril from above, remaining somewhat protected. This physical positioning reinforces her role as an affective agent, thus producing the intense mélange of her fears, desire to play, confusion, and awe. Annette Kuhn calls this kind of liminality that children practice 'going exploring,' specifying that 'the home's edges – its boundaries and its borders between inner and outer, its thresholds – may lastingly assume special emotional and imaginational weight' (2010: 86). Although this hut may not be considered the protagonist's 'home,' this moment also insists on perceiving the hut as an intricate terrain for Ceci's play.

This sequence also reminds us of Albertina Carri's *La rabia* (2008) and its child character's production of 'retributive affect' (Selimović 2015: 517). If the pampas' physical openness and size ironically communicate the sense of emotional enclosement for Nati and her mother in Carri's *La rabia*, then the ocean breadth in Markovitch's *El premio* threatens with a literal asphyxiation. In both cases, the inner selves of the child characters fight against their psychological capitulation through moments of play. Unintentionally, perhaps, their play-focused attempts generate not only their own affect bodily, but also an affective dissent before the adults' constraints. According to Massumi, a 'body is defined by what capacities it carries from step to step, [w]hat these are exactly is changing constantly. A body's ability to affect or be affected, its charge of affect is not something fixed' (2015: 4). Nati intensifies her autistic compulsions as well as drawings, while Ceci engages in play through jumps and laughs. As Ceci observes, rebels against, or attempts to collaborate with her mother as part of their new survival tactics, her non-autistic subjectivity actively fluctuates between the territories of vulnerable children and those of cunning adults. The child's age, mischief, and oneiric settings ultimately emphasize the non-absolutist social attributes that the filmmaker assigns to the feeling child in *El premio* as she seeks to affect her immediate circumstances, above all, with play.

Playing is nonetheless doubly scripted and performative in public spaces in *El premio* (Fig. 3.1). Play with Ceci's peers, in fact, becomes almost entirely scripted regarding her family matters. Play, for Ceci, is another dimension where her resocialized self must be displayed performatively. When Ceci begins to attend classes in a nearby village school, she is rigorously coached to share a prefabricated story about her absent father. In a rather frantic mode, before Ceci attends her first day of school, her mother grabs the little girl's face and demands that she memorize how to speak about her parents. The daughter

El premio: Affect and Political Resocialization   75

Figure 3.1 Ceci and Silvia play outside of class. © Paula Markovitch

accepts her scripted lines reluctantly, leaving the mother in a state of anguish and uncertainty. Yet this new responsibility also signals the engendering of Ceci's fragile agency. By being displaced from her own familiar living circumstances in Buenos Aires, but not officially in exile, Ceci is instantly compelled to adjust to new ways of being that are largely out of sync with her true familial identity. Somewhat like Ernesto/Juan's familial responsibilities in *Infancia clandestina*, Markovitch's child protagonist must perform the false-life narrative persuasively to protect her family.

The seriousness of the mother's demands stays intact in the girl's consciousness, especially when she is at play with her peers. Ceci's nascent friendship with one of the village girls, Silvia, accentuates the girls' social togetherness affectively because it remains besieged by Ceci's compulsory resocializations. The camera follows them to and from school as they spontaneously play in the dunes or quibble at school. Their interactions ooze with the potential for closeness, comfort, and cheerful intersubjective exchanges. When Silvia, toward the middle of the film asks 'Where is your house?', Ceci becomes robotically guarded and answers, 'My dad sells curtains and my mom is a housewife' ('¿Dónde está tu casa? Mi papá vende cortinas y mi mamá es ama de casa'). Ceci's insistence on repeating the same answer verbatim to Silvia's tweaked yet continuingly insistent questions, underscores Ceci's social courage as well as vulnerabilities.

The child's coached feelings must be well-established to make for a convincing performance during the award ceremony for her winning literary essay. These sequences in the film take the notion of resocialization to its extreme. Ceci's initially submitted draft to the teacher uproots her mother urgently and results in her inappropriate visit in the wee hours to the teacher's home. The adults, Ceci's mother and teacher, confront the little girl by simply urging her to change her essay and to filter in falsehood before it gets submitted to the military. Ceci's irreverent perceptions of the military in her essay compromise the teacher's security as well. The literary competition, which is instituted for the sake of praising the military, serves as the most overt platform for Ceci's resocialization in the film. The teacher, Rosita, welcomes Sergeant Estévez, who explains the reason behind the literary competition: 'the army organized a big competition. You will write pretty words about our army and will have to draw a picture of our flag' ('el ejército organizó un gran concurso. Deberán escribir las palabras bonitas sobre nuestro ejército y tendrán que hacer un dibujo de nuestra bandera'). The child's basic ethnography on repressive modes at home and school pours out into her initial essay draft in a way that is perilously uncensored. When Ceci's mother asks, 'How many times have I told you not to say it?,' Ceci responds candidly and in defense of what had not been rehearsed, 'I didn't say it, I wrote it. It's different to write than to say' ('¿Cuántas veces te he dicho que no lo dijeras. No lo dije, lo escribí. Es distinto escribir que decir'). By center-staging Ceci's rebellious piece, the filmmaker succeeds in showing that, as Karen Lury suggests in *The Child in Film: Tears, Fears, and Fairy Tales* (2010), 'children *want* and they *act*, and they should therefore be considered *agents* as well as subjects' (2010: 308, original emphasis). In addition to revealing tart humor, the child's distinction between saying and writing embodies the delicate sensibility of her agentic self, particularly as she attempts to understand her mother's coaching or lack thereof.

The corrected version ultimately positions Ceci at the heart of the school award ceremony, which the military representatives attend, where she accepts an award. Markovitch exposes the inner contradiction the little girl feels by focusing on her physical discomfort: she rarely smiles, her body is limp, and she lacks any genuine expression of happiness. 'Small children,' as Vicky Lebeau relevantly states, 'have many more perceptions than they have terms to translate them' (2008: 16). Much of the little girl's genuine state of mind in this sequence remains unavailable to those around her. Yet based on recent resocialization in the places she frequents, Ceci's judgement of social behavior must be equally appropriate. Ceci must know how to feel publicly. 'A feeling subject – not necessarily intentionally – selects from the coming information that affects him [or her],' observes Ed S. Tan and continues, 'something that matters, something that immediately and spontaneously strikes him [or her] as significant' (2011: 16). This social acuity in the film reinforces the protagonist's agency – that is, the 'responsibility of children facing a political situation of crime, perhaps regardless of their cognitive preparedness or emotional maturity ('responsibilidad de los niños frente a la situación política de crímen') (Markovitch 2015: n.p.).[2] During the award ceremony, the affective presence of the military, the mother's coaching, and the reasons for the competition keep Ceci's otherwise-mischievous spirit performatively focused, firm, and trapped. Yet the little girl ultimately knows that her award is as false as the topic she develops in her essay, for it functions simultaneously as an emotional punishment at home and as a farcical success at school. The submitted and prize-winning essay also becomes an indelible, even if fabricated, form of rebellion that she unwillingly instigates against, above all, the mother. Upon bringing the award home, Ceci can only ask her mother for forgiveness in sadness.

Although the child – and her mother – remain(s) at the heart of different psychological terrors in *El premio*, the film avoids falling into a clichéd trap of considering Ceci and her mother 'the most vulnerable victims of society' in violent times

(Rocha and Garcés 2010: xxix). Markovitch has straightforwardly remarked upon the opposite: 'when there is a situation of crime, it affects all of us' ('cuando hay una situación de crímen, nos atraviesa a todos') (Markovitch 2015: n.p.).[3] The filmmaker also does not leave the spectator with the impression of children 'as autonomous and outside of the reach of adults' (Wilson 2007: 170). On the contrary, through the failed or scripted playing, Ceci remains affected by – but also affects – the political shadows of the adult world. Brimming with a free-spirited subjectivity amid the political repression, Ceci's character facilitates the formation of an affective platform for revealing the political dreadfulness, trauma, and violence. Lury's remarks become relevant again for 'the child figure does not, or cannot, provide authority on the facts of war, yet the representations of its experience as visceral, as of and on the body, demonstrate how the interweaving of history, memory, and witness can be powerfully affective' (2010: 7). Keeping this in mind, Ceci's age, curiosity, play, and mischievousness nonetheless mediate the political climate in an imprecise yet affectively palpable way.

Although inspired by the filmmaker's childhood during Argentine state terror, the film omits any straightforward "remedial" materials about the era in question (Selimović 2016: 422). At the same time, *El premio* refuses to omit the contextual details that drive its plot potently, even when, as noted, the implied violence remains visually absent. Unlike Luis Puenzo's *La historia oficial*, Gastón Biraben's *Cautiva*, or Peter Sanders' *The Disappeared*, Markovitch's *El premio* is not about the well-known and ongoing reappropriations of political dissidents' kidnapped children, whose childhood had been illegally appropriated during the state terror era. Unlike Cristina/Sofía in Biraben's *Cautiva*, Ceci is not an illegally appropriated child. Yet Ceci's unavoidable resocializations in *El premio* might echo the ongoing complexities that reappropriation efforts have inevitably entailed in Argentina. Elaborating on the 1983 report, *Nunca Más/Never Again*, which specifies that close to 500 babies were illegally adopted from detained, tortured, and subsequently murdered female political dissidents, Michael Lazzara explains that

> most babies were taken at birth and the mother forced to write a letter with instructions to the 'adoptive' parents. Soon thereafter, the mother would be drugged and dropped into the ocean from military planes. The babies were subsequently placed either with military families or families sympathetic to the military's cause and given false names – and false documentation – that sought to erase any trace of their biological origins. (2013: 320)

Playing sinisterly with these children's biological origins was part of the Argentine state terror's campaigns of 'systemic nature' against the political opposition, just as recovering the same children's biological origins continues to unfold in complex, unfinished, and intricate ways. The Grandmothers of Plaza de Mayo/Abuelas de Plaza de Mayo, which has initiated legal dealings with the kidnapped children at home and internationally, has recovered (as of June 2025) 139 kidnapped children. Such political activism garnered additional support particularly in the mid-1990s when many members of the Sons and Daughters for Identity and Justice Against Forgetting and Silence (Hijos por la Identidad y la Justicia contra el Olvido (H.I.J.O.S.)) took on a more active role alongside the Abuelas de Plaza de Mayo in 'actively orchestrating media campaigns to find the stolen children' (Lazzara 2013: 322). As Lazzara insightfully argues, biological reunions have led to complex reactions among the reappropriated, including both those who have engaged wholeheartedly with their biological origins and those who have rejected such possibilities altogether or to various degrees.

Although infrequent, some resocialization processes among the reappropriated adults have ended fatally.[4] If 1982 marks the Abuelas de Plaza de Mayo's initial legal success regarding the illegal babies' reappropriations, 2011 and 2015 add another layer to these already complex resocialization processes through the revelation of suicides among the reappropriated adults or their biological family members. The loss of legally reappropriated adults, their siblings, or other family members – such as

Virginia Ogando, 38; Pablo Genmin Athanasiu Laschan, 39; and Heman Emilio Calogerópulos, 40 – provides another kind of insight regarding these individuals' resocializations publicly. Ogando committed suicide on August 16th, 2011 – that is, four years before her own brother Martin was finally reappropriated. Ogando's note before the suicide related her weariness from failing to find her brother.[5] Laschan was the 109th reappropriated grandchild, and his parents disappeared when he was five months old in 1974. Laschan's parents were Chilean militants and active against Augusto Pinochet in Chile before their arrival in Buenos Aires in March of 1974. Their militant involvement in Argentina was brief for they were kidnapped in April of 1976. Their only son, Laschan, was reappropriated in August of 2013. Two years later he was found dead in Buenos Aires, apparently by reason of suicide. Calogerópulos committed suicide in 2015. Like Ogando and her involvement with social justice movements, Calogerópulos was an active member of H.I.J.O.S. He was the son of Ramón Demetria Calogerópulos, who had disappeared in September of 1976. Calogerópulos repeatedly expressed his inability to integrate socially in his own town (Campana) given the public knowledge of his parents' political dissent.[6] Without falling into any reductive inference regarding the reasons for their deaths, one might contemplate the ways in which these suicides engender intricate responses to the dictatorial kidnappings, illegal appropriations of political dissidents' children, and brutal disappearances of political dissidents. Indeed, such cases have broadened the complexity of the Abuelas de Plaza de Mayo's ongoing human rights efforts, thus further expanding 'questions about whose human rights should be upheld in the aftermath of state-sponsored violence' (Lazzara 2013: 331).

These adults' suicides, which are intimately tied to the reappropriating processes, generate a peculiar instance of 'affective politics,' especially if the latter is 'an art of emitting the interruptive signs, triggering the cues, that attune bodies while activating their capacities differently' (Massumi 2015: 56). Legally obliged to respond to the National Commission for Identity Rights

(CONADI) and the 2007 DNA Law, the reappropriated children and their family members, such as Ogando, Laschan, and Calogerópulos, signal radically singular responses. Their suicides erect their absences rather affectively within 'the debate [that] pitted the rights to identity against the rights to privacy' (Lazzara 2015: 329). These newly stimulated deaths add an additional layer to the already intricate dealings with the human rights campaigns in question. 'Affective politics is inductive,' reiterates Massumi and clarifies, 'bodies can be inducted into, or attuned to, certain regions of tendency, futurity and potential, they can be induced into inhabiting the same affective environment, even if there is no assurance they will act alike in that environment' (Massumi 2015: 57). The differently manifested reactions among the reappropriated children and their family members indeed exemplify the lack of 'assurance' regarding a homogenous approach toward the ongoing resocializations.

The final sequences in *El premio* frame the child protagonist alone on a gray and windy beach day. The same sequences emblematically generate an affective clash between personal feelings and public demands as it zooms in on Ceci without her parents and after the multilayered resocialization processes she struggles to understand. 'Feeling,' Paul Ricoeur reminds us,

> is without doubt intentional: it is a feeling of 'something' – the loveable, the hateful, [...] But it is a very strange intentionality which on the one hand designates qualities felt on things, on persons, on the world, and on the other hand manifests and reveals the way in which the self is inwardly affected. (1967: 127)

The final moments of the film complexly clash feelings and affect through two emotionally wounded and interconnected selfhoods. More precisely, the spectator hears the mother crying uncontrollably in the background and sees the child facing away from the mother's sobbing in confusion. An affective clash seals the final moment of the film through the juxtaposition of the mother's irrepressible feelings (despair, anguish, and frustration), which paradoxically accompany – but also accentuate – the intensity of Ceci's confused self. This affective clash *cuts* beyond *El premio's* diegetic world, reminding spectators of broader national politics regarding the reappropriated children's resocialization and its necessary, overdue, but also angst-ridden manifestation.

Notes

1 Several critics have examined *El premio*. Geoffrey Maguire studies *El premio* in conjunction with contemporary Argentine films that attempt 'to endow the generational figure of the *hijo* with an independent agency against the backdrop of contemporary Argentine society' (2017b: 8). Similarly, in *Rethinking Testimonial Cinema in Postdictatorship Argentina: Beyond Memory Fatigue* (2019), Verónica Garibotto situates *El premio* alongside Pablo Agüero's *Salamandra* (2008), Nicolás Prividera's *M* (2007), Daniel Bustamante's *Andrés no quiere dormir la siesta* (2009), and Benjamín Ávila's *Infancia clandestina* (2012) because these filmmakers' 'fiction films [...] return to a child's or a teenager's perspective and to an "archaic" 1980s format' (141). More recently, Guillermo Severiche emphasizes the film's autobiographical elements as its thematic and aesthetic anchor. 'Markovitch's personal memories serve as a point of departure to construct this story [*El premio*],' he writes, 'and may also provide a general tone of mourning and impotence' (2023: 154). For Severiche, *El premio* 'relies on concomitant and dynamic relationship between the visual and the multi-sensory' (2023: 159). Erin Hogan also notes autobiographical resonances in *El premio*, while studying the child protagonist as 'the example of a *niña sacer* during the Dirty War through its semi-autobiographical tale of a young girl's civil death' (2018: 254).
2 See https://www.youtube.com/watch?v=ukrYNcOqWEM. Accessed 17 July 2015.
3 See the following interview with the filmmaker. https://www.youtube.com/watch?v=ukrYNcOqWEM. Accessed 17 July 2015.
4 See the Grandmothers' note on one of these suicides: http://www.minutouno.com/nolas/360120-gran-perdida-abuelas-se-suicido-el-nieto-recuperado-l09. Accessed 10 March 2017.
5 See 'Se mató en Mar del Plata una hija de desaparecidos,' *La Capital de Mar del Plata*, 16 August 2011, http://www.lacapitalmdp.com/noticias/Policialcs/2011/08/16/192365.htm. Accessed 5 September 2011.
6 See 'Se suicidó Pablo German Athanasiu Laschan, el nieto recuperado 109,' *Notas*, 13 April 2015, https://notasperiodismopopular.com.ar/2015/04/13/suicido-pablo-german-athanasiu-laschan-nieto-recuperado-109/. Accessed 15 April 2015.

4

Armando y Genoveva (2013): Vociferous Canvases

By 2001, Paula Markovitch had lost both of her parents. Armando Markovitch died in 1995 and Genoveva Edelstein passed away six years later. Markovitch's decision to incorporate their previously recorded voices into *Armando y Genoveva* (2013a/b) breathes new life into the posthumous images in the film. These images are also enveloped by the sepulchral sounds of Mexican composer and artist Sergio Gurrola. Having composed for other films by Markovitch – *El premio* (2011), *El actor principal* (2019b), and *Ángeles* (2025) – Gurrola has remarked that sound in her films often 'probes into the human voice as a sign of resistance' ('indaga en la voz humana como signo de resistencia').[1] In *Armando y Genoveva*, Gurrola's disquieting soundscape surrounds the protagonist's grief-stricken excavation of the parents' creativity. Gurrola's dissonant sounds moreover highlight *Armando y Genoveva*'s emotional tension and reinforce the film's somber mood. As the filmmaker unpacks, wraps, cleans, and caresses some of the approximately 400 art pieces, *Armando y Genoveva* also reaffirms itself as a unique artefact of intermedial mourning.

Armando y Genoveva draws on innovative aesthetic techniques to create a cinematic homage to Markovitch's parents as artists and political dissidents. The film's novelty stems not so much from Markovitch's focus on merging the political with the personal, but rather from her use of intermediality to peer into and document her parents' past. More specifically, *Armando y Genoveva*'s intermediality is primarily realized in the unpredictable connections between the parents' audio letters and their recovered artwork. These oscillations and interactions between media establish the film's structure as well as its multifaceted story right from the start. The result is what Ágnes Pethő (2011) conceptualizes as meaningfully capricious interconnections among and between different media in contemporary cinema that allow works to communicate in aesthetically novel ways. According to Pethő, such aesthetic tendencies foster a space 'of "in-between" that is continually constructed and deconstructed by the ebb and flow of the images, by their appearance and disappearance' (9). In *Armando y Genoveva*, intermedial relations are based on this 'in-betweenness' not solely to convey 'concrete, memorable images of formidable power' but also to shed light on the parents' past – a past that concurrently anchors as well as unsettles their present (Nichols 2017: 83). Such intermedial manifestations ultimately initiate an immortalization of the parents' unbroken commitment to artistic expression despite their life-long isolation because of Argentina's political violence (1976–83).[2]

This notion of intermedial mourning singularly unites the past and present, preventing their conceptualization as a binary or a dualism. It also recalls Homi Bhabha's notion of 'the third space.' In *The Location of Culture* (1994), Bhabha states that 'the third space' does not 'merely recall the past as social course or aesthetic precedent; it renews the past, refiguring it as a contingent 'in-between' space, that innovates and interrupts the performance of the present. The past-present becomes part of the necessity, not nostalgia of living' (7). Different degrees of this liminality and, more relevantly, Pethő's notion of 'in-betweenness,' are perceptible in *Armando y Genoveva* as the intermedial relationship between the parents' paintings and their audio missives intensifies. These intermedial intensifications engender new insights about the artists' intricate trajectories and their sociopolitical realities. By analyzing the interplay of intimate media from her parents' memorable lives, this chapter studies Markovitch's intermedial reconstruction of Armando Markovitch's and Genoveva Edelstein's public (in)visibility.

Although Markovitch has spent most of her adult life away from her parents' home in Argentina, her closeness to them permeates both her cinematographic and literary work. As various scholars have noted, *El premio* (2011) was inspired by the filmmaker's childhood in relation to her parents' political past.[3] *Cuadros en la oscuridad* (2017) was also largely based on her father and his struggles to engage with fellow artists beyond his immediate setting. In *Cacerías imaginarias* (2022), a collection of meditative essays, poetry, and aesthetic musings about film, Markovitch ruminates in detail about the anguish caused by her mother's death (Markovitch 2022: 100). In *Armando y Genoveva*, this kind of existential bewilderment resurfaces intermedially, but now concerns the life and death of both of her parents. The parents' political past also places the documentary's main argument into the larger context of Argentina's post-dictatorial cinema without aligning it entirely with the works of, among others, Albertina Carri's *Los rubios* (2003), María Inés Roqué's *Papá Iván* (2004), or Nicolás Prividera's *M* (2007). According to Gonzalo Aguilar's *New Argentine Film: Other Worlds* (2008), these filmmakers have been 'direct victims of state terrorism [...] and had begun to use film as a means of expression' to explore, question, and reflect on their parents' explicit involvement in the *montonero* movement and subsequent deaths (156).[4] Markovitch's *Armando y Genoveva*, in contrast, captures the consequences of her parents' *subdued* political dissidence (the parents were not directly imprisoned or tortured) through their social and economic decline, even after the return of democracy in Argentina.

Markovitch's intermedial layering unfolds temperately. The director contextualizes through voice-over alternatingly and layers in the parents' artwork and their recorded voices in various ways. In the opening moments of *Armando y Genoveva*, Markovitch's voice-over narration establishes the context for the making of the film: she has arrived in Córdoba, Argentina to recover her parents' art. The filmmaker's voice-over here clarifies the film's purpose, but it is the interconnectivity of the artworks with the audio missives, and subsequently her touch, that lends the film its aesthetic vitality. Such an approach to intermediality differs from Brazilian Jorge Furtado's in *O homem que copiava/The Man Who Copied* (2003). According to Cynthia Tompkins (2013), intermediality principally manifests in Furtado's film through the merging of 'cartoon panels, animated cartoons, television clips, and self-reflexive sections' (2013: 65). More specifically, the film's intermedial attributes are created principally through "pastiche" (2013: 65). In contrast, as Markovitch strengthens the connection between different media in *Armando y Genoveva*, she loosely turns her film into a unique multimedia topography without suspending each medium's intrinsic qualities. This is particularly evident if we consider Janna Houwen's *Film and Video Intermediality* (2017), which elucidates the production of intermedial settings without erasing their individual traits. By merging different media, clarifies Houwen, 'the distinction between two media can form a persistent yet productive gap in intermedial objects' (2017: 7).[5] These 'gaps' are particularly salient in *Armando y Genoveva* as the filmmaker's voice-over contextualizes but rarely comments on the discrete artworks she has unearthed. The filmmaker establishes an equally interesting paradox between her voice-over interventions and the parents' recorded missives: the voice-over does not establish a posthumous conversation with the recorded missives, even if they are structurally braided in the film.

Markovitch's hand-held camera remains haptically intimate from the outset within different storage spaces: wardrobes, bedrooms, and attics in her parents' home. We are consequently permitted close contact with abundant artworks as well as their condition: framed, rolled up, unframed, impeccably protected, or damaged.[6] By foregrounding hapticity, the film also implies experiences beyond the audiovisual realm. According to Laura Marks' seminal work, *The Skin of the Film* (2000), haptic images 'invite the viewer to respond to the image in an intimate, embodied way, and thus facilitate the experience of other sensory impressions' (2). For Marks, in other words, film and video can convey certain sensory experiences that transcend their audiovisual qualities; that is, their intrinsic traits. Appealing to touch in *Armando y Genoveva* reinforces the notion of 'haptic visuality,' but from a unique intermedial perspective (Marks 2000: xi). On the one hand, the intimate close-ups invite us to *feel* the canvases visually. On the other hand, the filmmaker's free hand enters the frame on several occasions to feel the discovered paintings lingeringly. The filmmaker's provocative touch also invites us to think 'how the sense of touch may embody memories that are unavailable to vision,' and to contemplate the likelihood of the filmmaker's familial remembrances during those moments (Marks 2000: 22). The presentation of the paintings in *Armando y Genoveva*, furthermore, contrasts sharply with what Pethő refers to as 'the Hitchcockian painting' – a 'painterly image [which] emerges as the medium of the unknown, threatening to throw the mind of the character (and implicitly of the viewer) into the abysmal depths of the uncanny and the unidentifiable' (2011: 7). Markovitch's intermedial process remains probing yet also elucidatory: her presentation of the found artworks is superimposed with the parents' voices. Consequently, the parents' audio recordings posthumously recreate their artistic impulses and make them known.

Recovered from a multi-year compilation of cassettes (from approximately 1992 to 1995), the audio recordings persistently yield different glimpses into the artists' everyday life.[7] The filmmaker explains in *Armando y Genoveva* how these recordings, above all, were an epistolary connection to her parents:

> When I came to live in Mexico, my parents and I often communicated through cassettes because in that era there was no email, and letters, well, the letters took a long time. We did communicate by letters too, but [cassettes] were a way to send me their voice. And, sometimes, I also answered them with cassettes. But those cassettes came and went, and we had forgotten about them until I found them.
>
> (Cuando vine a vivir en México, mis padres y yo a veces nos comunicábamos por casetes porque en esa época no había mails y las cartas, bueno, las cartas tardaban mucho. Me lo mandaban por cartas también, pero [casetes] eran una manera

de mandarme su voz. Y yo también a veces les contestaba con casetes. Pero esos casetes fueron y vinieron y se nos habían olvidado hasta que los encontré.)

By connecting several hundred artworks with these recordings in *Armando y Genoveva*, Markovitch essentially ensconces a haptic invitation not only to the parents' world of artistic exuberance but also to existential fragility. Viewed from Pethő's vantage point, such invitations appear to facilitate a sensation-based intimacy between the viewer and depicted settings. The 'sensual mode,' Pethő further specifies, 'invites the viewer to literally get in touch with a world portrayed not at a distance but at the proximity of entangled synesthetic sensations and resulting in a cinema that can be perceived in terms of music, painting, architectural forms or haptic textures' (2011:5). The notion of 'haptic textures' deepens as the filmmaker engages a variety of thematically distinct excerpts from a total of six hours of her parents' audio missives.

The interplay of the recordings and recovered art additionally opens a range of 'sensuous interfaces' wherein the filmmaker's physical presence and memory-oriented journeys intersect unpredictably (Pethő 2011:5).[8] This interaction brings us deeper into some of the most intimate crevices of the parents' lived and thwarted pathways, capturing intermedially that which Markovitch wrote in *Cacerías imaginarias*, 'we lived in hiding, my parents in internal displacement. At that time, it was important to live in some degree of seclusion. Any childish confidence could have engendered a tragedy' ('mis padres eran insiliados, vivíamos escondidos. En aquel tiempo era importante vivir en cierto grado de aislamiento. Cualquier confidencia infantil hubiera podido provocar una tragedia') (2022: 19). Unlike the text from *Cacerías imaginarias*, which addresses the daughter's anguish through the poetry of her writing, the images of her parents' found artworks are most emotionally potent as they commingle aesthetically with her voice-over, audio missives, and composed as well as natural sounds. According to Bill Nichols, voice-over narrations typically work in harmony with images to translate their conceptual and emotional value. 'Photographic images,' Nichols explains, 'do not present concepts: they embody them. [...] The commentary, as spoken language, can name and define poverty, affluence, or fear directly' (2017: 73). Although the director's voice-over principally contextualizes the parents' biographies, her life is inherently implied in theirs. In other words, her commentary also indirectly 'embodies' autobiographical elements. For Geraldo Sarno, the act of making documentaries involves the notion of inexorable invasion, since a 'documentary happens when something in my relation to the other is illuminated and, to some extent, the other invades me' (quoted in Avellar 2013: 17). Pablo Piedras likewise reminds us that at the start of the 21st century in Argentina 'autobiographical documentaries tend to use the voice-over of directors to narrate aspects of their experiences, to delineate the questions at the story's core as well as to refer retrospectively to personal history' ('los documentales autobiográficos suelen recurrir a la voz en off de los directores para narrar aspectos de sus vivencias, para trazar los interrogantes que se hallan en el núcleo del relato, así como para remitirse en forma retrospectiva a la historia personal') (1995: 83). Piedras' characterization is particularly relevant to *Armando y Genoveva*'s subtle intimations about the Argentine political turmoil that had long dominated the Markovitchs' lives. Intermediality, as 'a veritable art of in-betweenness,' moreover, not only facilitates but also solidifies the director's attempts to dissect what Piedras calls 'la historia personal' (Pethő 2011: 1; Piedras 1995: 83). Nichols identifies such documentary dissections as 'personal portrait films' because they 'place their focus on the individual rather than the social issue [...] [and] demonstrate an intimate connection between the personal and the political' (187). Markovitch appeals to intermediality to capture layers of this 'connection,' especially since the superimposed recordings can also be viewed as the parents' audio diaries. The recordings are thematically heterogenous and emotionally layered, but they nearly always return to the importance of the parents' artistic conviviality. As noted, Gurrola's soundtrack supports the intermediality, deepens the film's emotional tenor, and builds a singularly innovative 'question of the voice' in the film (Nichols 2017: 49).

Gurrola's disquieting sounds frame the parents' recorded voices and accentuate their confessional bent.

Genoveva and Armando often converse about their love of painting, but politics continues to lurk behind their seemingly lighthearted exchanges. Armando's subtle remarks on his country's past exemplify the idea of a 'historical world' that Nichols sees as an essential component of personal portrait films (2017: 82). In her own thoughts on her father's past, the filmmaker has commented on how the political repression and violence in Argentina rarely succeeded in curbing her father's search for inspiration and his production of art. Argentina, writes Markovitch,

> was going through a historical period of silence and repression. I think my father saw signs on the walls. He was dazzled by the subtle [pencil] strokes, the textures, the fragments he found anywhere. As if he could glimpse in them indications of a reality that no one could speak of directly. There were mysterious signs full of beauty and despair. (2016: 27)
>
> (atravesaba un período histórico de silencio y de represión. Creo que mi padre veía signos en las paredes. Se deslumbraba con los trazos sutiles, las texturas, los fragmentos que encontraba en cualquier parte. Como si pudiera atisbar en ellos indicios de una realidad de la que nadie podía hablar directamente. Eran signos misteriosos llenos de belleza y desesperación.)

This amalgam of 'beauty' and 'despair' permeates nearly all the recordings that interact with the artworks excavated in the film. When Genoveva addresses Armando in one of the included missives about his timid approach to promoting himself in the past – 'You have not always been a painter who has gone to, promoted across, exhibited at the galleries' ('Vos tampoco has sido un pintor que ha ido, ha expuesto, ha mandado siempre a los salones') – Armando responds by reflecting on broader political disappointments and personal impotence, and existentially lamenting in an ironic tone: 'This is a big mistake. [...] I had been brainwashed [...] since my youth. They lured me into a socialist world [...] and we were all going to be, if not equal, alike. But all of this resulted in a colossal nothing' ('Este es un gran error. [...] Me habían lavado el cerebro [...] desde chiquito. Me metieron en el mundo socialista [...] y que todos íbamos a ser, si no iguales, parecidos. Pero todo esto resultó en un gran nada'). While the father's comments touch on the broader significance of the historical period, the recordings also emphasize his deeply personal struggles with isolation, poverty, and solitude.

In *Listening* (2007), Jean-Luc Nancy distinguishes between hearing and listening. Hearing, in Nancy's contemplations, is mere receiving, while listening is 'to be straining toward a possible meaning, and consequently one that is not immediately accessible' (2007: 6). Listening therefore positions the listener 'on the edge of meaning' (2007: 7). This kind of listening gains significance in *Armando y Genoveva* due to the intersection of the parents' voices and their visual artwork, which are creatively and communicationally bonded but often incongruent. In other words, the parents' voices are not commenting directly on the paintings that the filmmaker touches, unpacks, or restores, and this incongruence of their voices and their paintings demands that we be doubly attuned to listening while watching.

This kind of listening is linked again to the filmmaker's touch. If 'the sense of touch [,] [...] is perceived as annihilating not only space, but also time,' as Constance Classen (2020) states, then Markovitch's film manages to bridge her present to her parents' past not only by melding their voices and images but also through different recalibrations of her touch (278). The intensity of the director's touch – prolonged, fleeting, recurring, inquiring, spirited, or laden – varies as she sifts through the artworks in different settings. In the film's last scene, we watch the filmmaker's hand dust one of the many framed paintings before she begins to caress it (Fig. 4.1).[9] The act of caressing is protracted, while the lightness of her fingers renders it an intricately nostalgic act. This haptic interaction also instantiates, as Marks mentions in another context, how 'residual nonverbal knowledges remain a bodily repository that can only be understood in its own terms' (2000: 71). The director's choice to engage with this portrait

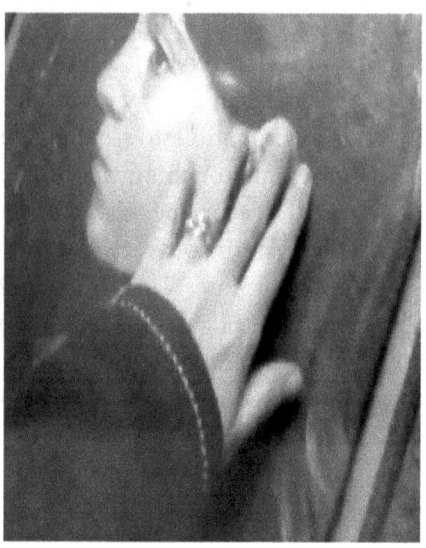

Figure 4.1 Markovitch haptically engages with an unnamed portrait. © Paula Markovitch

haptically and with intense absorption generates a number of queries: Could the portrait be of the artists' daughter, relative, friend, student, or someone else? Whose creative undertaking was this and when was it completed? Has the director seen it before? Was this a soothing surprise or a painful happenstance? These questions emerge primarily from the director's haptic disposition toward the piece – her complexly concentrated engagement with it. Seeing the filmmaker clean and caress this painting's surface is not enough; we also need to listen to her strokes and contemplate their implications.

Jacques Derrida's writing about touch is particularly relevant here. For Derrida, touch promises inimitability, since "[w]hat I see can be replaced. What I touch cannot, or in any case, we have the feeling, illusory or not, that touch guarantees irreplaceability: hence the thing itself in its uniqueness" (quoted in Pilar Blanco and Peeren 2013: 43). Running her fingers over the painting's surface in *Armando y Genoveva* has no simple or clear meaning; in fact, the act merely stimulates additional contemplations. One could read the haptic interaction with the portrait in relation to Marks' discussion of 'object and sense memory' (2000: 110). For Marks, an image 'insofar as it engages with memory at all, engages the memory of the senses. [...] the senses often remember when nobody else does' (2000: 110). Markovitch's act of caressing certain paintings might suggest a unique mélange of unuttered personal memories and compound emotional experiences. The same haptic interaction highlights the connection between objects and our bodies on a singularly personal level, showing us, as Sara Ahmed writes, 'how objects acquire value through contact with bodies' (2010: 23). The filmmaker's singular interaction (touching to engage memory with the senses) also simultaneously insists on a particular kind of listening to what is not directly communicated or might be emotionally implied in the amalgamated audio missives.

In *Sensuous Geographies: Body, Sense, and Place* (1994), Paul Rodaway underscores the importance of understanding all senses as not solely 'a medium' but also 'a kind of message, or a distinct perspective on the world' (26). As Markovitch's fingers touch the surface of the artworks, the viewer might also be prompted to think of her parents' creative vigor, gravitas, or inspiration at the most intimate and elemental level. Listening to these moments is additionally significant when we consider Saul Schanberg's key insights about touch: it is 'ten times stronger than visual or emotional contact' (quoted in Field 2014: 20). The intersection of listening and touch bolsters the intermedial attributes of the film for yet another purpose. According to Classen, touch rudimentarily facilitates interpersonal unification since it 'annihilates distance and physically unites the toucher and the touched' (2020: 77). Markovitch's touch not only provocatively disrupts the integrity of the shot but also generates a kind of intermedial union with the parents.

The filmmaker's selection of recorded missives is equally significant for these kinds of emblematic unifications. Listening to what the recordings say – and what they imply beyond the moment they were spoken – also bolsters for the filmmaker, and by extension for the viewer, what Edmund Husserl calls 'our near sphere' (quoted in Ahmed 2010: 24). For Husserl, this phenomenologically signifies 'a sphere of things that I can reach with my kinesthesis and which I can experience in an optimal form through touching, seeing' (quoted in Ahmed 2010: 24). Through the nexus of touching and listening, *Armando y Genoveva* creates 'our near sphere,' around the parents' art, drawing out the deeper emotional layers of their missives.

One missive does not immediately involve both parents but instead begins with Genoveva's timid confession. Before Genoveva's voice comes on assertively to explain that she will be recording alone for a few minutes, she experiences a literal loss of words, as though she has become petrified before the audio's blank page. Genoveva admits that she should have written a script to be better prepared for this engagement with her daughter. In her frustrated eagerness to express her thoughts, she becomes emotional and admits 'today marks exactly one year since I had seen you' ('hoy se cumple justamente un año que no te veo'). Even though this missive is ambiguous as to when it was recorded, it indirectly foregrounds a biographical element about the filmmaker, referring to her absence and new life in Mexico City.[10] If listening, as Nancy suggests, 'aims at – or is aroused by – the one where sound and sense mix together and resonate in each other, or through each other,' then listening is reinforced in Genoveva's missive by the mixing of 'sound' and conversational gaps (2007: 7). More concretely, what Genoveva does not communicate verbally seems to cry out indirectly through her hesitations, brief silences, and choppy attempts to articulate her deeply anguished state of being. She hesitates to express the void that her daughter's prolonged absences must have left in the parents' lives, and ultimately admits, 'I don't even know how I endured that year' ('No sé ni cómo lo pude aguantar a ese año'). If we listen and attune to Genoveva's 'sphere of things,' we might glean deeper meaning in what she only implies. Genoveva's despondency reverberates across each word she utters as she discloses, 'my dearest daughter, I love you so much, and I would like to be with you. This is the truth; the only truth. And nothing more' ('hijita, te quiero tanto, y quisiera estar con vos. Esta es la verdad; la única verdad. Y nada más'). When Armando enters Genoveva's physical and virtual space, he tries to suspend the recording so his wife can recompose herself. If we listen carefully, however, we can discern a complex mélange of forced humor and sedimented anguish about Genoveva's candid confessions. His concerns about how this missive might affect their daughter are also indisputably clear. Such concerns inhabit the interstices of Armando's nervous laughs, pauses, intonations, and words. These moments come across as easily consumed tokens of familial intimacy. Yet below the surface they intimate other unrevealed emotional states and yearnings.

Such intensely intimate moments among the family members cause us to reflect on what events had punctuated their lives and occasioned Markovitch's self-exile. Genoveva's comments allude to the parents' dissidence during the State terror (1976–83), Argentina's neoliberal tensions in the 1990s, as well as the country's colossal economic crisis (1998–2002). According to Nichols, documentaries' 'most social practices – from family life to social welfare, from military policy to urban planning – occupy contested territory' (2017: 77). The parents' intermittent, and seemingly nonchalant, reflections on their past are anchored in a particular kind of angst, which underscores 'contested territory' that is both social and political. The historical moments appear to be in the background of this missive (as well as others), erupting sporadically in the parents' nervous humor, explicit regrets, and uneasy confessions about their financial and existential struggles.

If we listen again to Armando's vocal entrance into Genoveva's missive with Nancy's contemplations in mind, we notice that his voice and the mother's nervous laughter communicate much more than his own attempts to offset their serious confessions in the missives. As we listen to the parents' voices and watch the director sift through their paintings, Markovitch's film instantiates anew what Pethő calls the 'unique configurations of intermediality and their sensuously perceivable excess, uncovering at the same time the way the poetics of intermediality can connect not only arts or media, but also art and life' (2021: 4). This intermedial configuration intensifies as Armando elevates their interrupted conversation to a sort of performative act, where conflicts and afflictions become a necessary theatrical device for ensuring that 'the audience returns' ('el público vuelva'). He then masterfully folds Genoveva's vulnerability into another lighthearted moment – 'we're messing around' ('estamos de joda') – so he may dispel any heavy emotional residue. When we listen to Armando's emotional maneuvering, we can discern a family that deeply longs for their only child during what turned out to be the last days of their lives. Although the audio missives swing between the parents' acutely sorrowful moments and those that brim with levity, they imply that the parents' acceptance of the filmmaker's absence must have been an onerous task.

Images of the painters' house in *Armando y Genoveva* – although brief and fragmented – allow us to enter the physical space that was the epicenter of their creativity as well as their confinement. Darkness, light, and haptics also intersect frequently in and around the house, both literally and metaphorically. The interior of the parents' house space is dark, which creates the differently calibrated moments of suspense about what might be discovered there. The darkness-imbued moments in *Armando y Genoveva* recall Michael Haneke's classic black-outs, particularly in *Le Temps du Loup / Time of the Wolf* (2003), although they were soft and served a different purpose. Haneke typically draws his viewer's attention to what frames the deliberately inserted blackouts, whereas Markovitch's focus on darkness signals a journey to the parents' life-long invisibility. Before the discovered artworks become 'objects for the eye,' to use Classen's words, the filmmaker moves through the darkness and interacts with the space, first through touch and then with sight (2020: 284). We suddenly see a hand attempting to turn on a lamp to vanquish the darkness. The room's lamp turns out to be broken, underscoring rather explicitly the parents' permanent absence. When the filmmaker finally opens one of the windows, natural sunlight allows the dilapidated interior to take center stage, thus bringing the parents' artwork to light.

As the interior grows clearer to the eye, so do its many uses over time by way of the filmmaker's voice-over. Markovitch helps the viewer to reimagine the house beyond its decaying state, telling us how, over the last twenty years of her parents' lives, the place was not only their home but also Armando's and Genoveva's atelier, Genoveva's workshop for more than seventy students, and the site that housed the family recordings that we hear intermittently in the film. This contextualization is supplemented by another recording. The latter takes place in the atelier, Armando describes Genoveva at work, revealing enthusiastically: 'We're in the studio, kiddo, your mother's sitting in front of the easel. [...] With the pastels. [...] I want the kiddo to hear it' ('Estamos en el taller, nena, tu madre sentada frente al caballete. [...] Con los pasteles. [...] Yo quiero que la nena escuche el pastel'). This is an intermedially vigorous moment. Genoveva's work with pastels is recorded in an audio form, and the moment is subsequently remediated as a reference in the daughter's cinematic work of art.

While initially *Armando y Genoveva* focuses on some of the most intimate spaces and moments of artmaking in the parents' home, the rest of the film sporadically branches out into their immediate community. Markovitch's engagements with other family members – in particular, Aunt Anita and several friends (Mario, Silvia, and the others who remain unnamed in the film) – depict the tender moments of communal mourning. Markovitch's choice to capture the commitment of these community members recalls, even if it does not strictly reproduce, 'the materiality of mourning' that Mary Schneider Enríquez (2016) finds in the work of Colombian artist Doris Salcedo. Most of Salcedo's installation art and sculptures, notes Schneider Enríquez, directly comment on certain outcomes of Colombian political violence and its consequences, which creates 'a material presence that evokes, without pictorializing, the absent, unnamed victims of civil war' (2016: 1). The community members in *Armando y Genoveva* – such as Mario and Silvia – embody an altruistic duty that comes closer to what Salcedo witnesses in *Acción de Duelo*, one of her public installations in Bogotá from 2007. This installation was communal and spontaneously interactive: during the installation of 24,000 candles, numerous unsolicited passersby ended up lighting the candles to commemorate the killing of twelve congressmen by the rebel group FARC.[11]

Public interventions in *Armando y Genoveva* likewise figure as communal forms of commemoration, though they are quieter, smaller, and focused on subtle ways of safeguarding the perished painters' works for posterity. Mario, the artists' friend, for instance, is shown in the film as a volunteer guardian of their paintings. In one of the sequences Mario sifts through numerous artworks and reports straightforwardly that 'several works are not signed' ('hay muchas cosas que no dicen nada'). His word ('cosas') refers to an abundance of the artists' surviving oil and watercolor paintings as well as engravings that are not always neatly signed. As an attentive guardian of their creativity, Mario yearns to honor the artworks' authorship and in so doing commemorates them informally. Throughout, his voice repeatedly registers concern for the damaged paintings. In one moment, however, his voice conveys a bit of delight when he picks up a painting and says 'it is signed' ('está registrado'). This interaction instantiates the 'in-betweenness of body and image [...] of life and art as a site where acute political, social, or psychological issues can materialize in a sensuously layered and intellectually complex [way]' (Pethő 2020b: 11). As the dust from the found paintings literally settles during these sequences of communal art excavation and protection, a small, local, and trustworthy community of the painters' friends comes into clear view.

The director's personal resolve to guard against the parents' obscurity as artists culminates with *Armando y Genoveva*'s debut but recurs across Markovitch's subsequent reflections and undertakings. 'Now, remembering my parents,' writes Markovitch in *Cacerías imaginarias* while transcending the familial immediacy and achieving universal significance,

I reflect on how curious and unyielding the artistic impulse is. There are, seemingly, no periods or places in which human beings have not felt the impulse to create. [...] How much beauty in the world will we have ignored, wasted, and abandoned? How many masterpieces will have gone unnoticed, unpublished, or forgotten? (2022: 41)[12]

(Ahora, al recordar a mis padres, reflexiono acerca de lo curioso e inquebrantable que es el impulso artístico. Al parecer, no existen períodos ni lugares, en que los seres humanos, no hayan sentido el impulso de crear. [...] ¿Cuánta belleza en el mundo habremos ignorado, desperdiciado, y abandonado? ¿Cuántas obras maestras habrán pasado desapercibidas, inéditas u olvidadas?)

These questions have been tackled intermedially beyond the film as well, most recently through an exhibition of the parents' artworks at the Museo Municipal Genaro Pérez de Bellas Artes / Genaro Pérez Municipal Museum of Fine Arts in Córdoba, Argentina in 2019. Curated by Gustavo Piñeiro, the exhibition, *Fantasmas Disfrazados*, included an ongoing screening of *Armando y Genoveva*. This effort might be a straightforward example of what Florencia Garramuño terms as '*una confluencia que se opone a la fusión*' (2015: 23–4, original emphasis). Garramuño's observation seems to lead us back to Houwen's theories about the rich aesthetic potentials when different media interact while also maintaining their discreate attributes. Garramuño's amalgamation allows for 'an understanding in which diverse materials meet without merging in a hybrid identity' ('un sentido en el que se encuentran diversos materiales sin que se busque su confusión o estabilización en una identidad híbrida') (2015: 24). Without naming it as such, Garramuño implies a particular kind of intermedial convergence that is also at the heart of *Fantasmas Disfrazados* and instantiates what Jørgen Bruhn and Beate Schirrmacher designate as 'a heterogeneous relation between different forms of meaning-making' (2022: 3–4). This is a renewed appeal to Pethő's 'in-betweenness' but now because of an intermedial interaction between the materiality of numerous paintings and the film in which they appear. Returning to the film itself, then, *Armando y Genoveva*'s intermedial modalities cathartically underscore the parents' past powerlessness as well as their quiet tenacity. Confronting fears of oblivion, the film's intermediality also enables the viewer to engage with the tensions between personal artistic pursuits and broader sociopolitical relations of power. As an intermedial work, *Armando y Genoveva* edifies as a meditative homage, a multisensory art catalog, and an intimate cultural sanctuary.

Notes

1 Sergio Gurrola, email exchange on 15 September 2021.
2 Argentina's military dictatorship led to the killings of approximately 30,000 left-wing political dissidents under General Jorge Rafael Videla's command.
3 See Geoffrey Maguire (2017b); Inela Selimović (2018a, 2022, and 2023b); Alessandro Rocco (2021 and 2023); and Guillermo Severiche (2023).
4 See Aguilar (2013) regarding additional remarks about the 'difficulties of reaching personal enunciation' when it comes to documentaries by the children of *desaparecidos* (209). Additionally, *Armando y Genoveva* may be closer aesthetically to some of the cultural expressions that Jordana Blejmar clusters epistemologically under the notion of 'playful aesthetics' (2016: 4). In *Playful Memories: The Autofictional Turn in Post-Dictatorship Argentina* (2017) Blejmar weds 'autofiction' with 'playful aesthetics' in order to explore how certain artists and filmmakers of the post-dictatorial generation 'are characterized by the use of humor and by an original interplay between imaginative investments of the past, the fictionalization of the self, visual collages, and artistic modifications of documentary archives' in order to respond to the Argentine era of political violence (4). Intermedial tendencies peer through much of Blejmar's concept as well as the works of many filmmakers and artists in her study, including those of Albertina Carri, Mariana Eva Pérez, Félix Bruzzone, Lucila Quieto, and Lola Arias.
5 Houwen seeks to understand the specificity of different media to define their unique intermedial bonding. She writes that 'if medium specificity is dependent on differences with other media, a medium cannot be regarded as an autonomous, isolated unit. It is specified by other media' (10).
6 Yapeyú is a neighborhood where the family lived. The parents used to gift paintings to their neighbors. Toward the end of the film, we enter one of

the neighbors' homes and encounter several paintings from both parents on their walls.
7 Interview with Markovitch on 8 March 2022. Although the parents' recordings do not address the specificities of their socio-economic context and survival, their old age coincided with Argentina's economically turbulent post-dictatorial era during and beyond the first democratically elected president, Raúl Alfonsín (1983–89); Carlos Menem's neoliberal policies-driven presidency (1989–99); Fernando de la Rúa's (1999–2002) leadership and ultimate resignation during the economic collapse; and the brief leadership of Adolfo Rodríguez Saá (2001). The filmmaker reconnects with the parents' home and artwork in 2006 after the presidency of Eduardo Duhalde (2002–3) and during Néstor Kirchner's government (2003–7).
8 Another significant intermedial layer is an online compilation of the parents' artwork, their biographies, and art arrangements, see www.armandoygenoveva.org. Accessed 10 May 2020.
9 For more information on the specificity of each piece, see www.armandoygenoveva.org. Accessed 22 May 2022.
10 In *Cacerías imaginarias*, Markovitch comments on her decision to self-exile: 'I fled from my own fear. My plan was to live in France and study film at La Fémis. But I had no money and the language was an obstacle. My dramaturgy teacher, Sergio Schmucler, had been a political exile and suggested that I travel to Mexico. There, according to him, I could get some job as a writer, just as I sought. I wanted to *live from my writing*' ('Huí de mi propio miedo. Decidí migrar. Mi plan era vivir en Francia y estudiar cine en La Fémis. Pero no tenía dinero y el idioma era un obstáculo. Mi maestro de dramaturgia, Sergio Schmucler, había sido exiliado político y me sugirió viajar a México. Allí, según él, yo podía lograr algún empleo de escritora, tal como me lo proponía. Yo quería *vivir de escribir*' (2022: 26, original emphasis).
11 The rebel group refers to the Revolutionary Armed Forces of Colombia (FARC). See 'Artist Doris Salcedo on Bogotá,' 26 July 2016. https://www.theguardian.com/cities/video/2016/jul/26/artist-doris-salcedo-bogota-forces-work-brutal-video. Accessed 22 May 2022.
12 Most of the parents' works (approximately 3,000 pieces) are in the filmmaker's conservatorship in Mexico City and several are still with family friends in Córdoba, Argentina. Interview with Paula Markovitch on 8 March 2022.

5

Unpretentious Specters in *Cuadros en la oscuridad* (2017)

Inspired by the creative tendencies and work of the filmmaker's father, Armando Markovitch (1936–95), *Cuadros en la oscuridad* (2017) focuses on its protagonist (Marcos) and his love of painting despite – and because of – the different and everyday forms of social erasure he endures.[1] The film takes place in 1995 in Córdoba, Argentina. When situated within Markovitch's oeuvre, *El premio*'s political context also shines through in various moments of *Cuadros en la oscuridad*. Just as the main characters in *El premio*, (Ceci and her mother) hide in an Argentine costal village from the military dictatorship (1976–83), Marcos' isolation in a shantytown of Córdoba in *Cuadros en la oscuridad* is not apolitical. Marcos' past political dissent – the same sort of dissent that killed Ceci's father and kept Ceci and her mother in hiding – has indelibly bruised his life. Unlike Ceci's family, Marcos lives in Argentina's post-dictatorial era and is not overtly characterized as among the haunted. Marcos' lasting and internalized political alienation, abject poverty, and poor health nonetheless render him with a specter-like presence in the film.

Markovitch's early notes about *Cuadros en la oscuridad* (2022) portray a character who is subtly haunted by his country's cruel recent past. This is most obvious in his enervated physique, for the filmmaker writes in her script, 'Marcos is pale, bright-eyed, with a despondent aura and a tormented soul. He seems preoccupied and frightened' ('Marcos es pálido, de ojos brillantes, tiene el aliento humeante y el alma atormentada. Parece absorto y asustado') (2022: 42). Although Marcos' daily priorities revolve around his paintings, aloneness, and very occasional social interactions, his sporadic comments subtly allude to his politically complex past and clarify his socially ostracized present. In thinking about the last two films (*El premio* and *Cuadros en la oscuridad*), Markovitch asks rhetorical questions about artists' endurance in the face of hindrances, including 'marginality, lack of resources, lack of time for art, absence of recognition by others. . . How do they affect the creativity of an artist? To what extent do the years of anonymity dishearten him? Do they perhaps take away the desire and impulse to create?' ('la marginalidad, la falta de recursos, la falta de tiempo para el arte, la ausencia de reconocimiento de los demás. . . ¿Cómo afectan la creatividad de un artista? ¿Hasta qué punto los años de anonimato lo desalientan? ¿ Le quitan tal vez las ganas y el impulso de crear?').[2] These questions overtly inquire about artists' archetypal tenacity to create despite obstacles, just as they covertly imply Markovitch's personal laments about insufficient public attention to her parents' artistic trajectories.

While Marcos resides firmly in *Cuadros en la oscuridad*'s fictional world, much of his life seems to emerge from the deeply personal experiences of Markovitch's haunting familial stories (Chapter 3 and Chapter 4). Yet unlike *El premio*, *Cuadros en la oscuridad* is not solely based on the filmmaker's contemplations of childhood. Rather, it unfolds into a more open-ended cinematic exploration of repugnance toward creative impulses that are ignored and unwelcomed but worthy of respect, and the hunger for freedom in a society with residues of repression. As noted in the previous chapters, Markovitch's *Cacerías imaginarias* (2022), which is a mélange of creative reflections, aspirations, and concerns regarding the filmmaker's completed and nascent work, becomes particularly significant when analyzing *Cuadros en la oscuridad*. The notebook describes the director's plans and struggles to represent cinematographically the depth of Marcos' alienation, angst, and isolation. Markovitch's notebook reminds us of both Ingmar Bergman's text-oriented notebooks as well as of Agnès Varda's and Federico Fellini's creative diaries because *Cacerías imaginarias* brims with intermedial juxtapositions of her writing, commentary, photographs, poetry, and self-reflection, to mention but a few. This chapter highlights the notebook's initial aspirations for and historical context of *Cuadros en la oscuridad* to examine the creation of a protagonist's ghostly presence as an embodied critical reflection on Argentina's recent past.

In *Cuadros en la oscuridad*, Marcos' infrequent social encounters oscillate between a street child (Luis) and a fruit vendor (Carmen). Aside from these encounters, Marcos' solitude and marginality abound in the film. Although we rarely see the protagonist paint extensively in the film, he is existentially entombed in his work. Nearly everything he does revolves around his commitment to his art: Marcos' modest home is also his atelier, his social interactions are facilitated by his art, and his impromptu urges to draw are interspersed with his unsatisfying day job at a nearby gas station. These moments precede Marcos' death on an unnamed street of the *villa*, and his copious and stored artwork comes to life posthumously in ways both accidental and indelicate.

Markovitch utilizes a unique and particular kind of spectrality in order to highlight the protagonist's alienation. Specters in *Cuadros en la oscuridad* are rarely present in otherworldly ways as they are, for instance, in both classic or relatively contemporary Latin American filmic and literary works, such as Julio Cortázar's 'La casa tomada' (1946), Gabriel García Márquez's *Cien años de soledad* (1967), Alfonso Arau's *Como aqua para chocolate* (1992), Mariana Enríquez's *Los peligros de fumar en la cama* (2009) as well as *Chicos que vuelven* (2010), Ernesto Semán's *Soy un bravo piloto de la nueva China* (2011), Félix Bruzzone's *Las chanchas* (2014), Lucrecia Martel's *Zama* (2017), Jayro Bustamante's *La llorona* (2019), to mention a few. Moreover, Markovitch's use of spectrality does not align with what scholars in *El pasado inasequible: desaparecidos, hijos y combatientes en el arte y la literatura del nuevo milenio* (2018) study under the phenomenon of 'lo espectral' (20). According to Jordana Blejmar, Silvana Mandolessi and Mariana Eva Pérez in *El pasado inasequible*, specters are evoked among Argentinian artists and writers of the new millennium 'to refer to the complex nature of the disappeared: shadows, monsters, silhouettes and ghosts, all united under the common denominator of "the spectral"' ('referirse a la compleja naturaleza del desaparecido: sombras, monstruos, siluetas y fantasmas, todas aunadas bajo el común denominador de "lo spectral"') (2018: 20). These critics elaborate that 'the spectral is also the sinister, what ("haunts us") from a dimension both familiar and unknown' ('lo espectral es también lo siniestro, lo que nos asecha ("haunts us") desde una dimensión a la vez familiar y desconocida') (2018: 20). However, *Cuadros en la oscuridad*'s main specter appears principally as a metaphor of Marcos' internalized distrust of the then newly reestablished – and still fragile – democratic forms of freedom. Spectrality in her third film also goes further as it encompasses and refers to the broader fears and existential states of those who stayed in the country during State terror (1976–83) as quieter dissidents. In one of her early musings about the film Markovitch writes, '[a]nd what happened to us? The internally displaced? Those of us who live hidden inside the country... Today I think we were hidden for too long, we had to pretend at existence. ('Y qué pasó con nosotros? ¿Los insiliados? Los que vivimos escondidos dentro del país... Hoy creo que estuvimos ocultos demasiado tiempo, tuvimos que disimular nuestra existencia. (Markovitch 2016: n.pag.). This intricate liminal state and space in *Cuadros en la oscuridad* teems with ghostly ways of life where self-erasure (or perhaps self-protection?) also sustains certain modes of artistic expression. In this context, Markovitch's film opts to highlight how such states of 'ocultamiento' and 'auto-negación' are inevitably plagued by existential anguish of various kinds. The filmmaker characterizes the protagonist from the start as a character who 'is tormented, confused' ('está atormentado, confundido') and subtly reveals the sources of his torment throughout the film (Markovitch 2016: n.pag.). In *Cuadros en la oscuridad*, the experience of home spaces for Marcos is at once intimate, solitary, and powerfully transformative.

In her published notebook, furthermore, the director explicitly links the protagonist's existential state to Argentina's socioeconomic and political situation prior to but also in the 1990s. In *Cacerías imaginarias*, the filmmaker elucidates:

> I [r]emember the nineties. The feeling of apparent democracy... Repression was still everywhere. I had the impression that the dead had become disproportionately present in memory, while the living seemed infected with absence, sick with emptiness. Marcos inhabits this context. [...] The 'dictatorship' has ended, but Marcos is still hidden. Hidden from whom? Maybe everyone and himself. Marcos is afraid. But afraid of what? Afraid of 'being,' of 'appearing,' of 'existing.' (Markovitch 2022: 45)[3]

> (recuerdo los noventa. La sensación de una democracia aparente ... La represión aún estaba en todas partes. Tenía la impresión de que los muertos se habían vuelto desmesuradamente presentes en la memoria, mientras que los vivos parecíamos contagiados de ausencia, enfermos de vacío. En ese contexto camina Marcos [...] La 'dictadura' ha terminado, pero Marcos sigue escondido. ¿Escondido de quién? Quizá de todos y de sí mismo. Marcos tiene miedo. ¿Pero miedo a qué? Miedo de 'ser', de 'aparecer', de 'existir.')

The filmmaker's statement that 'los muertos se habían vuelto desmesuradamente presentes en la memoria' applies to *Cuadros en la oscuridad* as well. This is particularly evident if we consider 'the ghost as no longer primarily a literal phenomenon requiring empirical verification [...], but a conceptual metaphor capable of bringing to light and opening up to analysis hidden, disavowed, and neglected aspects of the social and cultural realm, past and present' (Blanco and Peeren 2013: 21). Specters, as 'conceptual metaphors,' to further borrow from María del Pilar Blanco's and Esther Peeren's *The Spectralities Reader: Ghosts and Haunting in Contemporary*

Cultural Theory (2013), effectively mirror the protagonist's emotional states and experiences in *Cuadros en la oscuridad*; namely, his loneliness and fear but also subtle forms of rebellion. These emotional ambivalences furthermore appear to stem from the protagonist's internalized totalitarianism, which becomes clear in his conversations with Luis. Speaking with Luis on one occasion, Marcos reveals one of the reasons for his public invisibility regarding his art, 'Why don't I exhibit? I was in hiding. I was a communist.') ('¿Por qué no exhibo? Estaba clandestino. Yo era comunista.'). More than a decade after Argentina's dictatorship ended, sociopolitical brutalities are sedimented in Marcos' words and might continue to have him invisible. This calls to mind Margaret Crastnopol's *Micro-Trauma: A Psychoanalytic Understanding of Cumulative Psychic Injury* (2015) and her concept of 'little murders' or 'microtraumas that tear the fabric of relationships, corrode the quality of everyday life by communicating envy, hatred,' which can irrevocably bruise the psyche (2015: 26). When Marcos reflects before Luis on his past fears and present hesitations, he implies certain forms of social corrosion (political violence, repression, fear) that appear to have marked him indelibly.

In *Totalitarian Space and the Destruction of Aura* (2019), Saladdin Ahmed links the body to freedom as a defiant potential in totalitarian settings. Ahmed suggests that arguably the 'only way out of the totalitarianism is to use the body as the locus of spatial freedom to negate the apex of the spatial power pyramid' (2019: 168). In *Cuadros en la oscuridad*, Marcos' embedded existential discomfort with totalitarian tendencies is literally manifested through his body. Accustomed to past repression, Marcos' body in the film oscillates between inertia and dynamism. The film foregrounds Marcos' inactivity primarily through his daily social interactions or lack thereof: at the gas station he spends his working hours mostly waiting alone without any meaningful engagements. His regular and lonesome commute by foot to the gas involves movement yet those walks are also replete with uneasiness. We watch his unsure gaze become warily heavy as he has the feeling of being watched or followed. *Cuadros en la oscuridad* rather nonchalantly manages to demonstrate how the protagonist's political dissidence has transformed his existence into something irreversibly eerie: the viewer witnesses his solitude as well as his rare social interactions, which ultimately lead to his equally lonely death.

Marcos' ghostly presence in the film becomes more dynamic in random moments when he interacts with Luis and a neighborhood fruit vendor. The triangulation – Marcos, Carmen, and Luis – deepens our access to the protagonist's inner world, albeit in fragmented ways. Paradoxically, this access relies on a particular kind of silence among these characters. Indeed, the communicative power of silence reminds us of social engagements in *El actor principal* (Chapter 6), yet, in contrast to that film, the unsaid in *Cuadros en la oscuridad* has different sources. If Maricruz González sees the protagonist's artistic anonymity as an aftermath of the State terror in Argentina, Alessandro Rocco ties it to the repercussions of Argentina's neoliberalism. Rocco comments on Marcos' precarity and interpersonal loneliness, despite Luis' presence, and specifies that

> beyond his will, Luis is not able to hear the testimony, he cannot understand its scope nor play an active and participatory role in its reception. Therefore, the very expression of the testimony reinforces the sense of abandonment and social isolation of those who suffered the repression and persecution during the dictatorship. (Rocco 2023: 147–8)

> (más allá de su voluntad, no está en condiciones para recibir el testimonio, no puede comprender su alcance ni tener un papel activo y participativo en la recepción. Por lo tanto, la expresión misma del testimonio refuerza el sentido del abandono y del aislamiento social de quienes sufrieron la represión y persecución durante la dictadura.)

Rocco is right to connect Marcos' subjectivity to forms of indifference or an inability to comprehend the existential scars of survivors wronged during the military regime, particularly

Unpretentious Specters in *Cuadros en la oscuridad* 109

those who continue to live in the post-dictatorship era. Yet the protagonist's aloneness is multidimensional in this case and stems from his artistic drive. On the one hand, Luis and the neighborhood vendor heighten Marcos' aloneness because of their straightforward inability to understand the depths of his artistic compulsions. During one of his interactions with Carmen, Marcos expresses his desire to paint her portrait. He wishes to proceed instantly, thus showing his ungovernable impulses to create by seeking to touch her face as if to begin sketching it haptically. Committed to different modes of everyday life, however, the vendor declines to suddenly suspend her duties and unintentionally frustrates the painter's passion. Likewise, Marcos' attempts to demystify his intractable urges for painting before Luis come across awkwardly (Fig. 5.1). Luis listens but cannot truly comprehend the painter's passion. These interactions, above all, underscore Marcos' social ghostliness as well as the absence of any community with similar personal and professional affinities.

Figure 5.1 Marcos tries to engage with Luis about art multiple times. © Paula Markovitch

Marcos' ghostliness derives from his precarious existential state, which in the film also comes close to Fredric Jameson's interpretations of spectrality. For Jameson (2008), spectrality

> does not only involve the conviction that ghosts exist or that the past (and maybe even the future they offer to prophesy) is still very much alive and at work, within the living present: all it says, if it can be thought to speak, is that the living present is scarcely as self-sufficient as it claims to be; that we would do well not to count on its density and solidity, which might under exceptional circumstances betray us. (39)

As the film privileges Marcos' rituals of artmaking and acute social misunderstandings, the viewer is also rather quickly made aware of his fragile 'living present' visually across the ghostly settings – specifically, the vacated streets and scarcely populated neighborhoods. These scenes of dilapidated and poverty-ridden neighborhoods in Córdoba reinforce broader concerns obliquely present in the film, especially certain consequences of Menem's presidency in the 1990s (Rocco 2023). The visual elements of a ghost town in the protagonist's physical spaces nonetheless rarely remain static and on the surface. If, at the outset of *Cuadros en la oscuridad*, the film's spectrality remains Jamesonian, it also leans toward Jacques Derrida's notion of specters throughout the rest of the film. As Colin Davis explains, 'Derrida's specter is a deconstructive figure hovering between life and death, presence and absence, and making established certainties vacillate' (2013: 56). A mélange of Derridian and Jamesonian interpretations of specters invites a deeper understanding of the protagonist's unspoken struggles. As the film unfolds, moreover, Marcos' existence begins to embody the notion of "spectropolitics" which may be a politics *of* or *for* specters – designed to address how, in different parts of the world, particular subjects become prone to social erasure, marginality, and precarity' (2013: 19, original emphasis).[4] Indeed, the protagonist's extreme poverty and an almost complete (social and political) alienation are foregrounded persistently in *Cuadros en la oscuridad*, and reaffirm his status, above all, as a social specter.

Cuadros en la oscuridad's spectropolitics nonetheless manifests in paradoxical ways. For one, although Marcos remains permanently erased in social terms, his creative outbursts and abundant artwork insist on the vitality of his rebellious self. 'I think,' explains Markovitch, 'that Marcos' bewilderment is situated in the aftermath of the dictatorship. Repression not only leaves infinite corpses in its wake, it also omits, denies, confuses those who "survive"' ('Pienso que el aturdimiento de Marcos está situado en las secuelas de la dictadura. La represión, no sólo deja infinidad de cadáveres a su paso, también omite, niega, confunde a quienes "sobreviven"') (2022: 44). These remarks about Marcos' existential lessons might also hold broader cultural implications in *Cuadros en la oscuridad* – a subtle homage to all those who creatively and with more visibility marked the transition years toward democracy across the Southern Cone. This might include the works of Alicia Partnoy, Nora Strejilevitch, Ariel Dorfman, Diamela Eltit, and Raúl Zurita, but also writers from more recent generations, such as Mariana Enríquez, Andrés Neuman, Alejandro Zambra, and Agustina Bazterrica to name but a few. In writing about *Cuadros en la oscuridad*'s exploration of self-imposed invisibility, González (2017) specifies that the filmmaker's 'main objective of that production was to talk about artistic anonymity as a consequence of her country's dictatorship and that her father, author of more than a thousand artistic works, was never able to exhibit his work' ('objetivo principal en esa producción fue hablar del anonimato artístico como secuela de la dictadura de su país y es que su padre, autor de más de mil obras artísticas, nunca pudo exponer su trabajo') (2017: 1). Apart from reminding us of the purpose behind *Armando y Genoveva* (Chapter 4), as a solid thematic base for *Cuadros en la oscuridad*, González's notion of 'anonimato artístico' introduces another metaphorical layer of the spectral in *Cuadros en la oscuridad*: the notion of enduring mistrust in post-dictatorial social contracts (Feitlowitz 1998). While Marcos' distrust is even more evident because of his social isolation, his art of awe and versatility emerges, nonetheless, from, and stays locked in, this state of ghostly existence. The protagonist's most effective way of challenging the residue of repression is his compulsive creativity.[5] Although the protagonist is not shown at work (painting) for lengthy periods of time in the film, Marcos is not unproductively paralyzed or unable to create. That said, Marcos appears to subsist continuously between his high creative productivity and low social recognition from his community.

This disunion ultimately culminates in several anguish-ridden sequences as the other characters (children) and their destructive acts begin to erase Marcos' artistic traces, on the one hand, and reiterate his absence on the other. Painting stands out as Marcos' assertive form of unembroidered presence but also rebellion, yet Markovitch presents this rebellious presence in unexpected ways by the destruction of that which feeds his existence. When Luis and his street friends unearth Marcos' paintings accidently and out of mischievous curiosity toward the end of the film, they bulldoze through them and end up demolishing, damaging, and abandoning most of them. Rocco argues that the children's behavior 'stages a kind of symbolic death of Marcos' ('pone en escena una suerte de asesinato simbólico de Marcos') (2023: 157). At the same time, paradoxically, Marcos' art gains more visibility in the film precisely after his literal death and during the children's production of dystopian spaces at the painter's home.

Markovitch imagines this possibility unsentimentally and explains that Marcos 'dies unknown, but his legacy is not lost' ('muere inédito, pero su legado no está perdido') (Markovitch 2020: n.pag.). This 'legacy' in the film manifests as horror, creating what Gregory Claeys calls 'the stench of dystopia' or 'savagery, animality, and monstrosity' (Claeys 2016: 4). Yet such 'dystopia' both highlights the painter's absence and reinforces his presence through a formidable accumulation of 'cinematic emotions' after his passing. In *Feeling Cinema: Emotional Dynamics in Film Studies* (2011), Tarja Laine defines '[c]inematic emotions... as processes that are intentional in a phenomenological sense, supporting the continuous and dynamic exchange between the film's world and the spectator's world' (2011: 1). This 'exchange between' the two worlds is further and self-reflexively challenged in *Cuadros en la oscuridad*. In a ghostly way, one could argue that some of the children, who perpetuate these destructive discoveries and actions, are also their spectators. Some of them partake in the destruction, others seek to understand the found artwork. Still others simply observe. Marcos' absence therefore frees up the children's multisensorial curiosity – but also their monstrous conduct and spectatorship – as they break into his home and engage insensitively and destructively with his unexhibited art. 'Absence, when made present,' states Ahmed, 'forces one to think of the absent, and that which makes absence present has the power to determine the way in which one thinks of the absent' (2019: 162). The protagonist's absence rudimentarily grows more palpable as we visually riffle through this artwork at the children's destructive hands.

In *Managing Monsters* (1994), Marina Warner theorizes about children as transgressors due to their unique positionality in society. For Warner, 'children are perceived as innocent because they are outside society, pre-historical, no-social, instinctual, creatures of uneasiness primitive kin to unspoiled nature' (44). While being outside of the structures of power (alone and unwatched by adults), the street children in *Cuadros en la oscuridad* engage with that which Carolina Rocha and Georgia Seminet have discussed in *Screening Minors in Latin American Cinema* (2014) as 'their [minors'] impulse to become agents of their own desire' (xv). Markovitch's film presents minors whose everyday life is unpredictable and frequently transgressive principally due to their socioeconomic reality. The director's interest in the theme of street children's agency, transgression, and vulnerability is further explored in *Ángeles* (2025) but in extreme ways. In Markovitch's fifth film, street children make serious pacts with adults who are existentially inert (Chapter 7). The destructive acts in *Cuadros en la oscuridad* underscore the painter's absence but also emotionally shift 'our attention toward what cannot be seen, that which can only be detected by means of intersubjective sharing of experience' (Laine 2011: 4).[6] The destruction of his paintings reaffirms the protagonist's always already existential deadness as a dissident artist whose work sits somewhere between 'a protest against the impossibility of living beautifully, [...] [and] a form of mourning a loss of sorts' (Ahmed 2019: 169). This liminality in *Cuadros en la oscuridad* reminds us of the totalitarian forces that had labeled him as politically repulsive and have kept the painter figuratively incarcerated for decades.

These moments in the film also demarcate 'primitive and perceptual' spaces in accordance with Edward Relph's discussions in *Place and Placelessness* (1976). The primitive space, which the children in the film occupy during their destructive behavior, 'is the space of instinctive behavior and unselfconscious action in which we always act and move without reflection' (8). In contrast, 'perceptual spaces' are 'egocentric,' and 'perceived and confronted by each individual. This is a space that has context and meaning, for it cannot be divorced from experiences and intentions' (10). Markovitch's film questions such easy dichotomies, and after the protagonist's death, it succeeds at making them intersect. The director accomplishes this when she shows one of the street children in the painter's atelier, a curious young girl, engage with the paintings in a sensorially interpretative way. Riffling through the discovered paintings, which are subsequently hurled around and demolished, the little girl explains for Luis while engaging with one of the found artworks: 'This is the head. This is the eye. This is the eyebrow. This is the nose and this is the mouth. This is the forehead. This is the arm. This is the clothes. Got it?' ('Esta es la cabeza. Este es el ojo. Esta es la ceja. Esta es la nariz y esta es la boca. Esta es la frente. Este es el brazo. Esta es la ropa. ¿Entendés?'). In juxtaposing this moment with the destructive actions of the other minors at the same site evokes and then complicates the sole emergence of 'primitive spaces.' At this point in the film, the atelier entertains both spaces. This coexistence of 'primitive and perceptual spaces' poignantly creates a singular platform for Marcos' artistic remnants to be a public focal point – even if in fleeting and ghastly ways – before the repugnant handling of his art begins.

Disgust indeed resurfaces throughout *Cuadros en la oscuridad* with different emblematic implications. William Miller's seminal

The Anatomy of Disgust (1997) explains that disgust functions as 'an emotion that has large political and social theoretical consequences' (21). According to Miller, disgust

> must be accompanied by ideas of a particular kind of danger, the danger inherent in pollution and contamination, the danger of defilement, which ideas in turn will be associated with rather predicable cultural and social scenarios. [...] Some emotions, among which disgust and its close cousin contempt are the most prominent, have intensely political significance. They work to hierarchize our political order: in some setting they do the work of maintaining hierarchy; in other settings they constitute righteously presented claims for superiority: in yet other settings they are themselves elicited as an indication of one's proper placement in social order. Disgust evaluates (negatively) what it touches, proclaims the meanness and inferiority of its object. (8–9)

Almost unambiguously, the film throughout portrays the consequences of Marcos having been tagged in the past as a dangerous citizen and a political pollutant. The notion of danger and social menace, which governs Marcos' subjectivity and has sedimented beyond the dictatorial past, echoes Marguerite Feitlowitz's seminal discussion in *A Lexicon of Terror: Argentina and the Legacies of Torture* (1998). Feitlowitz explains how the military regime in Argentina viewed its political dissidents, 'the missing and the dead were not victims, nor merely enemies; they were demons. And so was anyone who *thought* otherwise' (Feitlowitz 1998: 27, original emphasis). Disgust, as a biopolitical mechanism, conveys sociopolitical demonization and the 'inferiority' of the protagonist and his existential struggles. Markovitch is not subtle about this, for her early script announces that 'Marcos is a marginal artist who has never been able to exhibit his paintings' ('Marcos es un artista marginal, que nunca ha podido exhibir sus pinturas'.) (2016: n.p.).

Yet Miller's theorizations also suggest that disgust can inspire success and wellbeing. According to Miller, 'disgust is also a necessary partner in the positive; love, as we know it, would make little sense without disgust being there to overcome. Our own commitment to virtues of moral and bodily cleanliness, to the loathing of cruelty and hypocrisy, depends upon it' (1997: 18). When the children leave the atelier in disarray, we watch several paintings float in water, others are torn apart, and still others are wrinkled and broken. Markovitch has called this moment in the film 'un *collage* truculento' ('a horrifying *collage*').[7] In the final scenes of the film, Markovitch uniquely blends destruction with discovery; ignorance with curiosity; carelessness with interest. These scenes further intensify the film's focus on the protagonist's art, albeit in a grotesque way. 'Disgust,' Miller reminds us, 'differs from other emotions by having a unique aversive style. The idiom of disgust consistently invokes the sensory experience of what it feels like to be put in danger by the disgusting, of what it feels like to be too close to it, to have to smell it, see it, or touch it. Disgust uses images of sensation or suggests the sensory merely by describing the disgusting thing to capture what makes it disgusting' (1997: 9). Indeed, the same scenes create a shocking texture, depth, and luminosity to counter the original source (the invisible but controlling forces in Marcos' mind and his past) that had prevented the protagonist, on political grounds, from enjoying social visibility and professional prosperity. The scenes of repugnant, senseless destruction of cultural production critique the original repressive forces that had paralyzed Marcos' spirit. In a parallel twist, the shantytown children simultaneously exhibit and ruin the protagonist's artwork through their multisensorial engagement with it: they touch, see, and ultimately smell it, as the unframed paintings rot away in the flooded house.

In her initial script drafts, Markovitch imagines a soul-crushed character living in an equally tired socio-economic setting but is ambivalent about how to represent his legacy.[8] These particular laments had begun to take root in *Armando y Genoveva* (Chapter 4) but grew deeper first in Markovitch's creative diary entries ('Escribir' in *Cacerías imaginarias*) on *Cuadros en la oscuridad* and then in the film itself. The entries are brief, but they are oriented toward, and illuminate, the filmmaker's creative processes for and thematic desire to depict the protagonist's complexity as precisely as possible. The filmmaker's notebook is a unique entry point into *Cuadros en la oscuridad*, for it describes Markovitch's contemplations of a dual purpose: an artistic reflection on her father's life-long identity as a shunned artist, and her own attempts to grapple with his public stagnation, notwithstanding his inexorable commitment to painting. As the film unfolds, the viewer also learns that the protagonist in *Cuadros en la oscuridad* appears to lead a life that falls somewhere between 'migratoriness' and 'displacement' in Mieke Bal's terms (2010: 3). For Bal, in *Of What One Cannot Speak: Doris Salcedo's Political Art* (2010), migratoriness 'characterizes the culture that both longer-term inhabitants and newcomers share' while 'displacement' occurs to 'people who are pushed around by powers' (3). Marcos' character embodies certain elements of both conditions: he comes across as a permanent newcomer in his immediate neighborhood because of his social isolation, and his displacement is undeniably political in nature and rooted in his dissident youth.

In *Adaptation Studies* (2013), Anna Sofia Rossholm contributes a chapter about directors' notebooks to reflect analytically on Ingmar Bergman's cinema. 'The artist's notebook,' in broad terms, explains Rossholm, 'is in itself a heterogeneous genre that can take many forms and have various functions: scrapbooks, creative diaries, drafts, sketches, photos, or other imprints' (Rossholm 2013: 205). For Rossholm, the artist's notebook's critical richness derives from its generic distinctiveness; in other words, 'the transgressive character of the genre: it is a text somewhere between the personal and the shared, between the fictional and the real, between aesthetic practice and reflection' (205). Markovitch's creative diaries on *Cuadros en la oscuridad* fit this characterization, for she frequently merges the personal and the historical to reflect on her aesthetic alignments, undertakings, hesitations, and creative impulses.

The ending of *Cuadros en la oscuridad* demands more focus on the personal and its ambivalence. This ambivalence is revealed in two related artistic sources: the director's published notebook but also another, and publicly less known, version of the film which the director entitled as 'Cuadros. Experimento Dramático.' Creatively, 'Cuadros. Experimento Dramático' could be viewed as an additional layer, albeit a digital one, to Markovitch's published notebook. More importantly, the other 'ending,' in the unofficial version of the film, signals the director's ambivalence about Marcos' legacy but also the role of her autobiographical details. Consequently, 'Cuadros. Experimento Dramático' elucidates 'the process of creation,' especially since it allows us to reimagine Marcos' legacy differently and through his family ties, inserting what the filmmaker has called 'dash of hopefulness' ('una pincelada de esperanza') (Rossholm 2013: 205).[9] The radically different version of the film reveals Markovitch's tense grappling with the protagonist's artistic tribute and legacy. In the alternative ending, the filmmaker envisions Marcos' daughter returning to collect, preserve, and potentially honor publicly her father's artwork. Such an ending straightforwardly prevents the posthumous extinction of the painter's work. More obviously, 'Cuadros. Experimento Dramático' echoes a similar commitment that *Armando y Genoveva* foregrounds through the filmmaker's autobiographical perspective (Chapter 4). In this artistic context, Markovitch exhibits another instance of 'auto-adaptation' which 'refers to a continuous movement of writing and transposition that takes place on two levels: first the materialization of the author's "self" in the process of writing, and then the transposition from one form of inscription, the notebook, to another, a film or a screenplay' (Rossholm 2013: 206). In Markovitch's case, though, 'Cuadros. Experimento Dramático' seems to suggest that certain creative processes resist closure and instead continually renew themselves in multiple directions.

The alternative ending suggests not only a glimpse of hope but also a particular kind of resilience. Resilience is not an unknown attribute to those around Marcos in *Cuadros en la oscuridad* but it more closely resembles the discussion in Robin James' *Resilience & Melancholy: Pop Music, Feminism, Neoliberalism* (2015). James illuminates paradoxical forms of resilience that are often at the mercy of different hegemonic entities, stating that '*[h]egemony actively incites death and damage; resilient populations recover and even profit from it, while precarious populations exhaust all their resources in their constant struggles to stay barely alive.* Resilience discourse is a biopolitical technology that reinforces the line between those fit to live, and those whose death is necessary for society's ongoing health' (2015: 9, original emphasis). By situating her film in a shantytown of Córdoba, Markovitch indirectly gestures at such 'struggles' without dwelling on them directly; we watch Marcos and Luis share a boiled egg; we watch them inhabit a cold and derelict home; we watch Marcos' occasional purchase of just one piece of fruit, to mention a few examples. The materialized yet failed intersubjectivities among those who must first privilege their sheer survival (Luis and Carmen) and those, who ground their bare survival, above all else, in creative acts (Marcos), reinforce the core paradox in the film. Their conviviality, which appears to be anchored more in the inability to understand each other rather than overt misunderstandings, culminates in disgust. 'Along with indignation,' states Miller, disgust 'gives voice to our strongest sentiments of moral disapprobation. It is bound up intimately with our response to the ordinary vices of hypocrisy, betrayal, cruelty, and stupidity' (1997: 20). *Cuadros en la oscuridad* invites the viewer to contemplate how Marcos' response to those who had tagged him as a political pollutant might have found its key in his artistic gift and expressions, namely – paintings as quiet expressions of political defiance. Yet such a defiance, ultimately, is both reaffirmed (through the discovery of his paintings) and rapidly extinguished (through the accidental destruction of his artwork). Marcos' defiance reinforces his own ghostliness. His art becomes fleetingly visible only to those whose struggle for mere survival also highlights their social spectrality.

Notes

1   Markovitch writes straightforwardly about her inspiration for *Cuadros en la oscuridad* in *Cacerías imaginarias* (2022: 40).

2 See Paula Markovitch, 'Armando y Genoveva.' <www.https://armandoygenoveva.org. Accessed 22 June 2022.
3 Markovitch continues to reflect on the 1990s in *Cacerías imaginarias* and writes that '[th]e year 1995 was unfolding in Córdoba, Argentina. One of the worst crises in the country's history was brewing. My dad worked at a gas station dispatching fuel. Like almost all intellectuals in the country, my parents had had to hide for many years. Many friends and family were killed. Today I believe that the military dictatorship had killed "people," but also dreams, creativity, hopes ... My parents, seemingly, had become used to solitude and anonymity' ('[t]ranscurría el año 1995 en Córdoba, Argentina. Se preparaba una de las peores crisis de la historia del país. Mi padre trabajaba en una estación de servicio despachando combustible. Como casi todos los intelectuales del país, mis padres habían tenido que ocultarse durante muchos años. Muchos amigos y familiares fueron asesinados. Hoy creo que la dictadura militar había matado "personas," pero también sueños, creatividad, esperanzas ... Al parecer mis padres se habían acostumbrado a la soledad y al anonimato') (2022: 41).
4 The figure of the ghost has held multifaceted implications historically across different cultures. According to del Pilar Blanco's and Peeren's discussions of the ghost through a cross-disciplinary lens, the figure of the ghost frequently functions as 'a conceptual metaphor capable of bringing to light and opening up to analysis hidden, disavowed, and neglected aspects of the social and cultural realm, past and present' (2013: 21).
5 We are reminded of Chilean Diamela Eltit's mother protagonist in *Los vigilantes* (1994), who writes compulsively to directly challenge a repressive familiar order, thus establishing an emblematic critique toward Pinochet's dictatorship in oblique ways. Markovitch's protagonist does not embody a confrontational mode of addressing the lingering consequences of Argentina's state terror through writing, but his commitment to painting could be viewed as a quiet form of resistance.
6 This is even more evident in the second version of the film in which the painter's daughter returns to the father's atelier to sort out his work.
7 Interview with Markovitch 1 August 2023.
8 Interview with Markovitch 28 July 2023.
9 Rossholm's remark is worthy of citing in its entirety: 'the notebook is beyond the realm of art [...]. On the one hand, it is a form where the author can write freely, test ideas and reflect on the creative process in an intimate sphere protected from the judgment of readers, audiences, and critics. On the other hand, the artistic diary turns the aesthetic process of rendering the subjective into a shared experience. As such, it makes the process of creation itself visible' (Rossholm 2013: 205).

6
El actor principal (2019): Emotional Gestures

Unspoken words, half-articulated thoughts, and broken proficiencies in English and Spanish elegantly hold together *El actor principal* (2019). From the outset, the film obliges the viewer to read the characters' emotions down to the most subtle detail, since their spoken exchanges fail them regularly. As the protagonists' engagement with personal past and present burdens grows increasingly dependent upon their gestures – and occasionally upon touch – their emotional closeness deepens in unpredictable ways. Indeed, their chance encounter in Berlin intersects a singular mélange of geography, emotion, and social interactions, just as it reveals how their interpersonal boundaries grow more porous despite their inability to understand each other with ease.

This paradox emerges as the film privileges a particular kind of spatial and emotional interconnectedness where, to borrow from Steve Pile, 'emotions, now, lie *between* individuals, and *between* individuals and perceptual environments' (2010: 13, original emphasis). While Pile's argument identifies the situatedness of emotions, Sara Ahmed goes further to underscore their complex dynamisms. In *The Cultural Politics of Emotion* (2015), Ahmed notes that 'emotions are not only about movement, they are also about attachments or about what connects us to this or that' (2015: 11). Pile's and Ahmed's takes on emotion are at work in Markovitch's film, for the director highlights the forceful interplay between the characters' basic emotions and the spaces they jointly occupy through their frequently gesture-based communication. Such an interplay consequently centers on what other critics have called the inevitable 'permeability of psycho-social boundaries' (Davidson, Bondi, and Smith 2005: 10). The latter notion simply stems from the idea that social settings, places, and geography in general are vigorously intertwined with emotions, which function as 'a relational, connective medium' (2005: 7). 'Emotion,' note the critics in *Emotional Geographies* (2005), 'has the power to transform the shape of our lives, expanding or contracting our horizons, creating new fissures or fixtures we never expected to find' (2005: 1). According to Joyce Davidson, Liz Bondi, and Mick Smith, emotions are manifestly 'situated within, and co-constitutive of, our working (as well as social) lives' (2005: 2). Their conceptualization of 'emotional geographies' is relevant to the present analysis for its mediation-focused role, particularly in 'understand[ing] emotion – experientially and conceptually – in terms of its socio-spatial mediation and articulation rather than as entirely interiorized subjective mental states' (2005: 3). *El actor principal*'s entire main argument relies on the nexus amongst the protagonists' socio-spatial circumstances, emotions, and gesture-based intimations.

El actor principal's emotional geography begins to take form when the protagonists' emotional gestures – the distinct nonverbal packaging of meaning through subtle and overt emotion-imbued bodily and facial expressions – intensify and in so doing bring to light their social marginality as well as transgressions. As a result, the characters' interpersonal connectedness becomes engendered not solely through what Laura Marks calls a 'personal sensorium,' or 'the bodily organization of sense experience,' (2000: 2), but also through what Ahmed and Jackie Stacey denominate as 'a skin-tight politics, a politics that takes as its orientation not the body as such, but the fleshy interface between bodies and worlds' (2001: 1). For these critics, in *Thinking through the Skin* (2001), the notion of 'inter-embodiment' signifies 'the mode of being-with and being-for, where one touches and is touched by others' (2001: 1). The seemingly simple emotional connectedness between Azra and Luis throughout the film initiates their inter-embodiment and reveals additional content of their subjectivities. In particular, we are allowed access to their pasts – namely, Azra's survival throughout the political violence in Kosovo (1998–99) and Luis' perseverance and autonomy through informal labor sectors (involving unregistered vendors and poverty) in Mexico.[1] This kind of inter-embodiment, which is based potently on emotional gestures, heightens Markovitch's complex aesthetic explorations of social marginality and transgression. This chapter studies the intersection of the protagonists' basic emotions, bold gestures, and defiantly occupied places in Markovitch's *El actor principal*, which, in turn, reveals the tensions between their precarious livelihoods and subtle forms of agency.

Azra is the driving force in *El actor principal*, for her presence allows us to make sense of Luis' wanderings. Luis, who has been randomly cast to star in a film entitled *Mirror*, is subsequently invited to participate in a film festival in Berlin. His arrival involves simple expectations. He must rest in his hotel room, then dress up and join the rest of the film crew at the festival. Instead, he mischievously embarks on a random exploration of the hotel spaces, ranging from its rooms, hallways, lobbies, and kitchens to its laundry facilities. The latter space, with its abundant piles of clean and dirty bedsheets, folded bedding, and industrial washing machines, lulls Luis into sleep until a hotel worker, Azra, stumbles upon his seemingly lifeless body. Unable to speak Spanish well, Azra is also unable to rid herself of Luis immediately. Their mutual linguistic frustration turns into a cross-cultural curiosity, which they attempt to explore with different degrees of success. Their encounter is accidental yet instantly emotionally charged, for we watch them experience – with varying degrees of sophistication and clumsiness – surprise, fear, erotic interest, and relief.

In thinking about broader Latin American cinema contexts, Markovitch's *El actor principal* could be linked, albeit to different degrees, to Lisandro Alonso's *Fantasma* (2006), Claudia Llosa's *La teta asustada* (2009), Adrián Caetano's *Bolivia* (2008), and Lola Arias' *Mucamas* (2011), to mention a few. This contextualization stems primarily from Markovitch's aesthetic approach to

Figure 6.1 Luis on the streets of Mexico City. © Paula Markovitch

the voices of historically marginalized, stereotyped, or simplified subjectivities in cinema (i.e., women, immigrants, minorities, indigenous groups, and children). These aesthetically diverse films moreover share a common attribute. Although they distinctly approach marginality, they also exemplify how 'reconfigurations of power become possible in places of struggle' (Lavander and Mignolo 2011:7).[2] *El actor principal* can be aligned with the aforementioned films also due to the director's enduring suspicion of representing personal and collective fortitude and afflictions in uncomplicated ways.[3] Indeed, different 'knowledges' as well as 'reconfigurations of power' are also at the heart of *El actor principal*, and they stem from those Gloria Anzaldúa calls the 'dark-skinned, the outcast, the persecuted, the marginalized, the foreign' (1987: 63–4). The two main characters, Azra and Luis, are foreigners in Berlin, and their social presences are both needed and vaguely respected. Their circumstances furthermore link the notion of social marginality to precarity but also to agentic potentials. As a result, the protagonists' multidimensionality is exposed rather quickly in the film, for they simultaneously come across as marginalized and invisible as well as transgressive and complex in their immediate settings and personal lives.

Complex juxtapositions of marginality and agency – sociopolitical (Maguire 2017a: 4; Selimović 2018b: 25; Rocco 2021: 499) and cultural (Garibotto 2015: 269) – interpenetrate Markovitch's cinema particularly in terms of intergenerational tensions involving historical memory and Argentina's dictatorship (1976–83).[4] By creating a story that highlights singular cross-cultural connections beyond solely Latin American contexts, however, Markovitch's film opens up a new space for exploring a particular kind of social navigations of marginality.[5] The filmmaker's story indeed might be a subtle nod to Néstor García Canclini's seminal discussion on shattering 'obsessions with the immaculate conception of authentic national [...] cultures' without disregarding the significant sociopolitical differences and cultural authenticities of the main characters (1992: 11–12). Indeed, in *El actor principal* Markovitch works with different forms of battered subsistence cross-culturally by engaging Azra's personal loss and difficult survival in Kosovo with Luis' economically precarious background from Mexico City (Fig. 6.1). While Luis' context alludes to contemporary issues that grow out of impoverished and crime-stricken areas of Mexico City, Azra's vocalized experiences might resonate with those familiar with Latin American sites and practices of political unrest and resistance, including those of Argentina's Mothers of Plaza de Mayo during the Argentine military dictatorship (1976–83) and H.I.J.O.S in the post-dictatorial era, Chile's Mujeres de Calama during and after Pinochet's regime (1973–90), or the more recent and equally devastating Ayotzinapa case (2014) in Mexico. Some of these Latin American contexts of violence and human rights-oriented quests indeed anchor many of Markovitch's stories in *El premio* (2011), *Armando y Genoveva* (2013a/b), and *Cuadros en la oscuridad* (2017). In *El actor principal*, Markovitch furthermore engages marginality and agency by focusing on the characters' cultural backgrounds, whose intricate political pasts, endured losses, and rebellious tendencies facilitate their interpersonal connectedness in paradoxical ways. In building an intimate cross-cultural geography of emotional gestures (and senses) between the main characters in *El actor principal*, Markovitch distinctly centers first their social marginality in order to amplify, critique, and disrupt other forms of exclusion – those that are cultural, racial, linguistic, gender-based, and professional. As a result, the film highlights the notion of marginality that is constantly embodied as well as contested by its main characters.

El actor principal is Markovitch's first film that does not take place entirely in Latin America. The film begins in the suburbs of Mexico City, yet it is primarily situated in limited places in Berlin. While much of the film unfolds in the hotel's basement away from the heart of the international gathering in question, several scenes, particularly the final ones, are filmed directly on the real and live red carpet of the 2017 Berlinale film festival. This juxtaposition of central and peripheral sites of the Berlinale space, as well as the mixing of genres (documentary and non-documentary), cuts symbolically beyond the immediacy of the characters' chance encounter and their singular modes of relating to each other in cross-cultural ways. Film festivals, notes Cindy Wong, constitute not solely 'vital nodes for global film industries' but also 'are crucial centers for the development of film knowledge and film practices' (2011: 1). When Luis leaves the central spaces of the Berlinale and roams into the less visible spaces of the hotel for much of the film, his agentic decision gains a broader symbolic dimension. Being in the peripheral spaces of the film festival building appears to shed light on 'the historical development and contested hierarchy of films, filmmakers, film languages, themes, and places' but also 'struggles for the right to define film taste and knowledge' (Wong 2011: 1 and 5). As a novice film-festival goer and a nonprofessional actor participant, Luis defies his director's demands and refuses to partake in a panel on *Mirror*, which paradoxically solidifies his autonomy. In this context, Markovitch creates a nuanced invitation to her viewers to contemplate those entities that shape 'what we as audiences and scholars will see' at film festivals (Wong 2011: 1).

The chance encounter in the peripheral sites of the hotel basement first mobilizes the protagonists' mutual openness to reveal the paradoxical side of their exclusion. Azra and Luis fleetingly shape the small walled-in space into a terrain of interpersonal freedom despite their linguistic incoherence. Both characters laugh, nudge each other to drink wine, and are gesturally inquisitive. The foreground and background constantly merge in the claustrophobic crevice that they occupy because of the director's decision to frame both characters in tight close-ups. In fact, one could argue that Markovitch's tight framing dominates during this encounter to emphasize the nature of their ambiguously fragile togetherness. More specifically, their fragility as well as agency are expressed in the ways the characters' bodies articulate their emotional affirmations, inquiries, and misgivings. We watch the characters' bodies engage in emotionally expressive but also unsettled ways: they fold in anxiety, animate in curiosity, come closer in trusting ways, and separate in fear. The mechanics of the camera and the increasing weight of emotion during their stay in the basement accentuate certain features of what feminist geographer Gillian Rose calls 'paradoxical spaces,' or the 'geography [that] describes that subjectivity as that of both prisoner and exile; it allows the subject of feminism to occupy both the centre and the margin, the inside and the outside' (1993: 155). The intricate notion of liminality, which is at the heart of Rose's definition of 'paradoxical spaces,' anchors the chance encounter between Azra and Luis: they are together physically and mostly apart linguistically; they are central discursively and marginal socially; and they are regarded as essential professionally but frequently disregarded on a personal level.[6]

Markovitch's focus on social spaces beyond the hotel basement walls moreover warrants further consideration. If much of the film takes place in the hidden site of the hotel laundry room, its beginning and a significant part of its end pull us into different, urban, and transient sites of order or unpredictability. This spatial juxtaposition creates strong emphasis on the main characters' development and emotional complexity.

Before Luis' communication with Azra unfolds, the audience watches him roam in seemingly aimless ways. With Luis, we enter a flea market and other urban corners of Iztapalapa, occupy small spaces of an aircraft, gaze through its narrow windows at a perfect amalgamation of cottony clouds, and wander through airport spaces. He also ventures into hotel lobbies, hallways, rooms, and, as already discussed, he lingers in the hotel's laundry room before exiting into the streets of Berlin. Luis strikes us as a free-spirited individual whose white hula hoop reminds the viewer of the spaces he used to belong to and even dominate on his streets of choice in Mexico. As a petty thief and a street entertainer, Luis is accustomed to roam the streets in search of opportunities. Brief, *in medias res*, sequences at the beginning of the film, highlighting Luis' precariousness but also his agentic attitude, allow us to see him cohabit casually with the urban poor, nomadic peddlers, and flea market bargainers in Iztapalapa. The focus on nomadic peddlers, street entertainers, and the homeless from a recognizable borough of Mexico City centralizes a particular reality in subtle ways, especially since approximately 60% of inhabitants in Iztapalapa participate in the city's informal economy.[7] Markovitch does it without sidelining its vibrant artistic expressions (i.e., street performers and artists), underscoring the latter alongside the borough's economic and social ills (i.e., gender-based violence, high crime, lack of potable water, to mention a few) (Brito 2011: n.p.). Such scenes manifest as a backstory to Luis' nomadic and street-focused existence but also as random shots from what might have inspired *Mirror* before Luis' arrival in Berlin.

In *Strange Encounters: Embodied Others in Post-Coloniality* (2000), Sara Ahmed defines the term 'encounter' as, above all, 'a meeting, which involves surprise and conflict' (2000: 6). The encounter between Azra and Luis does not lack these elements, but it also reaffirms their uniquely dignified autonomies. Given that identity gets constituted through encounters, the odd encounter in *El actor principal* ties the notion of autonomy to the complexities of the characters' identities. In essence, the encounter between Azra and Luis straightforwardly demonstrates how, as Ahmed notes in *Strange Encounters*, 'each encounter reopens past encounters,' allowing the viewer to cut deeper into the protagonists' intimate pasts (2011: 8). Despite the fragmented nature of Azra's confessions in English about her past, we gather with certainty that she had lived through a war. Just as the film does not directly name Iztapalapa's social and economic tribulations, neither does it name Azra's context but clearly refers to the relatively recent conflict in Kosovo. Luis, as already noted, comes from the underprivileged social class in which survival is based on petty theft and on a frail labor sector.[8] His involvement in *Mirror* appears to have been purely accidental, for he was spotted stealing car mirrors by a Mexican filmmaker and was invited to act out some of his life experiences in the film. While their displacements differ in radical ways – Azra's is war-caused; Luis' is shaped by feeble informal labor opportunities – their encounter reveals that they both have been thrown into new lives and professional roles abruptly. Although Azra appears to be a responsible worker, and Luis' role in *Mirror* has led him to a celebrated film festival abroad, their encounter alludes to the sense of vulnerability they both might feel in such roles. Yet such feelings of vulnerability do not cancel out their fragile forms of defiance. Both characters briefly suspend their work duties and engage in that which Howes and Classen denominate in a different cultural context as 'immersive social intimacy' (i.e., they play with the washing machines, dance, listen to Kosovar music, drink, play hide-and-seek, and chase each other frivolously) and act on their erotic impulses (2014: 84).

Certain degrees of encounter-based disclosure are found in the divergent ways Luis and Azra are committed to their films and footage, respectively. Luis' commitment to *Mirror* appears half-hearted from the outset. His playful indifference becomes further consolidated when he encounters a massive promotional poster for *Mirror* in a public space in Berlin toward the end of the film but simply shrugs the encounter off with an ingenuous smile. Azra's commitment to 'her movie,' however, is radically different. When she hears about Luis' film, she grabs her iPad, searches for a video, and responds in an energetic way: 'Me too. Me too, "film"' ("película"). And when Luis asks 'Are you that one?' ('¿Tú eres esa?'), pointing at the iPad screen, Azra answers, 'Me.' Irrespective of the two characters' level of commitment, these moments of broken language proficiencies and alert emotional attunement blend during their encounter to shed light on their paradoxical psycho-social bonding but also on additional layers of their complex selves. Azra associates the footage, which seemingly features her younger self within a crowd of displaced people, above all, with a profound loss – namely, the loss of her daughter during the war in Kosovo. 'In Kosovo was a war,' she explains to Luis, 'War.' This encounter does not solely allow more information about their innermost fears, losses, and expectations but also shows the ways in which the encounter, as Ahmed reminds us, 'always carries *traces* of those broader relationships' (Ahmed 2000: 8, original emphasis). Azra's sparse but significant references to the Kosovo war, which started in February 1998 under the directive of Slobodan Milošević in the area of Drenica, bring to mind 'broader' implications regarding its most gruesome consequences: ethnic cleansing, displacement, systematic killings, and rape.[9] Azra's presence inevitably 'carries' larger war-related implications; her comments, independence, and interactions with Luis particularly bring to mind women's rights against 'the unwelcomed re-traditionalization of gender roles' (Di Lellio 2016: 8). Azra's vocalized remembrance of the war atrocities in Kosovo in Albanian consequently juxtaposes her loss and guilt with her agency and voice in authentic ways. These scenes in the film spell out a memory-based geography of emotion in which 'the interconnected location of emotions in people and places' gains significant traction (Bondi, Davidson, and Smith 2005: 5). Luis' attention to Azra's fragmented narrative about affliction and survival is unwavering and makes him paradoxically at ease during what otherwise would have been an awkward encounter between two linguistically and culturally distanced strangers.

On an aesthetic level, the inclusion of documentary footage about the 2017 Berlinale, and especially the war in Kosovo, is a straightforward example of 'archiveology' at work. In *Archiveology: Walter Benjamin and Archival Film Practices* (2018), Catherine Russell explains this practice as 'the reuse, recycling, appropriation and borrowing of archival material' (2018: 1). Russell's study builds on the work of Walter Benjamin, Michel Foucault, and Jacques Derrida and broadens the direct connection between archival material and memory through different media, particularly film, which leads to the notion of archiveology 'as a mode of transmission [that] offers a unique means of displaying and accessing historical memory' (2018: 1). The inclusion of the footage – its indirect 'recycling' – adds additional content to Azra's subjectivity on her own terms. The footage draws our attention to Azra as a war survivor but also highlights her struggles to articulate the war afflictions meaningfully. By opting for mechanisms that go beyond language to communicate the bits and pieces of her characters' backgrounds, Markovitch challenges that which the authors of *Ways of Sensing* (2014) denominate as '[v]isual and auditory evidence [that] generally takes precedence over evidence based on other sensory experiences' (2014: 94). By the end of the film, Markovitch's focus on emotional gestures marks the encounter as 'strange,' but in empowering ways. Keeping in mind Ahmed's discussion in *Strange Encounters*, each shared story layer between the characters highlights additional details of their identities while also disallowing 'an erasure of difference' to take form (2000: 6).[10]

Such a story space, moreover, produces a unique 'relationality' of languages, cultures, and political pasts and unlinks the characters from reductive or simplified representations of their social selves (Mignolo and Walsh 2018: 1). This said, social difference typically solicits varied reactions of compliance and rebelliousness (Howes and Classen 2014: 7). 'Social groups,' explain David Howes and Constance Classen, 'can contest their sensory typing and challenge the boundaries of their social containment. This can happen outright, as when a group demands that its voice be heard, or, more subtly by manipulating symbols and constraints to a group's own advantage' (2014: 7).

Luis' social difference and audacity at the Berlinale is a case in point. And so is Azra's, even if in a different way. If Luis decides to break away from his professional duties to enhance his autonomy, Azra handles his intrusion into her workday in transgressive ways. Markovitch positions her characters, above all, to '*feel through*' their condensed, incomplete, and sensorially framed stories about loss, confusion, and death, all of which are related to their politically and economically devastating pasts (2014: 79, original emphasis).[11]

The filmmaker's stories, in fact, frequently feature characters who defy, question, and sometimes shatter their marginalized states beyond those presented in *El actor principal*. Unlike *El actor principal*, which traces the protagonists' attempts to articulate their personal afflictions to each other in more refined ways, *El premio* reflects on the dictatorial government in Argentina (1976–83) and political dissent from the child's perspective, thus aligning the film with Marcelo Piñeyro's *Kamchatka* (2002), Daniel Bustamante's *Andés no quiere dormir la siesta* (2009), and Benjamín Ávila's *Infancia clandestina* (2011), to mention but a few. Apart from underscoring 'la experiencia de la perplejidad infantil ante un mundo contradictorio y muchas veces cruel,' such interactions in *El premio* are reinforced in affective ways and for the sake of the main characters' sheer survival (Borobio 2011: n.p.). According to Alessandro Rocco, Markovitch, above all, blends her lived experiences with fiction in *El premio* (2021: 499). *Cuadros en la oscuridad* (2017), which is partly based on her father (Armando Markovitch), his political persuasions, and his passion for painting, takes the viewer to Córdoba's shantytown where little is spoken and too much endured, especially in the protagonist's immediate world.[12] In this film, poverty assaults the protagonist, Marcos, daily, as he fights back through his love of painting and a tenuous friendship with a local, indigenous, and street child, Luis. In her recently published collection of short stories, *El monstruo* (2014), Markovitch's exploration of marginalization is intimately linked to abandonment, mental illness, betrayal, and addiction.

El actor principal, however, goes a step further in highlighting the changeability of the main characters' marginalized states through evanescent togetherness. The notion of evanescent togetherness in this film manifests through the interpersonal awkwardness and touch of those who appear to have much in common socially and personally yet remain unable to communicate or understand the nuances of each other's complex stories linguistically. This communicative gap is lessened through tactility in the film, particularly when we recall what Ahmed and Stacey articulate, namely that 'through touch, the separation of self and other is undermined in the very intimacy or proximity of the encounter' (2000: 6). Given that emotions are 'intrinsically relational,' the notion of evanescent togetherness entails an emotionally layered and physically unifying – even if impermanent – state between both characters (Davidson, Bondi, and Smith 2005: 9). Markovitch therefore reveals Luis and Azra as distinct strangers whose transient togetherness affirms that interruptions, confusion, and fragmented existential paths have interpenetrated their lives, even if only certain layers of these paths manage to be expressed between the two of them. The characters' inter-embodiment becomes a fleeting antidote to their immediate loneliness. If, as Howes and Classen note, '[w]ithin every field of social endeavour, explicit or implicit significance is ascribed to different sensations and sensory practices, whether visual and auditory, or tactile, olfactory, and gustatory,' then much of the antidote to their loneliness stems from their emotional attunement and sensory communication (2014: 4).

The encounter also appears to be held together partly due to what Erin Manning calls 'a leaky sense of self' (2013: 1). Echoing Gilles Deleuze's and Félix Guattari's discussion on 'becoming,' Manning argues that such interactions are inter- and cross-sensorially singular, since 'a looking becomes a touching, a feeling becomes a hearing. But not *on* the skin or *in* the body. Across strata, both concrete and abstract, they constitute an assemblage. This assemblage is a sensing body in movement, a body-world that is always tending, attending to the world' (2013: 2, original emphasis). The main characters' 'leaky sense of self' manifests through different sensorial moments of interaction. Azra, for instance, invites Luis to explore – and quite literally feel – certain items from a pile of random things (perfumes, dolls, toys, bottles of wine) which were left behind in guest rooms and subsequently collected by her, to grasp the content of her secret space. This space serves as a platform where their haptic – and olfactory – engagement with the collected things brings them closer and strengthens their emotional geography, for it allows them to gain even more interpersonal courage in the claustrophobic space of the laundry room and engage imaginatively each other's personal strength, playfulness, and emotional openness. During these moments, the filmmaker centralizes the characters' sensations to underscore their interpersonal discoveries.

The protagonists' emotional gestures interpenetrate their encounter partly because it brims with unpredictable sensations. 'What makes sensations so forceful,' explain Howes and Classen, 'is that they are lived experiences' (2014: 7). As Luis touches the objects Azra shares with him, he mobilizes his own curiosity and begins to 'live' her sensorial world, even without understanding most of it. Luis' haptic discoveries, under Azra's firm guidance, deepen, which, in accordance with Peter Bieri, exemplifies how 'the heat of mutuality constitutes a committed encounter' (2017: 57). Azra's gestural guidance of Luis' haptic engagement with their shared space differs from Vero's perplexing gestures in Lucrecia Martel's *La mujer sin cabeza* (2008), since Vero's gestures only further complicate her social engagement and bewilder those around her.[13] Azra's gesture-based invitation, which she carries out by signaling with her hands, smiles, eyes, and body to Luis to touch her adopted things, renders as poetically feverish insofar as we recall Andrey Tarkovsky's remarks from *Sculpting in Time* (2003) [1986]. There, Tarkovsky reminds us that certain experiences come to life only through poetic expressions – that is, 'there are some aspects of human life that can only be faithfully represented through poetry' (2003: 30). *El actor principal* relies more on absurdist interactions than purely on dream-like moments for the characters to venture intermittently into each other's past by focusing on their gestural intimations. These ventures first privilege interpersonal 'movement and sensation *and then* language to inquire into our tendency to place language as the determinant of experience' (Manning 2013: 9, emphasis added).

Incongruent dialogues – in Albanian, English, Spanish, and particularly those that stem from affliction-ridden pasts – allow Markovitch to erect 'the feeling of strangeness' ('[la] sensación de extrañeza')[14] to accentuate the tension in the film. It is not surprising that the director chooses 'the laundry room...noisy and infernal' ('la lavandería... ruidosa e infernal') for much of Luis' and Azra's interactions, for the background noise and constant movement further heighten their already apprehensive intersubjectivity.[15] 'Tension in encounters,' writes Erving Goffman, 'arises when the official focus of attention is threatened by distractions of various kinds; this state of uneasiness is managed by tactful acts, such as the open expression in a usable way of what is distracting attention' (2013: 13). The key bewilderment in Luis' and Azra's encounter is, above all, linguistic and is hardly ever completely 'managed' or overcome. This interaction fleetingly locks them into an intricate past-oriented present, or what Byung-Chul Han calls 'intervals' in *The Scent of Time* (2017). Han's conceptualization of 'intervals' blends arguably opposite feelings, emotions, and states of being or 'zones of forgetting, of loss, of death, of fear and anxiety, but also of longing, of hope, of adventure, of promising and expecting. In many respects, an interval is also a source of suffering and of pain. Remembering becomes a passion if it battles against time's surrendering of the past to oblivion' (2017: 36). Yet this communication-related '*extrañeza*' paradoxically appears to open the characters emotionally, placing them into what Rose considers 'a fluid and multidimensional topography, doubled between two poles but finding that tension productive in the imagining of an elsewhere' (1993: 156). If emotions 'create relationships whether fleeting or lasting,' then these characters' 'elsewhere' manifests in a particularly complex emotional immediacy (Frevert 2014: 5). Such an immediacy pushes the characters to seek imaginative ways of communicating outside of their language-based deadlocks.

As noted at the outset of this chapter, representing personal and collective suffering and individual agency in tidy ways is viewed with persistent suspicion in *El actor principal*. The characters' storytelling in their native languages (Luis' references to his life in Iztapalapa and Azra's to her displacement from Kosovo) disables the possibility that Azra and Luis will rehearse 'crass caricatures of what they actually feel' (Pile 2010: 9). The characters' genuine states of basic feelings – their sensing of each other's discomfort and uneasiness but also their mutual sensing of reprieve – when they share their stories in Albanian and Spanish are unquestionably apparent: their gazes harden as they speak of the past horrors, endured loss, and future uncertainties. Both tell their stories regardless of the interlocutor's ability to understand, creating an affective bond and exemplifying '[o]ur ways of sensing affect [, that is] not only how we experience and engage with our environment, but also how we experience and engage with each other' (Howes and Classen 2014: 6). Markovitch indeed privileges the ways in which the characters *do* their confessions, whereby certain objects serve as their props in their attempts to render the unspeakable.

During such confessions certain objects indeed function as linguistically enlivening facilitators. According to Jeffrey Alexander's theorizing of 'iconic consciousness,' objects are endowed with life; they are 'living, not dead,' for two particularly multidimensional layers hold all objects together – their 'aesthetic surfaces and discursive depths' (Alexander 2020: n.p.). Alexander details the differences between these two spheres, stating that 'iconic objects,' and objects in general, are layered through their form but also their meaning, for 'the surface is something material; it is form as well as shape and it is a texture. . . . Inside the aesthetically formed surface are discursive meanings: moral associations, collective beliefs, and emotions – they are inside, of course, metaphorically. The discursive meaning is invisible to the senses' (Alexander 2020: n.p.). In Alexander's view, the connection between 'aesthetic form' and 'discursive meaning' also demonstrates that iconic objects are never unspoiled and their power 'depends on how surface and depth are experienced by the audience' (Alexander 2020: n.p.). This dependence is evident in Markovitch's film on a simpler scale, whereby (aesthetic) objects (film pamphlets, film festival posters, documentary footage, and gadgets), as facilitators of memory, connect the 'aesthetic form' to and beyond their 'discursive meaning,' primarily to facilitate the immediate communication between the two characters and strengthen their emotional geography. These objects are what the characters 'apprehend' and 'what [they] turn toward, or what is created as an effect of turning' (Ahmed 2014: 25). Azra shares a video segment on her war-torn homeland after Luis shows her a few pamphlets about *Mirror*. Both characters turn 'toward' certain objects that instantiate key layers of their subjectivities for their path to and encounter at the hotel – namely, a refugee status for Azra, a non-professional actor role for Luis.

The pamphlets' aesthetic surface shows Luis' face and remains in place, even when Luis leaves the hotel, never attending his panel. In this way the poster's effectivity surpasses Luis' agency or wants, for its role is to stay effective for passersby, film attendees, critics, film novices, and others. At the same time, the film pamphlet creates an instant – even if incomplete – meaning for Azra. As she touches it, she appears to have understood the pamphlet's *basic* significance – namely, Luis somehow and importantly belongs to the film that the poster heralds in public spaces. These objects remain anchored in gestures and isolated words in Spanish and English that both can recognize. Luis likewise understands Azra's war-related memories to a certain degree only. Although she can further contextualize the footage from her iPad, he is sporadically offered a few utterances in English to scaffold some of Azra's vocalized memories. The filmmaker's usage of different media (iPad-streamed videos on the conflict in Kosovo and printed promotional material for *Mirror*) sensorially supplement the characters' language and gesture-based gaps. These scenes in the film reaffirm that 'it *is* possible to experience a socially and symbolically meaningful world through touch [and that] ... ideas are communicated through sensory impressions all the time' (Howes and Classen 2014: 3, original emphasis). These objects' aesthetic form also constantly prompts Azra and Luis to 'imaginatively experience [them] in a sensuous manner via sight, touch, and hearing' (Alexander 2020: n.p.). Such scenes in the film suggest Ahmed's insistence on the intersection of histories, emotions, and subjects, since 'objects are often read as the cause of emotions in the very process of taking an orientation toward them' (Ahmed 2015: 6). The characters' sensory experiences in the film further anchor – but also complicate – their emotional ties.

Basic emotions – in particular fear, desire, and relief – become key signposts that bridge the unnatural moments of silence and remembrances of poverty-related hardships (Luis) and war-based losses (Azra). Although the characters' emotional investment during their encounter is hardly ever free from ambiguity, their fear, desire, and relief simultaneously anchor and unsettle their fortuitous encounter. Fear frames their initial interaction, for Azra accidentally stumbles upon Luis during her shift. They are both startled by and even terrified of each other's prolonged gaze. Azra pushes Luis after having said in English, 'Who are you? You must go. You cannot sleep here.' And Luis responds rather defiantly, 'Let me sleep here' ('Déjame dormir aquí'). Neither leave. In Goffman's terms, this moment in the film summarily exudes certain attributes of 'unfocused interaction.' In *Encounters: Two Studies in the Sociology of Interaction* ([1961] 2013), Goffman states that unfocused interaction 'consists of those interpersonal communications that result solely by virtue of persons being in one another's presence, as when two strangers across the room from each other check up on each other's clothing, posture, and general manner, while each modifies his own demeanor because he himself is under observation' (2013: 7). Both characters 'modify' their behavior shortly into their interaction. Azra repeatedly gestures to Luis to leave, but he negotiates his stay by offering her a few Euros. Azra reluctantly accepts. At this point, the characters enter into Goffmanian 'focused interaction,' which 'occurs when people effectively agree to sustain for a time a single focus of cognitive and visual attention, as in a conversation, a board game, or a joint task sustained by a close face-to-face circle of contributors' (2013: 7). Indeed, we watch Luis engage with Azra with childish curiosity, thus accepting the rules of the space he begins to co-occupy. He follows her around the washing machines and even helps her finish certain work duties. When Azra motions to Luis to follow her, saying, 'Come on. Come on,' he unquestioningly complies. Their focused interaction leads to a fragile trust rather quickly.

Critics have linked forms of personal trust fundamentally to wholesomeness in individuals' emotional connection. 'Personal trust,' write Lewis and Weigert, above all, 'involves an emotional bond between individuals' (1985: 974). As we watch Azra invite Luis into the deeper entrails of the building, the notion of an emotional bond becomes further anchored through an awkward interpersonal openness.[16] The intonation of Azra's voice is crucial, for it manages to communicate reassurance, excitement, and safety. Indeed, Azra and Luis commence to trust each other enough to relax, smile, and ultimately laugh in a crammed space beneath the heating pipes of the hotel. This gradual formation of interpersonal trust also succeeds in revealing new attributes of their complex subjectivities through their sensual pursuit.

The characters' deeper cathartic confessions, which they express in their native languages, take their interpersonal connection to the next level. They engage in an erotic encounter, which is quick, mutually desired, and ultimately allowed with Azra's nod. Azra's agentic engagement with Luis implicitly functions on a cultural level as well to expose and reject what Elizabeth Stanko calls 'the regulation of femininity,'[17] or, more specifically in Azra's context, 'a conservative order dependent on the Albanian traditionalist family structure' (Di Lellio 2016: 11). Their initial explorations of each other's bodies simultaneously enhance and puzzle their communicative interactions in unique ways particularly if we think about 'the erotics of tactile encounter that open up a different way of thinking the body' (Ahmed and Stacey 2001: 5). As the camera focuses on Luis' attempts to undress and subsequently engage with Azra's half-naked body with his hands and gaze, another ambiguous form of narrative emerges: the thickened and ruggedly healed surface of Azra's burnt skin begins to expose additional details about her past. Azra's jagged skin surface gains more potency visually and reminds us that '[w]hen the skin becomes not a container but a multidimensioned topological surface that folds in, through, and across spacetimes of experience, what emerges is not a self but the dynamic form of a worlding that refuses categorization' (Manning 2013: 125). The camera's focus on Azra's skin suspends the centrality of Luis and even sidelines their lovemaking, without dismissing Simone de Beauvoir's philosophical approach to touch – that is, touching the skin of the other signifies experiencing 'one's own and the other's desire' (quoted in Ahmed and Stacey 2001: 12). Instead, the camera privileges a particular skin-oriented sensorium, reaffirming that skin, echoing Ahmed's and Stacey's discussions in *Thinking through the Skin*, can 'signify anew. It can acquire new meanings, new forms, new shapes' (2001: 15). Consequently, the exposure of Azra's skin poses a compound question: Is Azra's body birthmarked, accidentally harmed, entirely war-affected, or a mélange of all of these possibilities? Azra's comfort in and with her own (new) skin reminds us also of Mariana Enríquez's young subway protagonist in one of the author's short stories from *Las cosas que perdimos en el fuego* (2016).[18] Although both women, Enríquez's 'metro girl' ('chica del subte') and Markovitch's Azra, are scarred permanently in different cultural and political contexts, they also resist easy social dismissals (2016: 185). Neither covers her burnt face, and they are present in public spaces frequently with different degrees of confidence. Indeed, desire for these characters functions as 'a multiple force,' which they appear to employ to confront certain modes of sociopolitical tyrannies (Martin and Shaw 2017: 23). Markovitch's and Enríquez's references to burnt or killed women in wartime or in peace – both of which are a consequence of gender-based violence – could be viewed as a subtle homage to the women war victims and survivors of Kosovo but also to those from political violence-based contexts across Latin America and beyond.[19]

Relief appears to be another ambiguously shared emotion between Luis and Azra. When the characters finally separate, we are left with their activated gazes that suggest several possible questions: Is Luis relieved to have admitted that he killed someone? Is Azra sharing her story about the loss of her daughter during the war for the first time in this secret site? Have other strangers been to Azra's secret enclave at the hotel? Is having narrated personal stories in their native languages, even if not entirely comprehensible for the interlocutors, a subtle form of personal relief? These and other questions linger in the film's diegetic space, even if Azra does not reappear after their encounter in the rest of the film. In addition to having survived war and a precarious economy, and to being survivors, immigrants, and foreigners, both are also complexly courageous narrators of their personal experiences, fears, and expectations. The same questions underscore Azra's and Luis' emotional geography – namely, their ad hoc sharing of duty and personal vulnerabilities after having borne witness to political turmoil, violence, and different forms of destruction. Such questions also reiterate that encounters incessantly reconstitute individuals, coinciding with the perception that 'it is only through meeting with an-other that the identity of a given person *comes to be inhabited as living*' (Ahmed 2000: 8, original emphasis). In so doing, the film ultimately highlights the characters who oscillate between being victims to being agentic subjects in unpredictable ways.

The unsaid, however, solidifies the chance encounter in *El actor principal*, just as it reveals the main characters to be subjects full of will. Despite the characters' will to engage with each other earnestly about their past, the impossibility of articulating the lived degree of brutality, loss, and affliction stays intact between them. This tension reiterates the classic stance that not only atrocities, traumas, afflictions, but also certain ways of survival, defy words. Markovitch achieves this implication innovatively in *El actor principal* by engaging two speakers in linguistically incongruous ways; speakers who gesturally express their basic emotions, generate their evanescent togetherness, and consequently complexify and challenge their social marginalization. The main characters' half-communications in Markovitch's *El actor principal* consequently accentuate differently paced movement of bodies and comprehension, thus upholding, above all, their interpersonal geography of emotional gestures.

Notes

1. See the 2021 Iztapalapa Report, which is issued by the United Nations Office on Drugs and Crime (UNODC) on early drug use, criminal behaviors, and different forms of violence. https://www.unodc.org/documents/Urban-security/210521_UGSA_Iztapalapa_Ingles.pdf; Andrea Noble, 'Introduction: Visual Culture and Violence in Contemporary Mexico.' *Journal of Latin American Cultural Studies* 24. 4 (2015): 417–33; 'Iztapalapa Report 2021' United Nations Office on Drugs and Crime (UNODC) (México: Center of Excellence, 2021); and Lucero Calderón, '*El actor principal*, filmada a la viva México,' *Excelsior* 22 July 2019. https://www.excelsior.com.mx/funcion/el-actor-principal-filmada-a-la-viva-mexico/1325819.
2. In most of said films, for instance, indigenous conversations, ritual practices, or voices often stand on their own – nearly always without explanation in or translation into Spanish – to privilege the authenticity of their voices, identities, and experiences.
3. The abovementioned films' approaches to historically simplified subjectivities evoke forms of symbolic reparations as a response to the consequences of the past horrors related to, in Cynthia Tompkins' words, 'the cultural genocide of Indigenous peoples' by means of revitalizing the multidimensionality of their presence in the cultural production of today in Latin America and beyond (2018: xxiii). Such aesthetic choices also emphasize Diana Taylor's recent delineation of epistemic and cultural shifts in the context of Latin America and its neighbors. Taylor focuses on the importance of the pluralistic contributions of 'knowledge(s)' so that 'instead of using singular knowledge for the powerful and plural knowledges for the subjugated, [we] recognize that we all produce knowledge, or knowledges' (2020: 26). By adding to contemporary decolonial debates from the Global South, Taylor highlights the significance of multiple

platforms of knowledge, a notion that 'includes revalorizing the autochthonous languages that allow us to know, think, communicate, and be outside the colonial framework' (2020: 27).

4 See Gonzalo Aguilar's *Otros mundos: Ensayos sobre el nuevo cine argentino* (Buenos Aires: Santiago Acros, 2010), 188 and Cecilia Sosa's 'Queering Kinship: The performance of blood and the attires of memory.' *Journal of Latin American Cultural Studies* 21, no. 2 (2021): 224.

5 Marina Gržinić, 'Southeastern Europe and the Question of Knowledge, Capital, and Power' in *The Global South* 5, 1: 51–65 and Inela Selimović, 'La marginación empoderada en *El actor principal* (2019) de Paula Markovitch,' 9 August 2021, https://ljz.mx/2021/08/09/la-marginacion-empoderada-en-el-actor-principal-de-paula-markovitch-2019/.

6 Azra is never seen in conversation with other co-workers. Luis is verbally and physically abused by his compatriot and *Mirror*'s panel member, which ultimately hastens Luis' resolve to break away from the festival.

7 See 'Informal employment in Mexico: Current Situation, Policies and Challenges,' Programme for the Promotion of Formalization in Latin America and the Caribbean (2014): 1. My analysis is responding to *El actor principal*'s contexts of marginality and poverty in Mexico City. For more information on recent figures of disappeared individuals (over 95,000) in Mexico, please see https://news.un.org/en/story/2021/11/1106762. *UN News*. 29 November 2021. Accessed 19 August 2022.

8 According to Iztapalapa Report 2021, '35% of inhabitants live in poverty' (22).

9 Julie Mertus, *Kosovo: How Myths and Truths Started a War* (Oakland: University of California Press, 1999); Tim Judah, *Kosovo: War and Revenge* (New Heaven: Yale University Press, 2000); and *Winning Ugly: NATO's War to Save Kosovo* (Washington: Brookings Institution Press, 2000). According to the Congressional Research from April 2021, during the conflict in Kosovo, '[a]bout 13,000 people were killed, and nearly half of the population was forcibly driven out of Kosovo. An estimated 20,000 people were victims of conflict-related sexual violence. Most of all victims were ethnic Albanians. On a smaller scale, some KLA fighters – particularly at the local level – carried out retributive acts of violence against Serb civilians' (10).

10 The footage that Azra shares with Luis, which is available to the viewer only fleetingly, reaffirms both her pre-war existence and her agentic present. Given that Azra speaks of her broken and eviscerated motherhood, *El actor principal* brings in the voices of different aspects of motherhood in contexts of heightened political violence, including one that is related to what Di Lellio identifies as 'a wall of silence among survivors of sexual violence' (2017: 10). In this context, the unsaid competes for our attention

during the encounter between Azra and Luis and underscores the impact of, in Erin Manning's words, '[s]ounds and images [that] are collected and recombined in ways that produce new insights into the past' (2013: 18). At the same time, the impossibility of articulating the lived degree of brutality, loss, and affliction creates tension between the two characters. The intensity of their chance meeting furthermore shifts the chief purpose for Luis' stay at the hotel, thus creating a half-wanted defiance on his behalf and letting us watch the character wander away from his responsibilities into the unknown streets of Berlin.

11 According to Howes and Classen in *Ways of Sensing*, '[s]ensory metaphors have played an important role in conceptualizing and justifying these different responses to social difference. [...] One common metaphor presents society as a body. This is a highly useful image for suggesting organic unity, interdependence, and hierarchy. It also offers the compelling feature of being an image with which everyone is intimately familiar: it is not, therefore, just something to think about, but something to *feel through*. In the social-class version of this model, the head represents the ruling class, and the feet or, as we saw above, the hands, represent the workers' (79, original emphasis).

12 See Maricruz González, 'Con ficción, Paula Markovitch reflexiona sobre la dictadura argentina,' *NOTIMEX*. 24 October 2017.

13 See Inela Selimović, *Affective Moments in the Films of Martel, Carri, and Puenzo* (London: Palgrave Macmillan, 2018a), 114.

14 Paula Markovitch, 'Conversations.' Message to the author. 31 December 2020. Email.

15 Paula Markovitch, Interview. 25 March 2020.

16 The affect that these characters' linguistic barriers engender evokes the opening scene from Andrey Tarkovsky's *Mirror* [*Зеркало*] (1975). While the communicative obstacles each film underscores differ greatly (Markovitch's characters do not suffer from any speech impediments the way Tarkovsky's adolescent does, for instance), both highlight an odd formation of interpersonal trust and bonding.

17 Elizabeth Stanko quoted in Ahmed, *Strange Encounters*, 33.

18 Enríquez's short story, 'Las cosas que perdimos en el fuego,' refers to the burnt protagonist's body as a site for her inner force, 185–6.

19 Argentina's contemporary feminist movement, *Ni una menos*, provides regular data on gender-based violence prevention: https://remezcla.com/features/culture/ni-una-menos-collective-argentina-founders/. In terms of the Kosovar context, a forthright link emerges by means of Isa Qosja's *Three Windows and a Hanging/Tri Dritare dhe një Varje* (2014). This is particularly relevant in conjunction with the Kosovo war- and gender-based violence, especially in terms of sexual trauma. While Qosja's

film deals primarily with wartime rape in Kosovo and the ways in which women survivors revisit their wartime abuses from a politically fragile post-war era, Markovitch's film treats Azra's burnt body as a unique site of personal post-war defiance. In terms of an art-focused homage in Kosovo's context, one thinks immediately of Alketa Xhafa Mripa's installation called *Thinking of You* (2015). The installation commemorates the women and girls who were systematically raped in the Kosovo conflict.

7

Ángeles (2025): Between Play and Suicide

Ángeles (2025), which at this writing is in post-production, takes the viewer across Córdoba, Argentina but begins near the banks of the Primero River (Río Primero) in one of the city's shantytown neighborhoods.[1] Littered and muddy roads and tired and decaying buildings frame the opening sequences. The drizzly, gray skies intensify the feel of the area's deprivation.[2] In the midst of this warscape of sorts in *Ángeles*, the viewer encounters one of the children-protagonists, Ángeles. The camera centers her seemingly aimless wandering, as she holds a plastic sheet over her head as flimsy rain protection. As we see her face – and indeed recognize the young actress, Ángeles Pradal, from *Cuadros en la oscuridad* (Chapter 5) – we also hear her shout 'Isa.' This moment rather instantly affirms the centrality and agency of the young girl, for her first words both express care and command obedience. Isa shortly joins Ángeles, and they walk together beneath the same plastic sheet-coat, with Isa holding onto Ángeles' shirt. Before the end of the film's first minute, *Ángeles* pulls us into a complex sequence of geographical and social glimpses of vulnerability, kindheartedness, and marginality. Just as we watch the sisters roam as candy peddlers across Córdoba, we also witness the beginning of their intimacy and mutual tending. The girls' closeness – Isa's complete dependence on her older sister and Ángeles' watchfulness – takes center-stage and comments on shantytowns but also child labor in contemporary Argentina.[3]

While the minors in *Ángeles* rarely appear completely safe, the film's most vulnerable character in the end appears to be an adult. David, who is a middle-aged, employed, and a failed cello performer, regresses emotionally and existentially throughout the film. His existential torments impinge on the two minors' nomadic life and forcefully draw them more deeply into his own self-destructive pursuits. David's awkward search for solitude – principally through alcohol addiction – also reveals the intricate fallibility of human nature. As the minors become his audience for existential despair, David mingles with and sometimes overpowers the girls' play, work, and mischief. This curious interplay manifests particularly through Ángeles' ability to oscillate between being an informal vendor and a burdened receptacle for David's wishes. David's emotional fragility becomes particularly discernable for the older sister, who understands the gravity of his yearning and decision to die, as he enters the sisters' physical and emotional space. While the girls look for short respites from the sweltering summer heat during their candy peddling beyond the *villa*, they stumble upon his decision to quit his job and commit suicide. David admits his inclination in an urban parking garage, where he appears to work and live, as he declares 'I am going to kill myself' ('Me voy a matar'). With half-hearted humor, Ángeles responds to his blunt confession first by minimizing it – 'you are feeling sad' ('estás triste') – and then by deciding to capitalize on his resolve. She persuades him to embark on a casual city tour in a stolen car. They begin their tour criss-crossing the city's central and marginal zones in search of joy and a suitable site for David's suicide. These rides create a small but intricate space for all but infinitesimal experiences of affliction and diversion. Ángeles' acute perception of David's existential struggles – and her willingness to listen to the adult's guilt-ridden soliloquy about his son's premature death and his own suicidal ideations – deepen their social bond and further illuminate Ángeles' maturity and decisiveness. *Ángeles* illuminates Argentina's economically precarious communities through the collision between self-absorbed and broken adults and curious and working street children. These children protagonists' curiosity and survival could be approached from Erin Manning's notion of 'prehensions' (2009: 7). For Manning, prehensions 'pull what become actual occasions from the extensive continuum of experience [...] with its unfolding into an event comes the expression of life in the making' (2009: 77). Given that 'prehensions are events of perception,' the girls' mobility through the city becomes illuminated through their sense-based attunement to face their struggles and reveal their feats (2009: 77). This chapter explores the film's focus on street children's sensorial readings and acumen to navigate and circumvent obstacles as urban peddlers in the early 2020s.

In *Ángeles*, Markovitch returns to an area that features heavily in *Cuadros en la oscuridad*. Alessandro Rocco writes of this attribute in the film (2023: 140). Markovitch indeed reconnects with this area but this time primarily from the dynamic perspective of two shantytown girls (Fig. 7.1). This perspective remains intact throughout the film and principally explores their multifaceted intersubjective world: namely, their curiosity, survival, inner conflict, and play. Speaking about the protagonists in *Ángeles*, the director recently elaborated her interest in working with marginal non-adults, specifying that 'the girls hold a lucid, furious, wild gaze. I like to talk of children not as docile or tender beings, but rather as otherworldly entities, with a healthy surprise at seeing everything for the first time' ('las niñas proyectan una mirada lúcida, furiosa, salvaje. Me gusta hablar de los niños, no como seres dóciles ni tiernos, sino que están recién llegados al planeta y tienen una saludable sorpresa y ven todo por primera vez') (Espinosa 2023: n.pag.).[4] Markovitch's words recall Béla Balázs' early reflections on the child in film as a uniquely captivating figure. According to Balázs, the 'naturalness of [their] unconscious expressions and gestures' reinforces their gripping presence (2011 [1924]: 61). It can be argued that the director privileges the children's voracious curiosity and innocent humor at the minutest level, above all, to explore their perceptive depth, even during some of the most

Figure 7.1 Isa and Ángeles at Córdoba's *villa*. © Paula Markovitch

frivolous interactions. While Markovitch's camera does not ignore the ghastly surroundings of her protagonists' social settings, it mostly illuminates the girls' smallest forms of agentic energy. Isa's presence, due to her age, curiosity, and a liveliness infused with innocence, leads to spontaneous mischief and silliness. Ángeles, on the other hand, presents as a hybrid of stamina, vulnerability, and pragmatism. During their spontaneous city exploration with David, which is continuously framed by his suicidal ideations that range from playful to solemn, the girls insist on, or simply create, modest forms of amusement.

The marginality and criminality linked to deprived childhoods and adolescences in the works of some of the most prominent Latin American pre- and post-1990s filmmakers and writers, are less visible in *Ángeles*. Drawing on the influence of Italian neorealist films on Latin American films of the 1950s, 1970s, and the late 1990s, Geoffrey Kantaris reminds us of how 'the social exclusion of juveniles poses a particular nexus of representational problems within cinema,' and clarifies that 'mostly deriving from the fact that in many Latin American societies, street children occupy an unacknowledged or disavowed representational space within the social imaginary itself' (2003: 178). Such social forms of exclusion become particularly linked to shantytowns from the 1930s onward. Glauber Rocha's seminal 'The Aesthetics of Hunger' (1965) enumerates these subjectivities as 'dirty, ugly, gritty characters who are eating dirt [...] eating roots [...] stealing to eat' ('personajes sucios, feos, descarnados que están comiendo tierra [...] comiendo raíces, [...] robando para comer') (quoted in Buttes and Niebylski 2017: 71). Similarly, Zygmunt Bauman, who seems to echo certain elements of Georg Simmel's seminal essay, 'The Stranger,' comments on social disavowals in *Postmodernity and its Discontents* (1997), explaining that 'all societies produce strangers; but each kind of society produces its own kind of strangers, and produces them in its own inimitable way' (17). *Ángeles*' strangers are the precarious child laborers, yet *Ángeles* does not seek to reproduce the depiction of sociocultural marginality characteristic of Argentina's early official discourses concerning *villas miseria* from the mid-twentieth century. Agnese Codebò emphasizes that Argentina's *Plan de emergencia: eliminación de las villas miseria de la Capital Federal* (1958) created discursively 'the *villa* as a degraded and unpleasant aesthetic space [which] coincided with a growing interest among writers, artists and filmmakers, and intellectuals in the mechanisms of poverty' (2020: 93). Codebò refers to the 1950s and 1960s when the *villas miseria* across Argentina (and across Latin America) became 'an ideal space from which to pose a critique of labour conditions, underdevelopment, and capitalist exploitation' (93). Such a 'critique' inevitably led to the official denomination of a particular kind of otherness and simultaneously instigated artistic explorations of the same. These revivals of the depictions of slums spread among 'militant artists and intellectuals in subjects related to poverty [and] grew so rapidly throughout Latin America that in its extremes it became a stereotype that easily lent itself to parody' (Codebò 2020: 93–4). In *Pobreza y precariedad en el imaginario latinoamericano del siglo XXI* (2017), Stephen Buttes and Dianna Niebylski highlight different cinematographic representations of poverty throughout the twentieth century in Latin America, reiterating that 'the *favelas* become the most favorable setting to film the marginalization and precariousness of these populations' ('[l]as favelas se convierten en el escenario más propicio para filmar la marginalización y la precariedad de estas poblaciones') (26). *Ángeles* challenges such stereotypes by featuring the *villeras*' multidimensionality as uniquely gifted urbanites.[5]

As noted, Markovitch features Córdoba's *villa* at the outset briefly as if to imprint this precarious reality on the viewer's mind. As Ángeles shuffles through the city trash in the film, we are also reminded of the scars inflicted across Argentina by the economic crisis (1998–2002). Gonzalo Aguilar writes of Buenos Aires from that era, stating that 'the poor would roam the city looking for cartons among the garbage. [...] the presence of the slum (with the poor as its synecdoche) was felt in the city, in all of its streets and in all its corners' ('los pobres [...] recorrían la ciudad buscando cartones entre la basura. [...] la presencia de la villa (con los pobres como su sinécdoque) se sentía en la ciudad, en todas sus calles y en todos sus rincones') (Aguilar 2015: 195). Markovitch's story is not set in 2002 but could be linked to what Aguilar considers to be the lasting aftermath of the economic crisis in and beyond the country's capital: 'the slums had "arrived" to stay and the dream of eradication [...] it was no longer possible' ('[l]as villas habían "llegado" para quedarse y el sueño de la erradicación [...] ya no era posible') (2015: 196). Unlike some of the films that centralize the interior space of the *villas* as their setting and 'protagonist,' including Federico León's and Marcos Martínez's *Estrellas* (2007) and Pablo Trapero's *Elefante blanco* (2012), *Ángeles* shifts to a singularly complex microcosm of the two young *villeras* beyond the shantytown, and how their interactions with the rest of the city become entangled through work but also playful distractions (Aguilar 2015: 197).[6] The young protagonists' contact with David, furthermore, most forcefully demonstrates their exclusion and could connote Argentina's struggles with child labor. Although Argentina has ratified 'all key international conventions concerning child labor,' since the United Nations Convention on the Rights of the Child in 1989, Argentinian children continue to be affected by it.[7] The International Labour Organization (ILO) reports that the 2016–17

National Survey of Activities of Children and Adolescents/ Encuesta de actividades de niños, niñas y adolescentes (EANNA) has indicated that '10 percent of children between 5 and 15 years and around 32 percent of adolescents aged 16 and 17 are engaged in child labour' (2023: n. p.).[8] To this end, and according to the Observatorio de Trabajo Infantil y Adolescente (OTIA), the Comisión Nacional para la Erradicación del Trabajo Infantil has implemented the *Plan Nacional para la prevención y erradicación del trabajo infantil y protección del trabajo adolescente 2018–2022*,' which specifies child labor laws (2022: 11).[9] Markovitch does not dwell on this socioeconomic issue directly in the film. Yet the few scenes that show the minors roaming through different urban sites in hope of selling candy recall children's rights in general and those from shantytowns in particular. The film addresses this issue obliquely, especially in their interactions with David. The children's dependency becomes visible through their friendship with David. His presence allows us to deepen our understanding of the girls' dependence on strangers' interest in buying their candy and to witness their homelessness beyond the *villas*. At the same time, their work-related roaming through the city challenges their spatial marginality, even as it interrogates their safety, education, and health.[10] In the midst of their socioeconomic vulnerabilities, Markovitch insists on illuminating the street children's dynamism and wonder.

This approach to the marginalized is deliberate on Markovitch's part. When she participated in a series at the Cineteca Nacional in Mexico City in 2023, Markovitch interspersed comments on her ethos in her introduction to the screening of her films. The viewer is expected 'to immerse oneself in the undertaking of an artist faithful to herself, to her freedom, to her critical stance about the current state of Latin American cinema, which often portrays misery, violence, and sordidness from prejudice and privilege' ('sumergirse en la propuesta de una artista fiel a sí misma, a su libertad, a su postura crítica acerca del estado del cine latinoamericano actual, en el que muchas veces se retrata la miseria, la violencia y la sordidez, desde prejuicio y el privilegio')

(*Jornada:* 2003: n.p). In 2023, furthermore, she reflected on the paradoxical intricacy of her characters in general, many of whom are minors:

> I want to present in my works characters who are not defined by their circumstances, who are mysterious, wild, inexplicable, and unique; characters who are not the illustration of a problem. I feel that Latin American filmmakers are constantly forced to talk about social issues and their crude realities. But we are not just our problems; we are much more than that: beings both unique and strange. Sometimes, European or *gringo* cinema allows for the creation of stories in which the characters do not necessarily respond to any issues; they are purely unique and extraordinary. Yet it seems that, as latinos [*sic*], we are invariably obliged to talk about our problems. (2023: n.p.)

> (Quiero presentar en mis obras a personajes que no están definidos por sus circunstancias y que son misteriosos, salvajes, inexplicables y únicos; personajes que no son la ilustración de un problema. Siento que a los cineastas latinoamericanos se nos orilla a hablar de temas realistas con problemas sociales. Pero nosotros no sólo somos nuestra problemática; somos mucho más que eso: unos seres singulares, extraños. A veces, el cine europeo o el gringo se permite la creación de historias en las que los personajes no responden a ninguna problemática, sólo son únicos y singulares, y parecería que nosotros, como latinos [*sic*], tenemos que hablar siempre de nuestros problemas.)

This approach undergirds almost all of her films, even those that feature minors at the mercy of adults' whims. Markovitch's interest in minors therefore aligns with other contemporary Latin American filmmakers including, among others, Lucrecia Martel, Jayro Bustamante, Albertina Carri, Julia Solomonoff, Ana Katz, Celina Murga, and Álvaro Delgado Aparicio, who approach the topic from a range of class, ethnic, gender-based, and racial angles and cultural settings. Several critics have examined the growing centrality of children and adolescents in recent Latin American films from different perspectives: as defenseless victims (Julia Tuñón and Tzvi Tal 2007 and Laura Podalsky 2008 and 2011), carriers of complex social meanings (Kantaris 2003 and Philippa Page, Inela Selimović, and Camilla Sutherland 2018), or as intricately bold subjectivities (Carolina Rocha and Georgia Seminet 2012 and 2014; Deborah Shaw 2013; Sophie Dufays 2014; Deborah Martin 2017 and 2019; Geoffrey Maguire and Rachel Randall 2018), to mention a few. Keeping these critics' discussions in mind, *Ángeles* exposes, above all, the girls' intricate subjectivities. Their young subjectivities are already aggregated from a myriad of paradoxical experiences of vulnerability, thievery, exultation, and desolation. Without romanticizing the young girls' background, *Ángeles* punctuates the minors' emotional lives and social conviviality in and beyond the *villa* by spontaneous moments of curiosity, play, and ploy. Markovitch's depiction of her child protagonists indeed aligns with Deborah Martin's interdisciplinary observation in *The Child in Contemporary Latin American Cinema* (2019). For Martin, as 'children have increasingly been seen as subject of legal and human rights (in discourse if not in practice), and as the sociology and studies of childhood have increasingly defined the child as agent, [...], certain films have begun to move away from the portrayal of children as (suffering) victims, producing more agentic representations' (2019: 24). The children in *Ángeles* are engaged urbanites in Manning's terms, specifically since '[e]very perception is already a thinking in action. Every act is a thought in germ' (Manning 2009: 2). The director's careful focus on the protagonists' agency in delightful pursuits is manifested most powerfully in their emotional attunements and their multisensorial experiences.

Such attunements to multisensoriality in *Ángeles* complicate the presumptions of minors' vulnerability as well as transgression. Markovitch affiliates multisensoriality with emotional states, thus conveying the power of 'nonaudiovisual sense experiences' (Marks 2000: 2). Ángeles perceives David's mood swings (from being relatively content to deeply despondent) in conjunction with getting clammy. These perceptions are nestled in their joyful moments when the girls eat their ice creams, swim or get wet clothed in the city river. For Manning, '[f]olding into perception is moving-with the virtual resonance of force taking form. Perception is in the folds, not of the folds' (2009: 81). These 'folds' in *Ángeles* are entrenched in-between their spontaneous play in the city river and David's forlorn leanings. Such sensorial pleats hold joy and terror simultaneously: the girls' wet, dirty, and sticky play communicates different forms of fleeting contentment and interpenetrate David's resolve to die.

David's tactile closeness to both girls brims with significance and ambiguity. Unlike Dr. Jano in Lucrecia Martel's *La niña santa* (2008), who deliberately seeks to rub against Amalia's body in public, David's closeness oscillates between protective and needy. Yet one could also approach it from Michel Serres' philosophical stance of 'mingled bodies' in his *Les cinq sens* (1998) via Steven Connor – namely,

> in the skin, through the skin, the world and the body touch, defining their common border. Continency means mutual touching: world and body meet and caress in the skin. I do not like to speak of the place where my body exists as a milieu, preferring rather to say that things mingle among themselves and that I am no exception to this, that I mingle with the world which mingles itself in me. The skin intervenes in the things of the world and brings about their mingling. (quoted in Steven Connor 2005: 322 [1998: 97])

If, as Connor explicates, Serres' postulations about the skin and touch indicate 'a way of being amidst rather than standing before the world, that is necessary for knowledge,' then such sensory experiences of their surroundings reveal weightier involvements (322). They indicate an active partaking in the city despite their ostensibly economic and social marginality. Marks calls such acquisition of knowledge in cinema 'tactile epistemologies,' which 'conceive of knowledge as something gained not on the model of vision but through physical contact' (2000: 138). When Ángeles becomes ill, David welcomes her and Isa into his home and seeks to nurture them. We watch David prepare Ángeles' tea to ease her fever. Both end up asleep next to each other, with David's hand over the girl's compress-covered forehead. Their tactile proximity brings about Connor's interaction with Serres' work, again, explaining that the 'skin encompasses, implies, pockets up all the other sense organs: but, in doing so, it stands as a model for the way in which all the senses in their turn invaginate all the others' (2005: 323). Multisensoriality indeed drives forward the characters' communication. Without speaking to each other, their interpersonal hapticity phenomenologically turns their bodies into 'the sources of meaning themselves,' and shows 'how the body encodes power relations somatically' (Marks 145 and 152). In this scene, the tactile interactions between Ángeles and David are rendered as tense, thus confounding the expected social hierarchies in this shared space. Furthermore, 'to touch a child,' suggests Karen Lury in *The Child in Film* (2019), 'is riddled with ambivalence – whilst physical affection and a caring touch are seen as essential for the child to become properly socialized and emotionally secure, to touch a child is also a sensual, possessive act' (55). As David cleans the girl's nails, the camera frames Ángeles' emotionally indeterminate facial expressions, which shift infinitesimally between surprise, delight, power, puzzlement, and mirth.

While the scenes of the children's jubilant togetherness suspend their reality on the most minute level, they also subtly instantiate the notion of 'environmental poetics and art projects' in accordance with Gisela Heffes' discussions in 'Toxic Legacies' (2023: 397). At the heart of the struggle for environmental justice,[11] suggests Heffes, is the idea of 'extending through the material ground of toxic worksites to the discursive nature of toxic narratives, environmental poetics and art projects allows us to trace the intersections of the local and global, from the body to the environment and conversely, as a continual material flow' (2023: 397). Such undertakings consequently illuminate an 'aesthetic of toxicity' that is 'grounded in discourses on exposure, environmental (in)justice, bodily experiences, and material entanglements' (406). Screening Markovitch's film in 2024 instantly recalls other classic and contemporary artistic works in addition to Verbitsky's *Villa Miseria también es América*. Ángeles evokes Antonio Berni's oil collage on wood *Juanito Laguna va a la ciudad* (1963), as well as more contemporary forms of urban realism that intersperse Mariana Enríquez's short story, 'Under the Black Water,' from her collection of short stories *Las cosas que perdimos en el fuego/ Things We Lost in the Fire* (2016). In Enríquez's writing the 'influx of toxic substances,' to borrow Heffes' words, is the story's driving force (397). While Markovitch subtly invokes these influxes in subtle ways in *Ángeles*, inviting us to think about different toxic dimensions on the emotional level (parental and social neglect) without explicitly naming them, Enríquez situates her story in the Riachuelo basin to urge us to 'understand how social structures, cultural differences, and power dynamics shape the production, distribution, conceptualization, and embodiment of industrial toxins generated at any point in the capitalist world system' (quoted in Heffes; Theriault and Kang 2021:6). Argentine photographer Alejandro Kirchuk has written about the Riachuelo basin, defining it as 'a toxic place to call home: twenty-five per cent of children living in the villas have lead in their bloodstreams, and an even higher portion suffers from respiratory and gastrointestinal illness' (quoted in Blitzer 2016: 1). Markovitch's depiction of children in conjunction with toxicity demonstrates how 'representations of the child are changing, especially in relation to their political meanings and aesthetic modes' (Martin 2019: 2). In *Ángeles*, the minors' presence also complexifies their vulnerability and fortitude from an environmental injustice standpoint. The minors' mélange of vulnerability and independence underscores their multidimensional subjectivities and interests but also shines light on the adult world in their immediate surroundings – adults who are only partly competent, mostly absent, or utterly unwilling to engage with their own curiosities, trepidations, and wants.[12]

Ángeles relatedly depicts violent moments in discrete ways. Such moments commingle with different forms of multisensorial attentiveness and experience. Toward the end of the film, Ángeles and David intermittently sit in silence and in an unresolved disagreement as the camera focuses on their dripping ice creams, thus symbolically capturing the absurd juxtaposition of their jovial outing with David's burdened 'self-being.' Byung-Chul Han discusses 'self-being' by way of Emmanuel Levinas' study of the existential burden of the I, which is 'already riveted to itself, its freedom is not as light as grace but already a heaviness, the ego is irremissibly itself' (quoted in Han, 2018: 66). In *The Expulsion of the Other* (2018), Han builds on Levinas' discussion and reiterates that 'self-being does not simply mean being free. The self is also a burden. Self-being is being-burdened-with-one-self' (66). David's presence simultaneously facilitates the girls' amusement, as he purchases these experiences, but is also a constant reminder of his self-imposed unfreedom and ultimate self-destruction. Returning to the subtleties of violence in the film, one could relatedly argue that it emanates from uneasy intersubjectivities, where uttered words about or shared thoughts of interpersonal harm, suicidal ideations, and existential dead ends parallel random incidents of merriment.

The triad's visit to an urban arcade abounds with such parallelisms through sensory alertness. The arcade setting is, above all, a cacophony of soundscapes. As the girls play different games and take carousel rides, Ángeles' awareness of David's burdened self simultaneously generates a deep sense of disquiet. Markovitch achieves this effect through Ángeles' emotionally layered ways of looking. Looking, states Ann Kaplan in *Looking for the Other* (1997),

> is constituted as the child learns the culture it finds itself in. It learns what to look at, what to avoid looking at; what is to be visible, what invisible; who controls the look, who is the object of the look. Subjects in a culture are also constituted as able to 'see' or not. But prior to that, as some psychologists have argued, the child engages in a look that, while on the literal level unavoidably a structural 'subject/object' look, may be experienced as *mutual*, as a process, a relation. (xvi, original emphasis)

Markovitch's close-ups on Ángeles' face also convey the protagonist's supple look as she interacts in multidimensional ways with those around her. Uneasy intersubjectivities that Ángeles generates as a candy peddler with random strangers and with

David, concerning his strange death requests, are conveyed in what might be termed as her socially *practiced* look. Such emotionally vivid implications call to mind Rachel Randall's observations in *Children on the Threshold in Contemporary Latin American Cinema* (2017), that is, 'the inseparability of children's vulnerability and intersubjectivity from their potential for agency' (xiv). Ángeles' looking in the film is a multilayered 'process,' in Kaplan's terms, and is deeply rooted in her urban nomadism: bashful and vulnerable (when discovered at the supermarket); insistent and serious (when she asks David for his money); attentive and protective (in most of her interactions with Isa); mystified and irked (when she learns about David's suicidal intentions); impish and sly (when she persuades him to take a city ride at the outset of the film).

Violent intentions are likewise vocalized amid cheerful activities throughout the film. In essence, the theme of harm and self-harm gains traction in the second half of the film, for David is not alone in confessing his thoughts related to harm. Ángeles admits her past attempts at harming herself but also someone else who might have been viewed as her foster mother: 'I also felt like killing at times. I was going to kill myself. Kill other people. My mom, who is not my mom, is a drunk. And I feel like putting a broken shard inside her glass so that she drinks it and dies' ('a mí también me daba ganas de matar a veces. Iba a matarme yo. Matar a otra gente. Mi mamá, quien no es mi mamá, está tomando cerveza. Y se me da por romper un vidrio y ponerle para que lo tome y se muera'). Her confessions reinforce the girls' boldness, pathology, and familial fragmentation. Toward the end of the film, Ángeles boldly finds David's suicide site to help him fulfill his intentions. As the camera briefly catches David's lifeless and intoxicated body on the edge of a skyscraper under construction, Ángeles and Isa appear to assist in his suicide. While the film leaves the outcome ambiguous, David does not reappear in the rest of the film. This moment reminds us of what Rocha and Seminet in *Screening Minors in Latin American Cinema* (2014) have discussed through the notion of 'alterity of children in cinema' (xii). According to Rocha and Seminet, the otherness of minors 'has been deployed for a variety of reasons:

to depict innocence, the monstrous, and even nostalgia for what may be irreversibly lost in modern life' (xii). Ángeles appears to be a curious hybrid of these meanings. The more we learn about her subjectivity and experiences, the more she is rendered inexplicable.

Being the youngest in this unusual triad, on the other hand, Isa sporadically eavesdrops. As the topics become increasingly onerous between David and Ángeles, the viewer is led to believe that Isa remains spared the gravitas of their implications. In fact, we often see Isa combining creativity with rubbish. She plays with whatever comes her way – scraps, trash, and other objects. Yet Markovitch's known ability to shock is clear when Isa suddenly interjects to tell a gruesome story she either witnessed personally or learned from others. Isa describes a stabbing, and the wounds and blood smears on the deceased body. Unfazed by the youngster's macabre account, Ángeles and David listen phlegmatically, as if accustomed or numbed to such occurrences.

The misconnection between minors and adults is another recurrent theme in Markovitch's films and is explored anew in *Ángeles*. Whether the misconnection is emotional, physical, based on class, or a combination of these, it adds to tacit manifestations of violence. The adult world in *Ángeles*, exposed most directly through the absence of the girls' parents and David's life adrift, is rendered volatile, callous, and dispirited. As discussed in Chapter 3, Ceci's relationship with her mother remains emotionally taxing for sheer survival. The friendship between Marcos and a neighborhood boy, Luis, in *Cuadros en la oscuridad*, is based on their incapacity to meaningfully balance each other's curiosities (Chapter 5). Returning to *Ángeles*, the minors' unusual friendship with David has transactional elements: he provides city rides for them, assists with comfort foods, ice cream and drinking outings, and houses both when Ángeles becomes ill. In return, Ángeles shoplifts alcohol on his behalf, lies, and agrees to collect his most intimate belongings after he dies (his cell phone and cash). Ángeles' shoplifting in a supermarket, for instance, reiterates her decisiveness, despite David's poor preparation for such an undertaking. When the girl is caught at the supermarket, she recounts a distressing story about her family to protect herself and the next customer in line, David, with his stolen goods: 'My mom is sick. They removed both of her tits. An uncle of mine was recently released from prison. And he returned even worse. He hits me with his belt' ('Mi mamá está enferma. Le sacaron las dos tetas. Un tío salió hace poco de la cárcel. Y salió más malo. Me pega con el cinto'). While much of her ad hoc confession is ambiguous regarding her own life, mother, uncle, and abuse, these statements absolve her from additional consequences and facilitate David's thievery. They also testify to her resourcefulness to avoid punishment.

The children's sensorial readings of the places they traverse and the people they encounter in *Ángeles* indicate their search for play amid different forms of precarity. Their vulnerabilities are never completely unmoored from ruse, albeit on a small interpersonal scale, and this prevents them from becoming easy targets for sly adults. If, as Lury states, 'the child, as a vivid and emotive presence, is all too often a vehicle for adult concerns and fears,' then Markovitch's insistence on highlighting the minors' smallest forms of personal strength is her refusal to idealize their precarity (109). The director reinforces the latter in the final scene of the film in which Ángeles and Isa presumably head back to the slums on foot along a busy highway. Their return – or rather their flow in and out of the *villa* – might be reinforcing what Aguilar calls the 'transformation of the urban landscape' ('transformación del paisaje urbano') because the shantytown poor 'questioned the notion of the slum's boundaries, thus calling visual attention to the presence of the shantytown and the poor as something urgent which no longer tolerates suppression' ('ponían en cuestión la idea de frontera, haciendo la presencia de las villas y de los pobres algo visualmente apremiante que ya no admite supresión' (2015: 196). Far from being reduced to unthinking victims, both girls mirror the symbolic embodiments of the most relevant adults in their surroundings: those who are often self-absorbed or existentially lost (David), others who appear unwilling to redirect them in ethical and social ways (the cashier), or still others who are apparently entirely absent (parents). Before helping Isa climb up a steep canal wall and return to the *villa*, a brief dialogue reaffirms their existential uncertainty.[13] The minors' intermittent joy reveals their emotional complexity without neglecting symbolically larger national (and Latin American) preoccupations, particularly concerning mental health, environmental injustice, and child labor among the poor.

Notes

1 Interview with the director, 14 June 2023.
2 These sequences bring to mind Bernando Verbitsky's novel *Villa Miseria es también América* (2003), even if the novel takes place across different *villas* of Buenos Aires (38). Verbitsky's focus on the interpersonal benevolence and amity in *villas* in general does not negate the infrastructural reality of such places whose streets seem to be a 'parody of a street' (2003: 72).
3 See: *Human Rights Watch*: https://www.hrw.org/legacy/children/street.htm.%20Accessed%2013%20July%202024. Accessed 13 July 2024.
4 See Danieska Espinosa, 'Paula Markovitch retomará la mirada sobre la infancia en *Ángeles*.' *Crónica*. https://www.cronica.com.mx/escenario/paula-markovitch-retomara-mirada-sobre-infancia-angeles.html. According to Juan José Olivares (2023), the director dedicated the film to the young Argentinian actress (Ángeles Pradal).
5 Agnese Codebò studies the cultural renaissance of *villas* in the capital of Argentina. According to Codebò, '[b]etween 1947–60 around two million people arrived in the Buenos Aires Metropolitan Area, a great portion of whom ended up in *villas miseria*' (88). See Codebò's analysis of different official approaches to shantytowns in Buenos Aires, including *Plan de emergencia: informe Elevado por la Comisión Nacional de la Vivienda al Ministerio de Trabajo y Previsión* (1956) and the *Plan de emergencia: eliminación de las villas miseria de la Capital Federal* (1958).
6 See Aguilar's chapter entitled 'Imágenes de la villa miseria en el cine argentino: un elefante oculto tras el vidrio' on other shantytown-oriented feature and documentary films at the outset of the twenty-first century (2015: 195–211).
7 See Aizpuru, Anahí et al. (2023: 1–35) and 'Convention on the Rights of the Child' https://www.ohchr.org/sites/default/files/crc.pdf. Accessed 30 May 2024.
8 See https://www.ilo.org/projects-and-partnerships/projects/map16-measurement-awareness-raising-and-policy-engagement-accelerate-action/map16-project-activities-argentina. Accessed 30 May 2024.
9 According to the UN Convention on the Rights of the Child, Article 36, 'State Parties shall protect the child against all other forms of exploitation

prejudicial to any aspect of the child's welfare.' https://www.unicef.org/child-rights-convention/convention-text. In conjunction with Article 36 of the 1989 Convention, Argentina enacted several laws since 2005 to prevent and eradicate child labor. In 2005, the country enacted Law 26.061 (Integral Protection of the Rights of Children and Adolescents). In 2008, Law 26.390 was enacted on the Prohibition of Child Labor and Protection of Adolescent Labor. Five years later, in 2013, Law 23.849 further specified the prohibition of child labor (9). Accessed 1 June 2024.
10 This paradox evokes the UN Convention on the Rights of the Child (Article 32) – namely, '(1) States Parties recognize the right of the child to be protected from economic exploitation and from performing any work that is likely to be hazardous or to interfere with the child's education, or to be harmful to the child's health or physical, mental, spiritual, moral or social development. (2) States Parties shall take legislative, administrative, social and educational measures to ensure the implementation of the present article. To this end, and having regard to the relevant provisions of the international instruments, States Parties shall in particular: (a) Provide for a minimum age or minimum ages for admission to employment; (b) Provide for appropriate regulation of the hours and conditions of employment; (c) Provide for appropriate penalties or other sanctions to ensure the effective enforcement of the present article' (https://www.unicef.org/child-rights-convention/convention-text). Accessed 5 July 2024.
11 Environmental justice is defined as 'the right of all people to share equally in the benefits bestowed by a healthy environment' (Adamson, Evans, and Stein 2002: 4).
12 Equally significant are several prominent contemporary writers whose novels have tackled the topic of *villa miseria*, including Sergio Chejfec's *El aire* (1992), César Aira's *La villa* (2001), Juan Diego Incardona's *Villa Celina* (2016), Leonardo Oyola's *Santería* (2008), among others.
13   Ángeles: '¡Isa!
    Isa: What?
    Ángeles: Let's go!
    Isa: Where?
    Ángeles: Home. Let's go!
    Isa: What home?'
    (Ángeles: '¡Isa!
    Isa: ¿Qué?
    Ángeles: ¡Vamos!
    Isa: ¿Adónde?
    Ángeles: A la casa. ¡Vamos!
    Isa: ¿Qué casa?').

Conclusion

In his prologue to Markovitch's *Cacerías imaginarias*, Pablo Dotta defines the director's artistic core as an inspiring mélange of (un)certainty and authenticity. 'Her uncertainties trap us' ('Sus incertidumbres nos atrapan'), writes Dotta, 'her certainties unnerve us, her sincerity spurs us to confront our specters but also the poetry we carry within' ('sus certezas nos sonrojan, su sinceridad nos empuja a salir al encuentro de nuestros espectros y también de la poesía que llevamos dentro') (Dotta 2022: 12). As these chapters have shown, such attributes of Markovitch's aesthetic paradigm are fundamentally anchored by sense-oriented interactions across a variety of marginal spaces, existences, and experiences. Given that, as Paul Rodaway states in *Sensuous Geographies: Body, Sense, and Place* (1994), 'the sense(s) is (are) both a reaching out to the world as a source of information and an understanding of that world so gathered' then the diversity and changeability of sensescapes across Markovitch's cinema pulsate subtly with sociopolitical implications from and about the margins (Rodaway 1994: 5).

The subtlety of such stories comes from the protagonists' sensorial attunements – all of which attest to what Judith Butler discusses in *Bodies that Matter* (1993) as those 'who form the constitutive outside of the domain of the subject' (3). Indeed, Markovitch's cinema almost always sheds light on the spaces and places that Butler denominates as 'the unlivable and uninhabitable zones of social life,' not so much to simply highlight them as 'densely populated by those who do not enjoy the status of the subject,' but more to engage such 'zones' sensorially in search of their broader and emblematic potential (Butler 1993: 3). After engaging with Markovitch's multifaceted exploration of marginality through sensorial modalities, we are reminded of Mieke Bal's *Of What One Cannot Speak* (2010) in which the critic writes that 'an oeuvre implies a retrospective temporal logic according to which each new work recasts the terms in which the previous work could be understood' (8). Markovitch cogitates in *Cacerías imaginarias* that her filmmaking began, above all, out of a particular kind of nostalgia. 'My need to direct' ('Mi necesidad de dirigir'), writes Markovitch, 'had nothing to do with my career, but rather with my longing to return to my childhood [...] The past had faded, but it was still possible to recover its disjoined remains and glue them together anew' ('no tuvo nada que ver con mi carrera, sino con mi anhelo de regresar a mi infancia [...] El pasado se había desvanecido, pero aún era posible recuperar sus restos desarticulados y pegarlos de un modo nuevo') (2022b: 32). Drawing on personal and collective experiences from Argentina's recent dictatorial past, including the consequences of neoliberalism since the 1990s and extending to Javier Milei's austere regime that began in 2023, Markovitch approaches deeply marginalized existences in bold thematic and aesthetic ways that show their tenacity and refusal to surrender.

Markovitch's films are not after simple depictions of what David Sibley calls 'geographies of exclusion' that emphasize how certain groups' social identities are rejected. In *Geographies of Exclusion: Society and Difference in the West* (1995), Sibley studies exclusion by focusing particularly on subjects who differ perceptibly from the norm; for example, those linked to age, ethnicity, gender, class, and race. These attributes generate experiences that Mary Douglas names as 'matter out of place' in her seminal *Purity and Danger* ([1966] 2003) (36). While Markovitch, indeed, situates her stories in several places where exclusion is differently manifested, she does this not merely for expository reasons. The choice aims to 'shock to thought' the viewer and highlights how such 'geographies' sensorially abound with agentic potential, subjectivities, and interactions (Deleuze 1989: 151). As such, the marginalized in Markovitch's films are not merely foregrounded as 'persons in marginal state ... [that is] ... people who are somehow left out in the patterning of society, who are placeless. They may be doing nothing morally wrong, but their status is indefinable' (2003: 198). Instead, the marginal subjectivities and phenomena that manifest across Markovitch's films are decidedly composite, imbued with multisensoriality that evokes Masiello's notion of 'sense work in culture' anew, which

> makes abject experiences experientially available; it helps us organize cultural politics through a bodily, material presence [...] sense perceptions situate us in a time and place; they position individuals in a particular context. And although we all see and hear, touch and taste—universal activities that might define us as one—the specific example of culture or context alters the nature of these perceptions. (Masiello 2018: 4)

The protagonists' marginality in Markovitch's films is not simply 'indefinable' but rather unambiguously multifarious and nearly always sensorially galvanized to provoke certain sociopolitical and cultural considerations. Markovitch's cinematic explorations of the fringes in the sociopolitical, economic, and cultural imaginaries of Argentina, Mexico and beyond therefore remain more appropriately aligned with the works by Lucrecia Martel, Ana Poliak, Jayro Bustamante, Lola Arias, Alvaro Delgado Aparicio, Alejandro Alonso, and Juan Andrés Arango, to mention a few. Although diverse in aesthetic, contextual, and thematic modes, these directors' films, like Markovitch's, have sought to break away from facile depictions of the marginalized self.

Some of the most singular interpersonal connections and sensescape attunements in Markovitch's films, for instance, seem to unify incongruous personal attributes; for example, the characters' enfeeblement and rebellion; defiance and meekness; autonomy and dependence as they oscillate across different sociopolitical and cultural contexts. By innovatively revitalizing the margins in her films, Markovitch's fundamental approach to filmmaking continues to rely on what Howes calls 'socialization of the senses' (2022b: 4). In comparing her camerawork to acts of painting, the director implies the power of the sensorial tacitly that engenders the 'pulsating moment, through improvisation and work with non-professional actors as well as the fluidity of the camera's movements: a camera that mimics the freshness of a brushstroke' ('momento vivo, ya sea a través de la improvisación y el trabajo con actores no profesionales, como en la libertad en los movimientos de cámara: una cámara que imita la frescura de una pincelada') (quoted in Juan José Olivares 2023: 1). By highlighting marginality through sensescapes the director aesthetically inquiries into how 'senses are historical, that they are not universal but, rather, a product of place and, especially, time so that how people perceived and understood smell, sound, taste, and sight changed historically' (Smith 2007: 3). Relatedly, Markovitch's focus on the sensorial at the margins is an aesthetic invitation to perceive and understand the layers of certain sociocultural territories in novel ways.

By her non-reductionist, complex centralization of the marginalized in her films, furthermore, Markovitch seeks to understand the deeper components of contesting marginality from within. Such an approach to marginality centralizes the depth of her protagonists' socio-emotional conviviality, struggles, and conflicts that, in some cases, can lead to different degrees of unsettling 'identity, system, order' (Kristeva 1982: 4). Julia Kristeva's *Powers of Horror: An Essay on Abjection* (1982) links such forms of usurpation to abjection, which signifies 'what does not respect borders, positions, rules. The in-between, the ambiguous, the composite' (4). Markovitch's cinematic explorations of marginality coincide, albeit paradoxically, with much of Kristeva's theorizations of abjection: by spotlighting ambiguous forms of transgressive potential in social, political, cultural, and other ways from the depths of the margins. In so doing, Markovitch's cinema questions the fact that 'today we [literary and cultural critics and certain artists alike] dredge the rivers of sorrow in order to sell scenes of abjection' (Masiello 2018: 11). Without romanticizing the fringes in and beyond Latin American contexts, Markovitch invites the viewer into vulnerable spaces, places, and circumstances on the margins (homeless encampments, hospice-like spaces, assisted-suicide intersubjectivities, political displacements) through characters and interactions that convey with equal force the possibility for contention and agentive aptitudes. Viewed from Lugones' vantage point, such subtle forms of power and agency at the margins reveal how in 'our colonized, racially gendered, oppressed existences we [resistant and oppressed subjectivities] are also other than what the hegemon makes us to be' (2010: 746). As explored in each of these chapters, the filmmaker's appeal to shock and absurdity through the senses works as a singularly creative repository for the exploration of contested marginality. Different sensory experiences across said settings and places, particularly through smell, touch, hearing, taste, and sight, constitute the political in Markovitch's films. The films conceive of fresh imageries of those who have been viewed historically as marginal subjects across and beyond Latin America.

Filmography

Markovitch as director

Perriférico, short film. Background Producciones-IMCINE, 1999.
Marilina, short film. Unreleased. Producción independiente, 2001.
Música de ambulancia, short film. Cinepantera, IMCINE, 2009.
El premio, film. Kung Works, STARON-FILM, Mille et Une Productions, NiKo Film, Foprocine, World Cinema Fund, IMCINE, 2011.
Armando y Genoveva, documentary film. Altamira Films, 2013.
Anita, short film. Twins Latin Films, 2016.
Cuadros en la oscuridad, film. Romanos Films, NiKo Film, Universidad de la Comunicación, Altamira Films, 2017.
El actor principal, film. Cine CANÍBAL, Le Petit Soldat Cinema, Altamira Films, EFICINE, Foprocine, 2019.
Ángeles, film. Altamira Films, Isla Bonita Films, Gualicho Cine, Avanti Pictures, EFICINE, Ibermedia, Polo Audiovisual Córdoba, INCAA, 2025.

Books, Scripts, and Other Collaborations

Books:

Las manos azules. Mexico City: Aristalia, 2025.
Cacerías imaginarias. Mexico City: Aristalia, 2022.
El monstruo. Mexico City: Buena Tinta, 2014.

Scripts:

'Tres minutos en la oscuridad' (1993), written by Paula Markovitch. *Tres minutos en la oscuridad* (1994), directed by Pablo Gómez Sáenz.

'La carta de amor' (1993), written by Paula Markovitch. *Sin remitente* (1995), directed by Carlos Carrera.
'Elisa antes del fin del mundo' (1993), written by Paula Markovitch. *Elisa antes del fin del mundo* (1997), directed by Juan Antonio de la Riva.
'Temperatura ambiente' (2003), written by Paula Markovitch. *Lluvia* (2023), directed by Rodrigo García Sáiz.
'Dos abrazos' (2004), written by Paula Markovitch. *Dos abrazos* (2007), directed by Enrique Begné.
'Un poco más de amor' (2004), written by Paula Markovitch. *Una pared para Cecilia* (2010), directed by Hugo Rodríguez.
'El documental' (2019), written by Paula Markovitch. *El despenador* (2021), directed by Miguel Kohan.

Television:

La periodista. TV Series (10 episodes). Show runner, writer, and director of two episodes. Avanti Pictures, Foprocine, (in post-production), 2024.
Por ese palpitar. TV Series. Canal 22. Writer, 1999.
Al borde. Pilot chapter. TV Series. Written by Paula Markovitch and directed by Antonio Zavala, 1998.

Collaborations:

Temporada de patos (2004) directed by Fernando Eimbcke, co-written with Paula Markovitch.
Lake Tahoe (2008) directed by Fernando Eimbcke, co-written with Paula Markovitch.
La caja (2021) directed by Lorenzo Vigas, co-written with Paula Markovitch.
Días borrosos (2022) directed by Marie Benito, co-written with Paula Markovitch.

Bibliography

Ackerman, Diane (1990), *A Natural History of the Senses*, New York: Random House.
Adams, Mags, and Simon Guy (2007), 'Editorial: Senses and the City,' *Senses & Society*, 2: 2, pp. 133–6.
Adamson, Joni et al. (2002), *The Environmental Justice Reader: Politics, Poetics, and Pedagogy*, Phoenix: University of Arizona Press.
Aguilar, Gonzalo (2008), *New Argentine Cinema: Other Worlds*, New York: Palgrave Macmillan.
— (2010), *Otros mundos: un ensayo sobre el nuevo cine argentino*. Buenos Aires: Santiago Arcos.
— (2013), 'The Documentary: Between Reality and Fiction, between First and Third Person,' in Jens Andermann and Álvaro Fernández Bravo (eds), *New Argentine and Brazilian Cinema: Reality Effects*, London: Palgrave Macmillan, pp. 203–15.
— (2015), *Más allá del pueblo: Imágenes, indicios y políticas del cine*, Buenos Aires: Fondo de Cultura Económica.
Agüero, Pablo (2008), *Salamandra*, JBA Production.
Ahmed, Saladdin (2019), *Totalitarian Space and the Destruction of Aura*, Albany: SUNY Press.
Ahmed, Sara (2000), *Strange Encounters: Embodied Others in Post-Coloniality*, New York: Routledge.
— (2010), *The Promise of Happiness*, Durham: Duke University Press.
— (2014), *Willful Subjects*, Durham: Duke University Press.
— (2015), *The Cultural Politics of Emotion*, New York: Routledge.
Ahmed, Sara, and Jackie Stacey (2001), 'Introduction: Demographies,' in Sara Ahmed and Jackie Stacey (eds), *Thinking Through the Skin*, New York: Routledge, pp. 1–17.
Aizpuru, Anahí et al. (2023), 'La construcción de conocimiento como política pública,' *Ciudadanías. Revista de políticas sociales urbanas*. UNTREF, pp. 1–5.

Alexander, Jeffrey (2020), 'The Performativity of Objects,' The Bar-Ilan Center for Cultural Sociology. Lecture delivered on May 6, 2020. YouTube video, 1:40:24. <https://www.youtube.com/watch?v=porymkHjwqQ> (last accessed 1 February 2022).

Alonso, Lisandro (2006), *Fantasma*, 4L Juramento.

Alvi, Farzad H., and Jorge Alberto Mendoza (2017), 'Mexico City Street Vendors and the Stickiness of Institutional Contexts: Implications for Strategy in Emerging Markets,' *Critical Perspectives on International Business*, 13: 2, pp. 119–35.

Amado, Ana (2009), *La imagen justa: Cine argentino y política (1980–2007)*, Buenos Aires: Colihue.

Andermann, Jens (2012), *New Argentine Cinema*, London: I. B. Tauris.

— (2013), 'December's Other Scene: New Argentine Cinema and the Politics of 2001,' in Jens Andermann and Álvaro Fernández Bravo (eds), *New Argentine and Brazilian Cinema: Reality Effects*, New York: Palgrave Macmillan, pp. 157–72.

Andermann, Jens and Álvaro Fernández Bravo (2013), 'Introduction,' in Jens Andermann and Álvaro Fernández Bravo (eds), *New Argentine and Brazilian Cinema: Reality Effects*, New York: Palgrave Macmillan, pp. 1–10.

Anzaldúa, Gloria (1987), *Borderlands/La Frontera: The New Mestiza*, San Francisco: Aunt Lute Books.

Avellaneda, Andrés (2006), 'El discurso de represión cultural (1960–1983),' *Revista Escribas*, 3, pp. 31–43.

Avellar, José Carlos (2013), 'Camera lucida,' in Jens Andermann and Álvaro Fernández Bravo (eds), *New Argentine and Brazilian Cinema: Reality Effects*, New York: Palgrave Macmillan, pp. 1–30.

Ávila, Benjamín (2011), *Infancia clandestina*, Argentina: TV Pública. DVD.

Bal, Mieke (2010), *Of What One Cannot Speak: Doris Salcedo's Political Art*, Chicago: University of Chicago Press.

Balázs, Béla (2011), 'Visible Man,' in (ed.) Erica Carter, *Béla Balázs: Early Film Theory: Visible Man and the Spirit of Film*, New York: Berghahn Books, pp. 1–90.

Barker, Jennifer (2009), *The Tactile Eye: Touch and the Cinematic Experience*, Berkeley: University of California Press.

Barthes, Roland (1989), *The Rustle of Language*, translated by Richard Howard, Berkeley: University of California Press.

— (2007), *The Neutral*, translated by Rosalind Krauss and Denis Hollier, New York: Columbia University Press.

Basile, Teresa (2019), *Infancias: La narrativa argentina de HIJOS*, Córdoba: Eduvim.

Bauman, Zygmunt (1997), *Postmodernity and Its Discontents*. Cambridge: Polity.

Beceyro, Raúl, et al. (2000), 'Estética del cine, nuevos realismos, representación,' *Punto de Vista* 67, pp. 1–9.
Bemberg, María Luisa (1985), *Camila*, GEA Producciones.
— (1990), *Yo, la peor de todas*. Buenos, Argentina: GEA Cinematográfica.
Benjamin, Walter (2004), *Selected Writings, Volume 1: 1913–1926*, Cambridge: Harvard University Press.
Bentes, Ivana (2003), 'The *sertão* and the *favela* in contemporary Brazilian film,' in (ed.) Lúcia Nagib, *The New Brazilian Cinema*, London: Palgrave Macmillan, pp. 121–37.
Berger, John (1980), *About Looking*, New York: Pantheon Brooks.
Bernini, Emilio (2003), 'Un Proyecto inconcluso. Aspectos del cine contemporáneo argentino,' *Kilómetro 111. Ensayos sobre cine* 4, pp. 90.
Bettendorff, Paulina and Agustina Pérez Rial (2014), 'Imagen y percepción. La apuesta por un realismo sinestético en el Nuevo Cine Argentino realizado por mujeres,' *Cinémas d'Amérique latine* 22, pp. 90–103. <https://doi.org/10.4000/cinelatino.800> (last accessed 12 July 2023).
Beugnet, Martine (2012), *Cinema and Sensation: French Film and the Art of Transgression*, Edinburgh: Edinburgh University Press.
Bhabha, Homi (1994), *The Location of Culture*, London: Routledge.
Bieri, Peter (2017), *Human Dignity: A Way of Living*, translated by Diana Siclovan, Cambridge: Polity Press.
Biraben, Gastón (2005), *Cautiva*, Argentina: Cacerolazo Producciones. DVD.
Blanco, María del Pilar and Esther Peeren (2013), 'Introduction: Conceptualizing Spectralities,' in María del Pilar Blanco and Esther Peeren (eds), *The Spectralities Reader: Ghosts and Haunting in Contemporary Cultural Theory*, London: Bloomsbury, 1–27.
Blejmar, Jordana (2014), '*Copyright* de la memoria, autoficción y novela familiar,' in '*Soy un bravo piloto de la nueva China*', *Kamchatka: Revista de análisis cultural*, 3, pp. 169–79.
— (2017), *Playful Memories: The Autofictional Turn in Post-Dictatorship Argentina*, Cham, Switzerland: Palgrave Macmillan.
Blejmar, Jordana, Silvana Mandolessi, and Mariana Eva Pérez (2018), *El pasado inasequible*, Buenos Aires: EUDEBA.
Blitzer, Jonathan (2016), 'Life Along a Poisoned River,' *The New Yorker*, October 25, pp. 1–16.
Bollig, Ben, and David M. J. Wood (2022), 'Introduction,' in Ben Bollig and David Wood (eds), *The Poetry-Film Nexus in Latin America: Exploring Intermediality on Page and Screen*, Cambridge: Legenda, pp. 1–31.
Borda, Pablo (2013), 'Reinterpretaciones generacionales. La mirada de los hijos de desaparecidos sobre la militancia de sus padres en la década del 70 en el contexto contemporáneo de la construcción de la memoria sobre

el pasado reciente de Argentina,' *X Jornadas de Sociología*, Buenos Aires: Universidad de Buenos Aires, pp. 1–22.

Bordigoni, Lorena and Victoria Guzmán (2011), 'Márgenes y periferia en la representación de lo social en el Nuevo Cine Argentino: Caetano, Stagnaro, Trapero y Martel,' in Ana Laura Lusnich and Pablo Piedras (eds), *Una historia del cine político y social en Argentina (1969–2009)*, Buenos Aires: Nueva Librería, pp. 575–607.

Borobio, Olga (2011), '"La impunidad genera parálisis en la sociedad": Paula Markovitch,' *NOTIMEX*, February 13, <https://www.proquest.com/docview/851481829/E736F4CE246B4A7EPQ/1.> (last accessed 30 March 2022).

Braidotti, Rosi (1994), *Nomadic Subjects: Embodiment and Sexual Difference in Contemporary Feminist Theory*, New York: Columbia University Press.

Brito, Luis (2011), 'La capital mexicana esconde su cara más violenta en Iztapalapa,' Expansión, January 22, <https://expansion.mx/nacional/2011/01/22/la-capital-mexicana-esconde-su-cara-mas-violenta-en-iztapalapa> (last accessed 19 December 2021).

Brombert, Victor (1978), *The Romantic Prison: The French Tradition*, Princeton, NJ: Princeton Legacy Library.

Bruhn, Jørgen, Anne Gjelsvik, and Eirik Frisvold Hanssen (2013), 'Introduction,' in Jørgen Bruhn, Anne Gjelsvik, and Eirik Frisvold Hanssen (eds), *Adaptation Studies: New Challenges, New Directions*, London: Bloomsbury Academic, pp. 1–16.

Bruhn, Jørgen, and Beate Schirrmacher (2022), 'Introduction,' in Jørgen Bruhn and Beate Schirrmacher (eds), *Intermedial Studies: An Introduction to Meaning Across Media*, Abingdon: Routledge, pp. 3–27.

Bruzzi, Stella (2006), *New Documentary*, New York: Routledge.

Buñuel, Luis (1929) *Un chien andalou*. Les Grands Films Classiques.

Burger, Peter (1984), *Theory of the Avant-Garde*, translated by Michael Shaw, Minneapolis: University of Minnesota Press.

Burke, Edmund ([1757] 1990), *A Philosophical Enquiry into the Origin of our Ideas of the Sublime and Beautiful*, Oxford: Oxford University Press.

Burt, Jonathan (2002), *Animals in Film*, London: Reaktion Books.

Burucúa, Constanza and Carolina Sitnisky (2018), 'Introduction: Forms of the Precarious in the Cinemas of the Americas,' in Constanza Burucúa and Carolina Sitnisky (eds), *The Precarious in the Cinemas of the Americas*, Cham: Palgrave Macmillan, pp. 1–15.

Bustamante, Daniel (2009), *Andrés no quiere dormir la siesta*. Argentina: Primer Plano Film Group. DVD.

Bustamante, Jayro (2019), *La llorona*. Guatemala City, Guatemala: La Casa de Producción.

Butler, Judith (2011), *Bodies that Matter: On the Discursive Limits of Sex*, London: Routledge.
Buttes, Stephen and Dianna Niebylski (2017), 'Narraciones y visualizaciones de la pobreza y la precariedad en la literatura y el cine latinoamericanos del siglo XXI,' in Stephen Buttes and Dianna Niebylski (eds), *Pobreza y precariedad en el imaginario latinoamericano del siglo XXI*, Santiago: Editorial Cuarto Propio, pp. 13–44.
Calderón, Lucero (2019), '*El actor principal*, filmada a la viva México,' *Excelsior*, July 22, <https://www.excelsior.com.mx/funcion/el-actor-principal-filmada-a-la-viva-mexico/1325819> (last accessed 3 July 2022).
Campany, David (2008), *Photography and Cinema*, London: Reaktion Books.
Campos, Luis, and Catherine Paquette (2021), 'Arte y Cultura en la transformación de barrios populares en América Latina', *IdeAs: Idées d'Amériques* 17. <https://doi.org/10.4000/ideas.10789> (last accessed 15 July 2024).
Camus, Albert (1955), *The Myth of Sisyphus and Other Essays*, New York: Vintage Books.
Canclini, Néstor García (1989), *Culturas híbridas: Estrategias para entrar y salir de la modernidad*, Mexico: Editorial Grijalbo.
— (1992), *Consumidores y ciudadanos. Conflictos multiculturales de la globalización*, Mexico: Editorial Grijalbo.
Capdevielle, Julieta, Diego Ceconato, and María Rosa Mandrini (2013), 'Segregación urbana y mercantilización del territorio en la ciudad de Córdoba, Argentina: El caso de Villa La Maternidad', *Revista Iberoamericana de Urbanismo* 9, pp. 47–71.
Carpenter, Edmund (1973), *Eskimo Realities*, New York: Rare Book Cellar.
Carral, Mabel (2019), 'Producción mural, elemento de empoderamiento y resistencia. Pensar con imágenes,' in Silvia García (ed.), *Aproximaciones políticas en el arte contemporáneo*, Buenos Aires: Universidad Nacional de La Plata, pp. 211–31.
Carri, Albertina (2003), *Los rubios*. Buenos Aires, Argentina: Cine Ojo.
— (2008), *La rabia*. Argentina: INCAA. DVD.
Carrillo Valles, Rodrigo, Patricia López Rodríguez, and Isidro Soloaga (2020), 'Dinámicas de pobreza en México, 2008–2018,' *EconoQuantum* 17: 2, pp. 7–32.
Carroll, Noel (1996), *Theorizing the Moving Image*, Cambridge: Cambridge University Press.
Cavarero, Adriana (2009), *Horrorismo nombrando la violencia contemporanea*, Mexico: Anthropos.
Cervio, Ana Lucía (2005), 'Expansión urbana y segregación socio-espacial en la ciudad de Córdoba (Argentina) durante los años '80,' *Astrolabio* 14, pp. 360–92.

Chion, Michel (2019), *Audio-Vision: Sound on Screen*. 2nd ed, translated by Claudia Gorbman, New York: Columbia University Press.

Claeys, Gregory (2017), *Dystopia: A Natural History*, Oxford: Oxford University Press.

Classen, Constance (1994), 'The Aroma of the Commodity: The Commercialization of Smell,' in Constance Classen, David Howes, and Anthony Synnott (eds), *Aroma: The Cultural History of Smell*. New York: Routledge, pp. 180–205.

— (1997), 'Foundations for an Anthropology of the Senses,' *International Social Science Journal* 49: 153, pp. 401–12.

— (2020), 'Touch in the Museum,' in (ed.) Constance Classen, *The Book of Touch*, New York: Routledge, pp. 275–86.

Codebò, Agnese (2020), 'Against the Grid: The Cultural Emergence of *Villas Miseria* in Buenos Aires,' *Journal of Latin American Cultural Studies* 29: 1, pp. 85–107. https://doi.org/10.1080/13569325.2019.1636365.

Comolli, Jean-Louis (2007), *Ver y poder. La inocencia perdida: cine, televisión, ficción, documental*, Buenos Aires: Nueva Librería.

Congressional Research Service (2021), *Kosovo Background and U.S. Policy*. Washington, DC: Congressional Research Service, <https://sgp.fas.org/crs/row/R46175.pdf> (last accessed 13 April 2022).

Connor, Steven (2005), 'Michel Serres' Five Senses,' in (ed.) David Howes, *Empire of the Senses: The Sensual Culture Reader*, Oxford: Berg, pp. 318–34.

'Convention on the Rights of the Child,' 20 November 1989. <https://www.ohchr.org/sites/default/files/crc.pdf> (last accessed 5 July 2024).

Cortázar, Julio (1951), 'La casa tomada,' *Bestiario*, Editorial Sudamericana, 12–20.

Crastnopol, Margaret (2015), *Micro-traumas: A Psychoanalytic Understanding of Cumulative Psychic Injury*, New York: Routledge.

Crenzel, Emilio (2015), 'Hacia una historia de la memoria de la violencia política y los desaparecidos en Argentina,' in Eugenia Allier Montaño and Emilio Crenzel (eds), *Las luchas por la memoria en América Latina: Historia reciente y memoria política*, Coyoacán, Mexico: Universidad Nacional Autónoma de México, pp. 35–62.

Crespo, Erick Baena (2016), '"Me fascinan las situaciones crueles y a la vez absurdas": Paula Markovitch,' *Plot Point – Revista*, January 19, <www.plotpoint.com.mx/peripecias/me-fascinan-las-situaciones-crueles-y-a-la-vez-absurdas-paula-markovitch> (last accessed 19 January 2022).

Cuerda, José Luis (1999), *La lengua de las mariposas*, España: Canal+. DVD.

Daney, Serge (2004), *Cine, arte del presente*, Buenos Aires: Santiago Acros.

Davidson, Joyce, Liz Bondi, and Mick Smith (2005), 'Introduction: Geography's "Emotional Turn",' in Joyce Davidson, Liz Bondi, and Mick Smith (eds), *Emotional Geographies*. New York: Routledge, pp. 1–16.

Davis, Colin (2013), 'État Présent: Hauntology, Specters and Phantoms,' in María Del Pilar Blanco and Esther Peeren (eds), *The Spectralities Reader*. London: Bloomsbury, pp. 53–60.
De Certeau, Michel (1984), *The Practice of Everyday Life*, Berkeley: University of California Press.
Deleuze, Gilles (1970), *Spinoza: Practical Philosophy*, San Francisco: City Lights Books.
— (1986), *Cinema 2: The Time-Image*, Minneapolis: University of Minneapolis Press.
— (2003), *Francis Bacon: The Logic of Sensation*, translated by Richard Howard. Minneapolis: University of Minnesota Press.
Deleuze, Gilles and Félix Guattari (2005), *A Thousand Plateaus: Capitalism and Schizophrenia*, translated by Brian Massumi, Minneapolis: University of Minnesota Press.
Delgado, María M., Stephen M. Hart, and Randal Johnson (2017), 'Introduction,' in María M. Delgado, Stephen M. Hart, and Randal Johnson (eds), *A Companion to Latin American Cinema*, Malden: Wiley Blackwell, pp. 1–18.
De Pablos, Emiliano (2014), 'Paula Markovitch Draws "Paintings in the Dark",' *Variety*. March 27, <https://variety.com/2014/film/global/paula-markovitch-draws-paintings-in-the-dark-1201149936/> (last accessed 4 March 2022).
Derrida, Jacques, and Bernard Stiegler (2013), 'Spectrographies,' in María del Pilar Blanco and Esther Peeren (eds), *The Spectralities Reader: Ghosts and Haunting in Contemporary Cultural Theory*, New York: Bloomsbury Academic, pp. 31–6.
'Despedida a un HIJO' (2015), *Página 12*. 10 July, <https://www.pagina12.com.ar/diario/elpais/1-276784-2015-07-10.html> (last accessed 12 July 2015).
Diaconu, Mădălina (2011), 'Matter, Movement, Memory. Footnotes to an Urban Tactile Design,' in Mădălina Diaconu, Eva Heuberger, Ruth Mateus-Berr, and Lukas Marcel Vosicky (eds), *Senses and the City: An Interdisciplinary Approach to Urban Sensescapes*, London: Transaction Publishers, pp. 13–32.
Di Lellio, Anna (2016), 'Seeking Justice for Wartime Sexual Violence in Kosovo: Voices and Silence of Women', *East European Politics and Societies* 30: 3, pp. 621–43.
Dos Santos, Danisa (2014), 'Biografías, testimonios y relatos de vida: Hacia una construcción estética de lo vivido,' in Diana Paladino (ed.), *Documental-ficción: Reflexiones sobre el cine argentino contemporáneo*, Buenos Aires: Eduntref, pp. 19–36.
Dotta, Pablo (2022), 'Prólogo,' *Cacerías imaginarias*. Mexico City: Aristalia, pp. 11–12.

Douglas, Mary ([1966], 2001), *Purity and Danger: An Analysis of the Concepts of Pollution and Taboo*, London: Routledge.

Drobnick, Jim (2005), 'Volatile Effects: Olfactory Dimensions of Art and Architecture,' in David Howes (ed.), *Empire of the Senses: The Sensual Culture Reader*, New York: Berg, pp. 265–80.

Durcan, Sarah (2021), *Memory and Intermediality in Artists' Moving Image*, Cham: Palgrave Macmillan.

Elleström, Lars (2010), *Media Borders, Multimodality and Intermediality*, London: Palgrave Macmillan.

— (2014), *Media Transformation: The Transfer of Media Characteristics Among Media*, Hampshire: Palgrave Macmillan.

Eltit, Diamela (1994), *Los vigilantes*. Santiago: Editorial Sudamericana.

Encina, Paz (2016), *Ejercicios de memoria*, Berlin, Germany: Autentika Films.

— (2022), *EAMI*, Silencio Cine, MPM Premium.

Enríquez, Mariana (2016), *Las cosas que perdimos en el fuego*, New York: Vintage Español.

Espinosa, Danieska (2023), 'Paula Markovitch retomará la mirada sobre la infancia en *Ángeles*.' *Crónica*. Crónica. 10 August, <https://www.cronica.com.mx/escenario/paula-markovitch-retomara-mirada-sobre-infancia-angeles.html> (last accessed 1 September 2024).

Farji, Sabrina (2010), *Eva y Lola*. Argentina: Primer Plano Film Group. DVD.

Feitlowitz, Marguerite (1998), *A Lexicon of Terror: Argentina and the Legacies of Torture*, Oxford: Oxford University Press.

Field, Tiffany (2014), *Touch*. Cambridge: MIT Press.

Flaxman, Gregory (2000), *The Brain in the Screen: Deleuze and the Philosophy of Cinema*, Minneapolis: University of Minneapolis Press.

Forcinito, Ana (2018), *Óyeme con los ojos. Cine, mujeres, visiones y voces*, La Habana: CASA.

Foucault, Michel (1972), *Power/Knowledge*, New York: Pantheon Books.

Fradinger, Moira (2014), 'Emilia Saleny,' in Jane Gaines, Radha Vatsal, and Monica Dall'Asta (eds), *Women Film Pioneers Project*, New York: Columbia University Libraries, <https://wfpp.columbia.edu/pioneer/emilia-saleny/> (last accessed 18 January 2023).

Frevert, Ute (2014), 'Defining Emotions: Concepts and Debates over Three Centuries', in (ed.) Ute Frevert, *Emotional Lexicons: Continuity and Change in the Vocabulary of Feeling 1700–2000*, Oxford: Oxford University Press, pp. 1–31.

Furtado, Jorge (2003), *O homem que copiava/The Man Who Copied*, Casa de Cinema de Porto Alegre.

García Márquez, Gabriel (1967), *Cien años de soledad*. Ashland: Blackstone Publishing.

Garibotto, Verónica Inés (2015), 'Private Narratives and Infant Views: Iconizing 1970s Militancy in Contemporary Argentine Cinema,' *Hispanic Research Journal* 16: 3, pp. 257–72.
— (2019), *Rethinking Testimonial Cinema in Postdictatorship Argentina: Beyond Memory Fatigue*, Bloomington: Indiana University Press.
Garramuño, Florencia (2015), *Mundos en común. Ensayos sobre la inespecificidad en el arte*, Buenos Aires: Fondo de Cultura Económica.
— (2023), 'Potencias de la vida anónima. Jonathas de Andrade y la sublevación de los cuerpos,' in Florencia Garramuño, Héctor Hoyos, and Romina Wainberg (eds), *Sujetos del latinoamericanismo*, Pittsburg: Iili, pp.1–23.
Gatti, Gabriel (2012), 'Imposing Identity Against Social Catastrophes: The Strategies of (Re)Generation of Meaning of the Abuelas de Plaza de Mayo (Argentina),' *Bulletin of Latin American Research* 31: 3, pp. 352–65.
Gemünden, Gerd (2019), *Lucrecia Martel*, Chicago: University of Illinois Press.
Giunta, Andrea (2014), 'Arte, memoria y derechos humanos en Argentina', *Artelogie* 6. https://doi.org/10.4000/artelogie.1420 (last accessed 4 November 2023).
Gleghorn, Charlotte (2017), 'Indigenous Filmmaking in Latin America,' in María M. Delgado, Stephen M. Hart, and Randal Johnson (eds), *A Companion to Latin American Cinema*, Oxford: Wiley Blackwell, pp. 167–86.
Goffman, Erving (1959), *The Presentation of the Self in Everyday Life*, New York: Doubleday.
— ([1961] 2013), *Encounters: Two Studies in the Sociology of Interaction*, Indianapolis: Bobbs-Merrill.
González, Alejandra Soledad (2014), 'Las artes en la última dictadura argentina (1976–1983): Entre políticas culturales e intersticios de resistencia,' *ERAS: European Review of Artistic Studies*, 5: 2, pp. 60–84.
González Iñárritu, Alejandro et al., (2002), *Amores perros*, Lion's Gate Home Entertainment. DVD.
González, Maricruz (2017), 'Con ficción, Paula Markovitch reflexiona sobre la dictadura argentina,' *NOTIMEX*, 24 October <https://www.20minutos.com.mx/noticia/288595/0/con-ficcion-paula-markovitch-reflexiona-sobre-la-dictadura-argentina/> (last accessed 8 March 2022).
'Gran pérdida para Abuelas: se suicidó el nieto recuperado 109' (2015), *MinutoUno*, 12 April, <http://www.minutouno.com/notas/360120-gran-perdida-abuelas-se-suicido-el-nieto-recuperado-109> (last accessed 10 March 2017).
Greco, Monica and Paul Stenner (2008), 'Introduction: Emotion and Social Science,' in Monica Greco and Paul Stenner (eds), *Emotions: A Social Science Reader*. New York: Routledge, pp. 1–21.

Gregg, Melissa and Gregory J. Seigworth (2010), 'An Inventory of Shimmers,' in Melissa Gregg and Gregory J. Seigworth (eds), *The Affect Theory Reader*, Durham: Duke University Press, pp. 1–25.

Guerrero, Felipe (2006), *Paraíso*. Colombia: Felipe Guerrero – Paraíso.

Gurrola, Sergio (2021), email exchange, 15 September.

Han, Byung-Chul (2017), *The Scent of Time: A Philosophical Essay on the Art of Lingering*, translated by Daniel Steuer, Cambridge: Polity Press.

— (2018), *The Expulsion of the Other*, Cambridge: Polity Press.

Haneke, Michael (2003), *Le Temps du Loup/Time of the Wolf*, Les Films du Losange.

Hart, Heidi (2018), *Music and the Environment in Dystopian Narrative: Sounding the Disaster*, Cham: Palgrave Macmillan.

Heffes, Gisela (2023), 'Toxicity,' in Jens Andermann, Gabriel Giorgi, and Victoria Saramago (eds), *Handbook of Latin American Environmental Aesthetics*, Berlin: de Gruyter, pp. 395–408.

Herman, Judith (1992), *Trauma and Recovery: The Aftermath of Violence – from Domestic Abuse to Political Terror*, New York: Basic Books.

Hogan, Erin (2018), 'Girls and Dolls: The Biopolitics of Gender and Race in Lucía Puenzo's *Wakolda*,' *The Comparatist* 42, pp. 246–63.

Holland, Patricia (2004), *Picturing Childhood: The Myth of the Child in Popular Imagery*, London: I. B. Tauris.

Houwen, Janna (2018), *Film and Video Intermediality: The Question of Medium Specificity in Contemporary Moving Images*, New York: Bloomsbury.

Howes, David (2005a), 'Introduction,' in David Howes (ed.), *Empire of the Sense: The Sensual Culture Reader*, New York: Berg, pp. 1–17.

— (2005b), 'Architecture of the Senses,' in Mirko Zardini, Wolfgang Schivelbusch, Norman Pressman, et al. (eds), *Sense of the City: An Alternative Approach to Urbanism*, Toronto: Lars Muller Publishers, pp. 322–31.

— (2022), *The Sensory Studies Manifesto: Tracking the Sensorial Revolution in the Arts and Human Sciences*, Toronto: University of Toronto Press.

Howes, David and Constance Classen (2014), 'Introduction: Ways and Meanings,' in David Howes and Constance Classen (eds), *Ways of Sensing: Understanding the Senses in Society*, Oxon: Routledge, pp. 1–13.

Iacopino, Vincent et al. (2013), 'A Population-Based Assessment of Human Rights Abuses Committed Against Ethnic Albanian Refugees from Kosovo,' *American Journal of Public Health* 91: 12, pp. 2013–18.

International Labor Organization (ILO) (2019), 'Map16 Project Activities in Argentina', <https://www.ilo.org/projects-and-partnerships/projects/map16-measurement-awareness-raising-and-policy-engagement-accelerate-action/map16-project-activities-argentina> (last accessed 26 July 2024).

James, Robin (2015), *Resilience & Melancholy*: Pop Music, Feminism, Neoliberalism, Winchester: Zero Books.

Jameson, Fredric (2008), 'Marx's Purloined Letter,' in Michael Spinker (ed.), *Ghostly Demarcations: A Symposium on Jacques Derrida's Specters of Marx*, London: Verso, pp. 26–67.
Kantaris, Geoffrey (2003), 'The Young and the Damned: Street Visions in Latin American Cinema,' in Stephen Hart (ed.), *Contemporary Latin American Cultural Studies*, London: Arnold, pp. 177–89.
Kaplan, Ann (1997), *Looking for the Other: Feminism, Film, and the Imperial Gaze*, New York: Routledge.
— (2016), *Climate Trauma: Foreseeing the Future in Dystopian Film and Fiction*, New Brunswick, New Jersey: Rutgers University Press.
Kjeldsen, Jens (2013), 'Virtues of visual argumentation: How pictures make the importance and strength of an argument salient,' *OSSA Conference Archive* 10, pp. 89.
'Kosovo Background and U.S. Policy' (2021), Congressional Research Service. 8 April, <https://sgp.fas.org/crs/row/R46175.pdf> (last accessed 22 May 2022).
Kozloff, Sarah (2000), *Overhearing Film Dialogue*, Berkeley: University of California Press.
Kristeva, Julia (1982), *Powers of Horror: An Essay on Abjection*, New York: Columbia University Press.
Kuhn, Annette (2010), 'Cinematic Experience, Film Space, and the Child's World,' *Canadian Journal of Film Studies* 19: 2 (Fall): pp. 82–98.
Laine, Tarja (2011), *Feeling Cinema: Emotional Dynamics in Film Studies*, London: Continuum.
Lang, Jamie (2017), 'Morelia: Writer-Director Paula Markovitch Discusses "Paintings in the Dark," Art Under Dictatorships, Upcoming Projects,' *Variety*. October 29. <https://variety.com/2017/film/festivals/morelia-writer-director-paula-markovitch-paintings-in-the-dark-1202601855/> (last accessed 12 June 2018).
Larraín, Pablo (2016), *Neruda*, Santiago, Chile: Fabula.
Lash, Kenneth (1948), 'A Theory of the Comic as Insight,' *The Journal of Philosophy* 45: 5, pp. 113–21.
Lazzara, Michael (2013), 'Kidnapped Memories: Argentina's Stolen Children Tell Their Stories,' *Journal of Human Rights* 12: 3, pp. 319–332.
Lebeau, Vicky (2008), *Childhood and Cinema*, London: Reaktion Books.
León, Christian (2005), *El arte de la marginalidad. Realismo sucio y violencia urbana*, Quito: Ediciones Abya Yala.
León, Melina (2019), *Canción sin nombre*, Lima: La Vida Misma Films.
Levander, Caroline, and Walter Mignolo (2011), 'Introduction: The Global South and World Dis/Order,' *The Global South* 5: 1, pp. 1–11.
Lewis, J. David, and Andrew Weigert (1985), 'Trust as a Social Reality,' *Social Forces* 63: 4 (June), pp. 967–85.

Llosa, Claudia (2009), *La teta asustada*, España: Institut Català de les Empreses Culturals. DVD.
Longoni, Ana (2013), 'Incitar el debate, a una red de colaboraciones, a otro modo de hacer,' *Afuera: Estudios de crítica cultural* 8: 13 (September), pp. 1–6.
Losada, Matt (2018), *The Projected Nation. Argentine Cinema and the Social Margins*, Albany: SUNY Press.
Lugones, María (2003), *Pilgrimages/Peregrinajes: Theorizing Coalition Against Multiple Oppressions*, Lanham: Lexington Press.
— (2010), 'Toward a Decolonial Feminism,' *Hypatia*, 25: 4, pp. 742–59.
Lury, Karen (2010), *The Child in Film: Tears, Fears and Fairy Tales*, London: I. B. Tauris.
Maguire, Geoffrey (2015), 'The Adolescent Image in Southern Cone Cinema: Memory and Utopia,' Paper presented at the Latin American Studies Association (LASA), Puerto Rico, May 27–30.
— (2017a), 'Playing in Public: Domestic Politics and Prosthetic Memory in Paula Markovitch's *El premio/The Prize* (2011),' *Studies in Spanish & Latin American Cinemas* 14: 1, pp. 3–21.
— (2017b), *The Politics of Postmemory: Violence and Victimhood in Contemporary Argentine Culture*, Cham: Palgrave Macmillan.
Mandoki, Luis (2006), *Voces inocentes*, Switzerland: Pelican Films. DVD.
Manning, Erin (2012), *Relationscapes: Movement, Art, Philosophy*, Cambridge: MIT Press.
— (2013), *Always More Than One: Individuation's Dance*, Durham: Duke University Press.
Markovitch, Paula (2011), *El premio*, Argentina: Elite Studios. DVD.
— (2013a), *Armando y Genoveva*, Altamira Films, armandoygenoveva.org, (last accessed 22 June 2022).
— (2013b), *Armando y Genoveva*, Vimeo. Online Video.
— (2013c), 'Paula Markovitch, directora de la película *El premio*,' Cuadro TV. 7 February, <https://www.youtube.com/watch?v=ukrYNcOqWEM> (last accessed 4 March 2022).
— (2014), *El monstruo*, Mexico City: Buena Tinta.
— (2015), 'Interview,' https://www.youtube.com/watch?v=ukrYNcOqWEM (last accessed 17 July 2023).
— (2016), *Anita*, Twins Latin Films.
— (2016), 'Cuadernos,' unpublished notes.
— (2018), *Cuadros en la oscuridad*, Morelia: Universidad de la Comunicación. DVD.
— (2019a), *Cacerías imaginarias*, unpublished script.
— (2019b), *El actor principal*, Mexico City: Cine Caníbal, DVD.
— (2020), 'Conversations,' Message to Author, 31 December 2020, email.
— (2022), *Cacerías imaginarias*, Mexico City: Aristalia.

Marks, Laura (2000), *The Skin of the Film: Intercultural Cinema, Embodiment, and the Senses*, Durham: Duke University Press.
Martel, Lucrecia (2001), *La ciénaga*, Madrid: Wanda Visión S. A.
— (2008), *La mujer sin cabeza*, Argentina: Argentina Video Home. DVD.
Martin, Deborah (2016), *The Cinema of Lucrecia Martel*, Manchester: Manchester University Press.
— (2019), *The Child in Contemporary Latin American Cinema*, London: Palgrave Macmillan.
Martin, Deborah and Deborah Shaw (2017), 'Introduction,' in Deborah Martin and Deborah Shaw, (eds), *Latin American Women Filmmakers: Production, Politics, Poetics*, London: I. B. Tauris, pp: 1–28.
Masiello, Francine (2018), *The Senses of Democracy: Perception, Politics, and Culture in Latin America*, Austin: University of Texas Press.
Massey, Doreen (2005), *For Space*, London: Sage.
Massumi, Brian (2002), *Parables for the Virtual: Movement, Affect, Sensation*, Durham: Duke University Press.
— (2015), *Politics of Affect*. Cambridge: Polity Press.
McLuhan, Marshall (1962), *The Gutenberg Galaxy*, Toronto: University of Toronto Press.
Mignolo, Walter (2012), *Local Histories/Global Designs: Coloniality, Subaltern Knowledges, and Border Thinking*, Princeton, NJ: Princeton University Press.
Mignolo, Walter, and Catherine Walsh (2018), *On Decoloniality: Concepts, Analytics, Praxis*, Durham: Duke University Press.
Milanich, Nara (2017), 'Daddy Issues: "Responsible Paternity" as Public Policy in Latin America,' *World Policy Journal*, 34: 3, pp: 8–14.
Miller, William (1998), *The Anatomy of Disgust*, Cambridge: Harvard University Press.
Mirzoeff, Nicholas (1999), *An Introduction to Visual Culture*, London: Routledge.
Morguen, Paula (2014), 'Representación de la pobreza: señales de cambio,' in Diana Paladino (ed.), *Documental/ficción. Reflexiones sobre el cine argentino contemporáneo*, Buenos Aires: Eduntref, pp. 69–84.
Morreall, John (2011), *Comic Relief: A Comprehensive Philosophy of Humor*, Wiley: Kindle Edition.
Mulder, Tavid (2014), 'Desencuentros of Postdictatorship Argentina: History, Politics, and Realism in Juan José Sear's *Glosa*,' *Revista hispánica moderna*, 67: 2, pp. 183–203.
Mullaly, Bob and Marilyn Dupré (2018), *The New Structural Social Work: Ideology, Theory, and Practice*, Oxford: Oxford University Press.
Nail, Thomas (2017), 'What is an Assemblage,' *Assemblages: (Pre)Political, Ethical and Ontological Perspectives*, *SubStance* 46: 1 (142), pp. 21–37.

Nancy, Jean-Luc (2007), *Listening*, translated by Charlotte Mandell, New York: Fordham University Press.

Nebbia, Gerardo (1999), 'Zedillo government Spurns Victims of Mexico Storm and Mud Slides,' *World Socialist Web Site*. October 16, <https://www.wsws.org/en/articles/1999/10/mex-o16.pdf> (last accessed 29 May 2024).

Nichols, Bill (2017), *Introduction to Documentary*, Bloomington: Indiana University Press.

Nixon, Rob (2009), 'Neoliberalism, Slow Violence and the Environmental Picaresque,' *Modern Fiction Studies* (Fall), 55: 3, pp. 443–67.

Noë, Alva (2004), *Action in Perception*, Cambridge: MIT Press.

Nouzeilles, Gabriela (2000), *Ficciones somáticas. Naturalismo, nacionalismo y políticas médicas del cuerpo (Argentina 1880–1910)*, Rosario: Beatriz Viterbo Editora.

Nussbaum, Martha (2013), *Political Emotions: Why Love Matters for Justice*, Cambridge: The Belknap Press of Harvard University Press.

Olivares, Juan José (2023), 'Paula Markovitch propone "hacer un cine descolonizado que trate los problemas de AL," *La Jornada Zacatecas* (2023): 7, <https://www.jornada.com.mx/2023/08/03/espectaculos/a07n1esp> (last accessed 23 June 2024).

Oubiña, David (2007), *Estudio crítico sobre* La ciénaga, Buenos Aires: Picnic Editorial.

— (2013), 'Footprints: Risks and Challenges of Contemporary Argentine Cinema,' in Jens Andermann and Álvaro Fernández Bravo (eds), *New Argentine and Brazilian Cinema: Reality Effects*, New York: Palgrave Macmillan, pp. 31–41.

Page, Joanna (2009), *Crisis and Capitalism in Contemporary Argentine Cinema*, Durham: Duke University Press.

Paladino, Diana (2014), 'Presentación,' in (ed.) Diana Paladino, *Documental-ficción: Reflexiones sobre el cine argentino contemporáneo*, Buenos Aires: Eduntref, pp. 11–12.

Paska, Roman (1995), 'Pensée-marionnette, esprit-marionnette: Un art d'assemblage,' *Puck* 8, pp. 63–6.

'Paula Markovitch's *El premio* Tops Mexico's Ariel Awards' (2013), *Cinema Tropical*, May 28, <https://www.cinematropical.com/cinema-tropical/paula-markovitchs-el-premio-tops-mexicos-ariel-awards> (last accessed 30 July 2015).

Peller, Mariela (2016), 'La historia de las niñas: Memoria, ficción y transmisión en la narrativa de la generación de la post-dictadura argentina,' in Luis A. Escobar, Juan Pablo Giordano, and Roberto Pittaluga (eds), *Figuraciones estéticas de la experiencia argentina reciente*, Ciudad de Santa Fe: María Muratore Ediciones, pp. 115–41.

Pethő, Ágnes (2011), *Cinema and Intermediality: The Passion for the In-Between*, Newcastle: Cambridge Scholars Publishing.
— (2012), *Film in the Post-Media Age*, Newcastle: Cambridge Scholars Publishing.
— (2013), 'The Vertigo of the Single Image: From the Classic Narrative "Glitch" to the Post-Cinematic Adaptations of Paintings,' *Acta Universitatis Sapientiae* 6: 1, pp. 65–90.
— (2015), *The Cinema of Sensations*, Newcastle: Cambridge Scholars Publishing.
— (2020a), *Caught In-Between: Intermediality in Contemporary Eastern European and Russian Cinema*, Edinburgh: Edinburgh University Press.
— (2020b), 'Introduction: The Art of In-Betweenness in Contemporary Eastern European Cinema,' in Ágnes Pethő (ed.), *Caught In-Between: Intermediality in Contemporary Eastern European and Russian Cinema*, Edinburgh: Edinburgh University Press, pp. 1–24.
Piedras, Pablo (2014), *El cine documental en primera persona*, Buenos Aires: Paidós.
Pijanowski, Bryan, Almo Farina, Stuart H. Gage, Sarah L. Dumyahn, and Bernie L. Krause (2011), 'What is soundscape ecology? An Introduction and Overview of an Emerging New Science', *Landscape Ecology* 26: 9, pp. 1213–32, <https://doi.org/10.1007/s10980-011-9600-8>.
Pile, Steve (2010), 'Emotions and Affect in Recent Human Geography,' *Transactions of the Institute of British Geographers* 35: 1 (January), pp. 5–20.
Piñeyro, Marcelo (2002), *Kamchatka*, Menemsha Films.
Pinto Veas, Iván (2008), 'Conversación con Gonzalo Aguilar,' *laFuga*, 7 (January), <http://2016.lafuga.cl/conversacion-con-gonzalo-aguilar/16> (last accessed 25 Jan 2024).
Podalsky, Laura (2004), *Specular City: Transforming Culture, Consumption, and Space in Buenos Aires, 1995–1973*, Philadelphia: Temple University Press.
— (2007), 'Out of Depth: The Politics of Disaffected Youth and Contemporary Latin American Cinema,' in Timothy Shary and Alexandra Seibel (eds), *Youth in Global Cinema*, Austin: University of Texas Press, pp. 109–30.
— (2008), 'The Young, the Damned, and the Restless: Youth in Contemporary Mexican Cinema,' *Framework: The Journal of Cinema and Media* 49: 1, pp. 144–60.
— (2011), *The Politics of Affect and Emotion in Contemporary Latin American Cinema: Argentina, Brazil, Cuba, and Mexico*, New York: Palgrave Macmillan.
Porteous, Douglas (1986), 'Intimate Sensing,' *Area* 18: 3, pp. 250–51.
— (1990), *Landscapes of the Mind*, Toronto: University of Toronto Press.
Prividera, Nicolás (2007), *M*, Argentina: Cinemargentino.
Pucciarelli, Alfredo Raúl (2011), *Los años de Menem: la construcción del orden neoliberal*, Buenos Aires: Siglo Veintiuno Editores.

Puenzo, Lucía (2007), *XXY*, Film Movement.
Puenzo, Luis (1985), *La historia oficial*, Argentina: Video Home. DVD.
Qosja, Isa (2014), *Three Windows and a Hanging/Tri Dritare dhe një Varje*, Kosovo: CMB Production. DVD.
Quintín (2002), 'De una generación a otra: ¿hay una línea divisoria?,' in Horacio Bernades, Diego Larer, and Sergio Wolf (eds), *El nuevo cine argentino: Temas, autores y estilos de una renovación*, Buenos Aires: Ediciones Tatanka, pp. 111–18.
Rajewsky, Irina (2005), 'Intermediality, Intertextuality, and Remediation: A Literary Perspective on Intermediality,' *Intermédialités* 6, pp. 43–64.
Rancière, Jacques (2015), *Dissensus: On Politics and Aesthetics*, New York: Bloomsbury.
Randall, Rachel (2017), *Children on the Threshold in Contemporary Latin American Cinema: Nature, Gender, and Agency*, Lanham: Lexington Press.
Ranzani, Oscar (2020), 'Paula Markovitch finalmente estrena "El premio" en la Argentina,' *Página12*, September 11, <https://www.pagina12.com.ar/291181-paula-markovitch-finalmente-estrena-el-premio-en-la-argentin> (last accessed 3 November 2022).
Relph, Edward (1976), *Place and Placelessness*, Toronto: University of Toronto Press.
Renov, Michael (1993), *Theorizing Documentary*, New York: Routledge.
Restrepo Sánchez, Gonzalo (2019), *Breve historia de los cineastas del Caribe colombiano*, Santa Marta, Colombia: Editorial Unimagdalena.
Rich, Rubi (1997), 'An/Other View of New Latin American Cinema,' in Michael Martin (ed.), *New Latin American Cinema*, Detroit: Wayne State University Press, pp. 273–97.
Ricoeur, Paul (1967), *Fallible Man: Philosophy of the Will*, Chicago: Henry Regnery Co.
Riedel, Friedlind (2019), 'Atmosphere,' in Jan Slaby and Christian von Scheve (eds), *Affective Societies: Key Concepts*, New York: Routledge, pp. 85–95.
Robben, Antonius (2005), *Political Violence and Trauma in Argentina*, Philadelphia: University of Pennsylvania Press.
Rocco, Alessandro (2021), '"¿Qué significa pesimista?" Infancia e insilio durante la dictadura argentina (1976–1983) en el filme *El premio* (2011) de Paula Markovitch,' *Kamchatka: Revista de análisis cultural* 17, pp. 497–527.
— (2023), '"A veces pienso en esos hombres . . .". Memoria, arte y marginación durante la dictadura y la postdictadura argentina en *Cuadros en la oscuridad* (2017) de Paula Markovitch,' in Jorge González del Pozo and Inela Selimović (eds), *Encuentros fortuitos: Agencialidad en conflicto y poder en movimiento en el cine hispano*, Madrid: Iberoamericana, pp. 135–61.
Rocha, Carolina (2017), *Argentine Cinema and National Identity (1966–1976)*, Liverpool: Liverpool University Press.

Rocha, Carolina and Elizabeth Montes Garcés (2010), *Violence in Argentine Literature and Film (1989–2005)*, Calgary: University of Calgary Press.

Rocha, Carolina and Georgia Seminet (2014), 'Introduction,' in Carolina Rocha and Georgia Seminet (eds), *Screening Minors in Latin American Cinema*, Lanham: Lexington Books, pp. xi–xx.

Rodaway, Paul (1994), *Sensuous Geographies: Body, Sense, and Place*, London: Routledge.

Rodríguez, Laura Graciela (2010), 'La educación artística y la política cultural durante la última dictadura militar en Argentina (1976–1983),' *Arte, Individuo y Sociedad* 22: 1, pp. 59–74.

Roman, Paska (2015), 'Pensamiento-títere, Mentalidad-títere. Un arte de ensamblaje,' unofficial translation by Javier Swedzky, Buenos Aires: UNA, pp. 1–5.

Roqué, María Inés (2004), *Papá Iván*, Zafra Difusión, S. Am.

Ros, Ana (2012), *The Post-Dictatorship Generation in Argentina, Chile, and Uruguay: Collective Memory and Cultural Production*, New York: Palgrave Macmillan.

Rose, Gillian (1993), *Feminism and Geography: The Limits of Geographical Knowledge*, Cambridge: Polity Press.

Rossholm, Anna Sofía (2013), 'Auto-adaptation and the movement of writing across media: Ingmar Bergman's Notebooks,' in Jørgen Bruhn, Anne Gjelsvik, and Eirik Frisvold Hanssen (eds), *Adaptation Studies: New Challenges, New Directions*, New York: Bloomsbury, pp. 203–22.

Russell, Catherine (2018), *Archiveology: Walter Benjamin and Archival Film Practices*, Durham: Duke University Press.

Saleny, Emilia Josefina (1919), *El pañuelo de Clarita*, Archive: Private Collection.

Sanders, Peter (2007), *The Disappeared*, New York: Eight Twelve Productions. DVD.

Scarry, Elaine (1985), *The Body in Pain: The Making and Unmaking of the World*, Oxford: Oxford University Press.

Schneider Enríquez, Mary (2016), *Doris Salcedo: The Materiality of Mourning*, New Haven: Yale University Press.

Schroeder Rodríguez, Paul (2016), *Latin American Cinema: A Comparative History*, Berkeley: University of California Press.

'Se mató en Mar del Plata una hija de desaparecidos' (2011), *La Capital de Mar del Plata*, August 16, <http://www.lacapitalmdp.com/noticias/Policiales/2011/08/16/192365.html> (last accessed 5 September, 2011).

'Se suicidó Pablo Germán Athanasiu Laschan, el nieto recuperado 109' (2015), *Notas: Periodismo Popular*, April 13, <https://notasperiodismopopular.com.ar/2015/04/13/suicido-pablo-german-athanasiu-laschan-nieto-recuperado-109/> (last accessed 15 April 2015).

Seggiaro, Daniela (2012), *Nosilatiaj. La belleza*, Argentina: Vista Sur Films. DVD.
Selimović, Inela (2015), 'The Social Spaces in Mutation: Sex, Violence, and Autism in Albertina Carri's *La rabia* (2008),' *Journal of Latin American Cultural Studies* 24: 4, pp. 517–33.
— (2016), 'Gastón Biraben's *Cautiva* (2005): An Instance of Enduring Grief,' *Bulletin of Hispanic Studies* 93: 4, pp. 421–38.
— (2018a), *Affective Moments in the Films by Martel, Carri, and Puenzo*, London: Palgrave Macmillan.
— (2018b), 'Coached Feelings and Political Resocializations in Paula Markovitch's *El premio* (2011),' in Philippa Page, Inela Selimović, and Camilla Sutherland (eds), *The Feeling Child: Affect and Politics in Latin American Literature and Film*, Lanham: Lexington Books, pp. 25–48.
— (2018c), 'Sensorial Youths: Gender, Eroticism, and Agency in Lucrecia Martel's *Rey muerto*,' in Geoffrey Maguire and Rachel Randall (eds), *New Visions of Adolescence in Contemporary Latin American Cinema*, Cham: Palgrave Macmillan, pp. 81–98.
— (2021), 'La marginación empoderada en *El actor principal* (2019) de Paula Markovitch,' *La Jornada Zacatecas*. August 9, <https://ljz.mx/2021/08/09/la-marginacion-empoderada-en-el-actor-principal-de-paula-markovitch-2019/> (last accessed 30 October 2023).
— (2023a), 'Entrevista a Paula Markovitch,' *Mistral: Journal of Latin American Women's Intellectual & Cultural History* 3: 1, pp. 119–22.
— (2023b), 'Sepulchral Intermediality in Paula Markovitch's *Armando y Genoveva* (2013),' *Mistral: Journal of Latin American Women's Intellectual & Cultural History* 3: 1, pp. 100–14.
Serres, Michel (1998), *Les cinq sens*, Paris: Hachette.
Severiche, Guillermo (2023), 'They Are All Around Us: Pain, Memory, and Multisensory Images in Paula Markovitch's *El premio* (2011),' in Mirna Vohnsen and Daniel Mourenza (eds), *Contemporary Argentine Women Filmmakers*, Cham: Palgrave Macmillan, pp. 147–61.
Shaw, Deborah (2018), 'Cómo estudiar el cine hecho por mujeres iberoamericanas: un manifiesto,' in Annette Scholz and Marta Álvarez (eds), *Cineastas emergentes: mujeres en el cine del siglo XXI*, Madrid: Iberoamericana/Vervuert, pp. 31–42.
Sibley, David (1995), *Geographies of Exclusion: Society and Difference in the West*, New York: Routledge.
Slaby, Jan and Rainer Mühlhoff (2019), 'Affect,' in Jan Slaby and Christian von Scheve, *Affective Societies: Key Concepts*, New York: Routledge, pp. 27–41.
Smith, Mark (2019), *Sensing the Past: Seeing, Hearing, Smelling, Tasting, and Touching in History*, Berkeley: University of California Press.
Solnicki, Gastón (2011), *Papirosen*, Argentina: Filmy Wiktora.

Solomonoff, Julia (2009), *El último verano de la boyita*, Travesía Producciones.
Sontag, Susan (1966), *Against Interpretation and Other Essays*, New York: Picador USA.
— (1977), *On Photography*, New York: Farrar, Straus and Giroux.
Soria, Carolina (2014), 'Reflexiones sobre realistas y no realistas,' in Diana Paladino, *Documental/Ficción. Reflexiones sobre el cine argentino contemporáneo*, Buenos Aires: EDUNTREF, pp. 37–56.
Sosa, Cecilia (2012), 'Queering Kinship: The Performance of Blood and the Attires of Memory,' *Journal of Latin American Cultural Studies*, 21: 2, pp. 221–33.
Southworth, Michael (1967), 'The sonic environment of cities,' thesis. Cambridge: MIT.
Spivak, Gayatri (1999), *A Critique of Postcolonial Reason: Toward a History of the Vanishing Present*, Cambridge: Harvard University Press.
Stagnaro, Bruno and Israel Adrián Caetano (1998), *Pizza, birra, faso*, Buenos Aires, Argentina: Palo y a la Bolsa Cine.
Stanko, Elizabeth (1997), 'Safety Talk: Conceptualizing Women's Risk Assessment as a "Technology of the Soul",' *Theoretical Criminology* 1: 4 (November), pp. 479–99.
Stephens, Sharon (1995), 'Introduction: Children and the Politics of Culture in "Late Capitalism,"' in (ed.) Sharon Stephens, *Children and the Politics of Culture*, Princeton, NJ: Princeton University Books, pp. 3–48.
Sternberg, Meir (1999), 'The "Laokoon" Today: Interart Relations, Modern Projects and Projections,' *Poetics Today* 20: 2 (Summer), pp. 291–379.
Svampa, Maristella (2004), *La brecha urbana*, Buenos Aires: Capital Intelectual.
— (2005), *La sociedad excluyente: La Argentina bajo el signo del neoliberalismo*, Buenos Aires: Taurus.
Swedzky, Javier (2012), 'Las arrugas del saco,' *Saverio: Revista cruel de teatro* 5: 18, pp. 7–9.
— (2014), 'Le silence,' *Puck. Humain/Non humain* 20 (June), 1–5, <https://www.librairie-gallimard.com/livre/9782355391682-revue-puck-n-20-humain-non-humain-la-marionnette-et-les-autres-arts-revue-puck/> (last accessed 20 July 2024).
— (2018), 'Escribir para las cosas. Elementos para pensar la dramaturgia para títeres, objetos y materiales,' in (ed.) Ana Alvarado, *Cosidad, carnalidad y virtualidad: cuerpos y objetos en escena*, Buenos Aires: UNA, pp. 47–99.
Swistun, Débora Alejandra and Javier Auyero (2009), *Flammable: Environmental Suffering in an Argentine Shantytown*, Oxford: Oxford University Press.
Tan, Ed (1996), *Emotion and the Structure of Narrative Film: Film as an Emotion Machine*, New York: Routledge.
Tarkovsky, Andrey (1975), *Mirror*, Mosfilm.

— (2003), *Sculpting in Time: Reflections on the Cinema*, translated by Kitty Hunter-Blair, Austin: University of Texas Press.
Taylor, Diana (2020), *¡Presente!: The Politics of Presence*, Durham: Duke University Press.
Tierney, Dolores (2018), *New Transnationalisms in Contemporary Latin American Cinemas*, Edinburgh: Edinburgh University Press.
Tompkins, Cynthia (2013), *Experimental Latin American Cinema: History and Aesthetics*, Austin: University of Texas Press.
— (2018), *Affectual Erasure: Representations of Indigenous Peoples in Argentine Cinema*, Albany: SUNY Press.
Tuan, Yi-Fu ([1977] 2014), *Space and Place: The Perspective of Experience*, Minneapolis: University of Minnesota Press.
United Nations Convention on the Rights of the Child (1989), <https://www.unicef.org/child-rights-convention/convention-text> (last accessed 5 July 2024).
United Nations Office on Drugs and Crime (Mexico) (UNODC) (2021), *Report of the Urban Safety Governance Assessment in Iztapalapa*, Mexico City: UNODC. <https://www.unodc.org/documents/Urban-security/210521_UGSA_Iztapalapa_Ingles.pdf> (last accessed 15 April 2022).
United Nations Office on Drugs and Crime (Mexico) (UNODC) (2021), 'Iztapalapa Report,' Mexico City: UNODC. <https://www.unodc.org/documents/Urbansecurity/210521_UGSA_Iztapalapa_Ingles.pdf> (last accessed 5 February 2022).
Usubiaga, Viviana (2012), *Imágenes inestables: Artes visuales, dictadura y democracia en Buenos Aires*, Buenos Aires: Edhasa.
Velarde Bernal, Genaro (2019), 'El "pibe chorro" y su escena delictiva,' *Psicoanálisis* 41: 1–2, pp. 191–206.
Verbitsky, Bernardo (2003), *Villa miseria también es América*, Buenos Aires: Sudamericana.
Viñar, Marcelo (2005), 'Niños fuera de la ley,' in Mario Torres (ed.), *Niños fuera de la ley: niños y adolescentes en Uruguay: exclusión social y construcción de subjetividades*, Montevideo: Trilce, pp. 37–53.
Viola, Bill (1986), *I Do Not Know What It Is I Am Like*, New York: EIA.
Vohnsen, Mirna and Daniel Mourenza (2023), 'Introduction. Women Filmmakers in Argentina: Reworking Cinematic Practices,' in Mirna Vohnsen and Daniel Mourenza (eds), *Contemporary Argentine Women Filmmakers*, Dublin: Palgrave Macmillan, pp. 1–23.
Walden, Victoria Grace (2019), *Cinematic Intermedialities and Contemporary Holocaust Memory*, Cham: Palgrave Macmillan.
Warner, Marina (1994), *Managing Monsters: Six Myths of Our Time*, London: Vintage.

Williams, Raymond (1977), *Marxism and Literature*, Oxford: Oxford University Press.
Wilson, Emma (2007), 'Miniature Lives, Intrusion and Innocence: Women Filming Children,' *French Cultural Studies*, 18: 2, pp. 169–183.
Wong, Cindy Hing-Yuk (2011), *Film Festivals: Culture, People, and Power on the Global Screen*, New Brunswick: Rutgers University Press.

Index

Note: Page numbers in *italics* indicate figures. The index is sorted by word-by-word alphabetization.

abjection, theorizations of, 167
About Looking (Berger), 42–3
absence, in *Cuadros en la oscuridad*, 112, 113
Abuelas de Plaza de Mayo, 67–8, 79, 80
Acción de Duelo (installation), 98
Ackerman, Diane, 58–9
'active subjectivity,' 10
El actor principal (2019, Markovitch), 6–7, 21, 24, 121–45
  Berlin setting, 126, 128
  cinematic context, 123–4
  close-ups, use of, 127
  defiance, 129
  desire, 140
  documentary footage in, 130–1
  economic precarity, 128
  'emotional geographies,' 122, 130, 134, 141, 142
  encounters, 123, 128–30, 141
  erotic encounter, 139–40
  fear, 138
  gestures, emotional, 122, 134–5
  hotel setting, 126, 127
  'iconic objects,' 136–8
  'immersive social intimacy,' 129
  inter-embodiment of Luis and Azra, 122–3, 133
  iPad video footage, 137
  Luis' role in *Mirror*, 129, 137
  marginality, 124–6, 133
  Mexico City, 124, 125
  peripheral spaces, 126–7
  power, re-configurations of, 124
  relief, 141
  sensorial interaction, 133–4, 138
  sexual encounter, 139–40
  skin-oriented sensorium, 140
  social difference and audacity, 132

El actor principal (cont.)
  spatial and emotional interconnectedness, 121, 122
  spatial juxtaposition, 127–8
  storytelling in characters' native languages, 136
  strangeness, 135
  togetherness, 133, 142
  touch, 133, 134, 138, 140
  trust, 139
  unfocused and focused interaction, 138–9
  the unsaid/unspeakable, 136, 141–2
  war atrocities, remembrance of, 130
adult world, in *Angeles*, 160, 161
affect
  affective clash, 81–2
  affective politics, 81
  and the body, 70, 72, 74, 81
  and disruption, 71
  and feelings, 66
  and play, 74, 78
  as relational dynamics, 67
agency
  of children, 76, 77, 113, 149
  and resistance, 10
  sensescapes of, 14–18
Aguilar, Gonzalo, 12, 85, 151
Ahmed, Saladdin, 107, 113
Ahmed, Sara, 93, 121, 128, 129, 138
Alexander, Jeffrey, 136–7
alienation, in *Cuadros en la oscuridad*, 110

Amado, Ana, 3
Amaral, Suzana, 9
ambivalence, and touch, 156
Andermann, Jens, 3, 60
Ángeles (2025, Markovitch), 20, 24, 146–63
  adult world in, 160, 161
  agency of child-protagonists, 149, 154
  existential despair, 147
  homelessness, 152
  looking, multilayered process of, 158–9
  misconnection between minors and adults, 160
  multidimensional subjectivities, 154, 157
  multisensoriality, 154–5, 156
  precarity, 147–8, 161
  'prehensions,' 148
  'self-being,' 157–8
  shantytown setting, 146, 149–50, 151, 161–2
  shoplifting sequence, 160–1
  suffering, 147
  suicidal ideation/suicide, 147, 149, 158, 159
  touch, 155–6
  toxicity, 156–7
  violence, depiction of, 157, 158, 159, 160, 161
animals
  cross-species solidarity, 43
  cruelty toward, 33
  marginalization of, 37
  and otherness, 42–3
'archiveology,' 131

Argentina
  child labor, 151–2
  economic crisis (1998–2001), 3, 151
  environmental pollution, 157
  kidnapping/illegal adoption of political dissidents' babies and children, 78–9
  Menem government, 3
  military dictatorship (1976–83), 67, 71, 78–9, 90, 115
  New Argentine Cinema, 12, 13, 14–15
  political violence, 67, 71, 78–9, 90
  poverty, 151
  resocialization processes, 79–80
  shantytowns, 150–1
  suicides of reappropriated adults and family members, 79–81
  women filmmakers, 7, 14–15
Armando y Genoveva (2013, Markovitch), 5–6, 23, 83–101
  artmaking process, 97
  audio recordings of Armando and Genoveva, 87–91, 93–6, 97
  communal commemoration, 97–8
  darkness, 96
  Genoveva's confession, 94–5
  haptic interaction, 86–7, 88, 91–3
  images of painters' house, 96–7
  'in-betweenness,' 84
  incongruity, 91
  listening, 91, 94
  paintings, contact with, 86–7, 88, 91–3
  political dissidence, 85
  'sensuous interfaces,' 88
  soundscape, 83, 89–90
  touch, 86–7, 88, 91–3
  voice-over narration, 85, 86, 89, 97
artistic anonymity, in *Cuadros en la oscuridad*, 104, 108, 111, 115
artists, creative resilience of, 103
artworks, haptic images of, 86–7, 88, 91–3
atmosphere
  Riedel's notion of, 36–7
  and social relations, 50
  of strangeness, 49–50
audacity, in *El actor principal*, 132
audio recordings, in *Armando y Genoveva*, 87–91, 93–6, 97
auditory space, 40–1

babies, illegal adoption of in Argentina, 78–9
Bal, Mieke, 117, 165
Balázs, Béla, 148
Barker, Jennifer, 51
Barthes, Roland, 66
Bauman, Zygmunt, 150
beach setting, in *El premio*, 68–70, 73–4, 81
bedbound characters, 59–60
Bemberg, María Luisa, 9

Benjamin, Walter, 71–2
Berger, John, 42–3
Berlin setting, in *El actor principal*, 126, 128
Berlinale film festival, 126
Bhabha, Homi, 84
black-outs, in film, 96
the body, and affect, 70, 72, 74, 81
Buenos Aires, 151
Buñuel, Luis, 33
Burt, Jonathan, 33
Burucúa, Constanza, 9
Butler, Judith, 164

Cacerías imaginarias (Markovitch), 1, 2, 25, 85, 88, 98–9, 165
director's notes on *Cuadros en la oscuridad*, 103–4, 106, 116–17
Calogerópulos, Heman Emilio, 80
camerawork, painting analogy, 167
Canclini, Néstor García, 38, 40, 125
caregiving, terminal illness in *Música de ambulancia*, 55–63
Carpenter, Edmund Snow, 40–1
Carri, Albertina, 33, 74
cat, appearance in *El actor principal*, 33–4
Un chien andalou (1929, Buñuel), 33
child labor, in Argentina, 151–2
children
  agency of, 76, 77, 149, 154
  destructive behavior, 112, 113, 114
  friendship, 75
  'going exploring,' 73–4
  kidnapping/illegal adoption of, 67–8, 78–9
  otherness of, 159–60
  portrayal of in Latin American cinema, 65, 148, 153–4, 159–60
  resocialization of, 65–82
  street children, 20, 113, 146–63
  subversiveness of, 72–4
  as transgressors, 113
Chile, 80, 125
La ciénaga (2001, Martel), 60
the city
  as 'theater,' 37–8
  video clip analogy, 40
  see also urban settings
Claeys, Gregory, 112
Classen, Constance, 56–7, 93
close-ups, in *El actor principal*, 127
Codebò, Agnese, 150
colonial domination, 10
communal commemoration, in *Armando y Genoveva*, 97–8
Connor, Steven, 18, 39, 61
contested marginality, 17, 18–26
Córdoba
  in *Ángeles*, 20, 146, 149, 151
  in *Armando y Genoveva*, 5, 6
  in *Cuadros en la oscuridad*, 110, 119
Fantasmas Disfrazados exhibition, 99

Cortés, Busi, 9
Crastnopol, Margaret, 107
creativity, compulsive, 109, 112
cruelty, towards animals, 33
Cuadros en la oscuridad (2017, Markovitch), 4–5, 23, 102–20, 132
   absence and presence, 112, 113
   artistic anonymity, 104, 108, 111, 115
   children's destructive behavior, 112, 113, 114
   compulsive creativity, 109, 112
   'Cuadros. Experimento Dramático' version of, 118
   cultural implications, 111
   defiance, 119
   destructiveness, 112–14, 116
   director's notes on, 103–6, 116–17
   disgust, 114–16, 119
   ending/s of, 117–18
   existential discomfort, embodiment of, 107
   internalized totalitarianism, 107
   legacy, manifestation of, 112, 118
   liminality, 105
   primitive and perceptual spaces, 114
   resilience, paradoxical forms of, 118–19
   shantytown setting, 110, 119
   silence, 108
   social isolation of central protagonist, 104, 108–9, 117
   spectrality, 104–7, 109–10, 119
   spectropolitics, 110, 111

Daney, Serge, 12
darkness, in *Armando y Genoveva*, 96
de Certeau, Michel, 61, 62
death drive, 60
'decolonial feminism,' 10
defiance
   in *El actor principal*, 129
   in *Cuadros en la oscuridad*, 119
Deleuze, Gilles, 8, 17, 25
   'nomadic assemblages,' 21–2, 24
Derrida, Jacques, 92, 110
desire, in *El actor principal*, 140; *see also* erotic encounters
despair, in *Ángeles*, 147
destructiveness, in *Cuadros en la oscuridad*, 112–14, 116
Diaconu, Mădălina, 36
directors' notebooks, genre of, 117
the 'disappeared,' 67–8, 80, 105; *see also* military dictatorship, Argentina
disgust, in *Cuadros en la oscuridad*, 23, 114–16, 119
displacement, in *El premio*, 71
disruption
   and affect, 71
   of play, 73–4

documentaries
    'contested territory' of, 95
    documentary footage use
        in *El actor principal*,
        130–1
    and the other, 89
    voice-over narration, 5, 6
    see also *Armando y Genoveva*
        (2013, Markovitch)
dog, protagonist's relationship
    with in *Perriférico*, 19, 34,
    37–8, 41, 42, 43, 44
Dotta, Pablo, 164
Douglas, Mary, 165
Drobnick, Jim, 59
the dying
    act of dying, 61
    dignity in dying, 59
    in *Música de ambulancia*,
    55–63
dystopia, 112

economic marginality/precarity,
    12–13
    in *El actor principal*, 128
    in *Ángeles*, 20, 147–8,
    161
Edelstein, Genoveva, 2–3, 83;
    see also *Armando y Genoveva*
    (2013, Markovitch)
'emotional geographies,' 122,
    130, 134, 141, 142
emotional incongruity
    in *Marilina*, 47
    in *Música de ambulancia*, 47,
    61–2
emotions
    and attachments, 121
    situatedness of, 121

encounters, in *El actor principal*,
    123, 128–30, 141; see also
    erotic encounters
Enríquez, Mariana, 140,
    157
environmental justice, 156
erotic encounters
    in *El actor principal*, 139–40
    in *Música de ambulancia*, 55,
    61–2
essay-writing prize/award
    ceremony, in *El premio*,
    76–7
essentialism, 11
existential discomfort,
    embodiment of, 107

false-life narrative, in *El premio*,
    74–6
Fantasmas Disfrazados
    (exhibition), 99
father–daughter interactions, in
    Marilina, 51
father figure
    in *Marilina*, 48, 49, 50, 51,
    55, 63
    in *El premio*, 67, 68
favelas see shantytowns
fear, in *El actor principal*,
    138
feelings
    and affect, 66, 81–2
    structure of, 66
Feitlowitz, Marguerite, 115
feminism, 'decolonial
    feminism,' 10
film festivals, 126
Fuchs, Thomas, 50
Furtado, Jorge, 86

Garramuño, Florencia, 99
Genaro Pérez Municipal Museum of Fine Arts, Córdoba, 99
gender, in caregiving, 59
gender-based violence, 140–1
gendered marginality, 9
'geographies of exclusion,' 165
geophony, in *Perriférico*, 36
gestures, emotional, in *El actor principal*, 122, 134–5
ghosts *see* specters; spectrality
Goffman, Erving, 135, 138
González, Maricruz, 111
Grandmothers of Plaza de Mayo, 67–8, 79, 80
Gregg, Melissa, 66
Guattari, Félix
  'nomadic assemblages,' 21–2, 24
  politics, 25
Gurrola, Sergio, 83, 89–90

Han, Byung-Chul, 135, 157–8
Haneke, Michael, 96
haptic imagery
  in *Armando y Genoveva*, 86–7, 91–3
  in *Música de ambulancia*, 56
haptic textures, 88; *see also* 'tactile epistemologies'; touch
hearing, and listening, 91
Heffes, Gisela, 156
Hijos por la Identidad y la Justicia contra el Olvido (H.I.J.O.S.), 79
'Hitchcockian painting,' 87
homelessness
  in *Ángeles*, 24, 152
  in Mexico, 39
  in *Perriférico*, 19, 34, 35, 36, 37, 40
hospice setting, in *Música de ambulancia*, 59
hotel setting, in *El actor principal*, 126, 127
Houwen, Janna, 86
Howes, David, 15, 16, 17, 22, 50
  'geography of the senses,' 36, 43
  olfactory values, 58
human sensorium, 17, 18
Husserl, Edmund, 94

'iconic objects,' 136–8
'immersive social intimacy,' 129
'in-betweenness,' in *Armando y Genoveva*, 84
Iñárritu, Alejandro, 33
incongruity
  in *El actor principal*, 135
  in *Armando y Genoveva*, 91
  in *Marilina*, 47
  in *Música de ambulancia*, 47, 61–2
  theory of, 23
informal economy, 128
inter-embodiment, in *El actor principal*, 122–3, 133
interaction, unfocused and focused, 138–9
intermediality, in *Armando y Genoveva*, 83–101
International Short Film Festival, Berlin, 34
interpersonal atmospheres, 50
interpersonal trust, 139

intersensoriality
  notion of, 22
  in *Perriférico*, 35–6, 37
intersubjectivities, agentic, 20–1
'intervals,' conceptualization of, 135
intimate sensing, in *Perriférico*, 42
iPad-streamed videos, in *El actor principal*, 137
Italian neorealism, 8, 12, 13, 149
Iztapalapa, 128

James, Robin, 118–19
Jameson, Fredric, 110
jump cuts, in *Perriférico*, 39–40

Kantaris, Geoffrey, 149
Kaplan, Ann, 158
Kirchuk, Alejandro, 157
Kosovo war (1998–99), 123, 130, 141
Kristeva, Julia, 167
Kuhn, Annette, 73–4

Laine, Tarja, 112
Laschan, Pablo Genmin Athanasiu, 80
Lash, Kenneth, 47
Latin America
  paternity reforms, 48–9, 50
  shantytowns, 150–1
Latin American cinema
  bedbound characters, 59–60
  children's portrayal in, 65, 148, 153–4, 159–60

marginalization, portrayal of, 152–3
New Latin American Cinema, 8–9
  spectrality in, 104
laughter, in *Música de ambulancia*, 62–3
Lazzara, Michael, 79
lead pollution, Argentina, 157
legacy, in *Cuadros en la oscuridad*, 112, 118
León, Christian, 11
Levinas, Emmanuel, 158
liminality
  in *Cuadros en la oscuridad*, 105, 114
  paradoxical space, 127
listening
  in *Armando y Genoveva*, 91
  Nancy on, 41
  and touch, 93, 94
looking, multilayered process of in *Ángeles*, 158–9
Lugones, María, 10, 168

Manning, Erin, 133, 154–5
'prehensions,' 24, 148
marginality
  in *El actor principal*, 124–6, 133
  in *Ángeles*, 149
  of animals, 37
  contested marginality, 17, 18–26
  economic marginality, 12–13, 20, 128, 147–8, 161
  essentialist visions of, 11
  gendered forms of, 9

marginality (cont.)
  'geographies of exclusion,' 165
  Latin American cinema's portrayal of, 152–3
  marginalized subjectivities, 7–14
  Markovitch's cinematic exploration of, 164–8
  and multisensoriality, 166
  and place, 15–16, 39
  and sensescapes, 167
  sensory engagement with, 14–18
  social exclusion, 15
  transgressive protagonists, 13–14
Marilina (2001, Markovitch), 19–20, 23, 47–55
  emotional incongruity, 47
  father figure, 48, 49, 50, 51, 55, 63
  puppet theater, 49, 52–4
  silence, 53–5
  single motherhood, 54–5
  strangeness, atmosphere of, 49–50
  suprises, 47, 48, 52
  touch, 51
Markovitch, Armando, 2–3, 83, 102, 117; see also *Armando y Genoveva* (2013, Markovitch)
Markovitch, Paula
  aesthetic paradigm, 164
  approach to filmmaking, 165, 166–7
  'auto-adaptation' method, 118
  childhood of, 2
  self-exile of, 3, 6, 95
Marks, Laura, 18, 93, 122
  'haptic visuality' of film, 56, 86–7
  'tactile epistemologies,' 155
Martel, Lucrecia, 14, 33
  La ciénaga, 60
  La mujer sin cabeza, 134
Martin, Deborah, 60, 154
Masiello, Francine, 16, 21, 166
Massey, Doreen, 15
Massumi, Brian, 66, 70, 74, 81
memory, and touch, 93
Menem, Carlos, 3
Mexico, 39, 125
Mexico City, 3, 19, 34, *124*, 125, 128
'microtraumas,' concept of, 107
Milei, Javier, 20
military, affective presence in *El premio*, 76, 77
military dictatorship, Argentina, 67, 71, 78–9, 90, 115
Miller, William, 114–16, 119
El monstruo (Markovitch), 132
Morguen, Paula, 12–13
Morreall, John, 47
mother–daughter relationships
  in *Marilina*, 20, 47
  in *Música de ambulancia*, 20, 47, 55–63
  in *El premio*, 65–82
motherhood, single, in *Marilina*, 54–5
mothering, theme of, 19

La mujer sin cabeza (2008, Martel), 134
Mulder, Tavid, 65
multisensoriality
 in *Ángeles*, 154–5, 156
 'haptic visuality' of film, 56
 and marginality, 166
 puppet theater, 53
 in urban settings, 36–7, 38, 51–2
Mumford, Lewis, 37
Museo Municipal Genaro Pérez de Bellas Artes, Córdoba, 99
Música de ambulancia (2009, Markovitch), 19–20, 23, 55–63
 emotional incongruity, 47, 61–2
 haptic imagery, 56
 laughter, 62–3
 opening scene, 56
 setting in, 60–1
 sexual encounter, 55, 61–2
 smell, 57, 58–9, 63
 surprises, 47, 55
 touch, 56, 61
 videogame-playing, 56
 vomiting, 56–7

NAC *see* New Argentine Cinema
Nancy, Jean-Luc, 41, 91
narrator, reliablity of, 43
Nebbia, Gerardo, 39
neoliberalism, 3
neorealism, 8, 12, 13, 149
Never Again/Nunca Más report, 78–9
New Argentine Cinema (NAC), 12, 13, 14–15

New Latin American Cinema, 8–9
Nichols, Bill, 88–9, 90, 95
Nixon, Rob, 34
'nomadic assemblages,' 21–2, 24
Nunca Más/Never Again report, 78–9

objects, aesthetic form of, 136–8
'ocular-centricity,' and urban settings, 38
Ogando, Virginia, 80
olfactory imagery, in *Música de ambulancia*, 57, 58–9, 63
'othering,' and the nomad, 22
otherness, 13
 of animals, 42–3
 of children, 159–60
 and documentaries, 89
Oubiña, David, 60

Page, Joanna, 12
pain, language for, 57–8
paintings, haptic imagery, 86–7, 88, 91–3
El pañuelo de Clarita (1919, Saleny), 7–8
paradoxical space, 127
Paska, Roman, 52–3
paternity reforms, in Latin America, 48–9, 50
peripheral space, 126–7
Perriférico (1999, Markovitch), 19, 22–3, 33–46
 geophony, 36
 homelessness, 19, 34, 35, 36, 37, 40
 intersensoriality, 35–6, 37

Perriférico (cont.)
  intimate sensing, 42
  jump cuts, 39–40
  opening scene, 34
  playfulness, 44–5
  reliable/unreliable narrator, 43
  sensing, types of, 42
  stray dog, protagonist's relationship with, 34, 37–8, 41, 42, 43, 44
  transformation of space into place, 44
  urban soundscape, 34, 35, 38, 39, 41, 44
personal trust, 139
Pethő, Ágnes, 84, 87, 95–6
photographic images, and voice-over narration, 88–9
physical pain, language for, 57–8
Piedras, Pablo, 6, 89
Pile, Steve, 121
place
  marginalized sites, 39
  and space, 15–16, 44
play/playfulness
  and affect, 74, 78
  Benjamin on, 71–2
  constraints upon child's play, 68–9, 71
  disruption of, 73–4
  as performative, 74
  in *Perriférico*, 44–5
  in *El premio*, 68–70, 74
political dissidence
  in *Armando y Genoveva*, 85
  in *Cuadros en la oscuridad*, 102, 108, 115
  in *El premio*, 67, 68, 78–9, 80

political resocialization, in *El premio*, 65–82
political violence
  Argentina, 67, 71, 78–9, 90
  Colombia, 97–8
  Kosovo, 123, 130, 141
  Latin America, 125
politics, Deleuze and Guattri, 25
pollution, Riachuelo River, Argentina, 157
Porteous, Douglas, 17–18
postcolonial theory, 11
poverty
  in Buenos Aires, 151
  in Córdoba, 110
  in Mexico, 39
  see also economic marginality/precarity; shantytowns
power, re-configurations of, 124
powerlessness, and dying, 61
Practice of Everyday Life, The (de Certeau), 61
precarity, 12–13
  in *El actor principal*, 128
  in *Ángeles*, 20, 147–8, 161
'prehensions,' Manning's notion of, 24, 148
El premio (2011, Markovitch), 4, 23, 65–82, 132
  absent father/husband, 67, 68
  affect, 66, 71, 72, 81–2
  agency of child-protagonist, 76, 77
  beach setting, 68–70, 73–4, 81
  children's friendship, 75
  disruption and displacement, 71
  essay competition and award ceremony, 76–7

false-life narrative, 74–6
military, affective presence of, 76, 77
political context, 78
self-censorship, 72
social dependence, inversion of, 70
subversiveness of child-protagonist, 72–4
primitive space, 114
psycho-social boundaries, 122
Pucciarelli, Alfredo Raúl, 3
puppet theater, in *Marilina*, 49, 52–4

La rabia (2008, Carri), 74
Randall, Rachel, 159
relief, in *El actor principal*, 141
Relph, Edward, 114
resilience, in *Cuadros en la oscuridad*, 103, 118–19
resistance, agency and, 10
'resistant subjectivity,' 10
resocialization, in *El premio*, 65–82
'responsible paternity,' 48–9
Riachuelo River, pollution of, 157
Rich, Rubi, 8, 9
Ricouer, Paul, 81
Riedel, Friedlind, 36–7
Rocco, Alessandro, 5, 108, 112
Rocha, Glauber, 150
Rodaway, Paul, 18, 93, 164
roller-blading, in *El premio*, 68–9
Rose, Gillian, 127, 135

Rossholm, Anna Sofia, 117
Russell, Catherine, 131

Salcedo, Doris, 97, 98
Saleny, Josefina Emilia, 7–8
Sarno, Geraldo, 89
Scarry, Elaine, 57–8
Schanberg, Saul, 93
Schneider Enríquez, Mary, 97
Seigworth, Gregory, 66
'self-being,' 157–8
self-censorship, in *El premio*, 72
sensation, Deleuze's notion of, 25
senses
  as 'cultural systems,' 16
  'geography' of, 36, 43
sensescapes, 14–18, 164, 166, 167
sensing, types of, 42
sensorial interaction
  in *El actor principal*, 133–4, 138
  in Markovitch's oeuvre, 21, 25, 26
'sensuous experience,' 18
'sensuous interfaces,' 88
sexual encounters
  in *El actor principal*, 139–40
  in *Música de ambulancia*, 55, 61–2
shantytowns, 12
  in *Ángeles*, 146, 149–50, 151, 161–2
  in *Cuadros en la oscuridad*, 110, 119
  in Latin America, 150–1
shoplifting scene, in *Ángeles*, 160–1

Sibley, David, 165
silence
　in *Cuadros en la oscuridad*, 108
　in *Marilina*, 53–5
Sitnisky, Carolina, 9
skin, and touch, 155, 156
skin-oriented sensorium, 140
slums *see* shantytowns
smell, in *Música de ambulancia*, 57, 58–9, 63
social dependence, inversion of
　in *El premio*, 70
social exclusion/isolation, 15, 165
　in *Cuadros en la oscuridad*, 104, 108–9, 117
　see also economic marginality/precarity
social groups, resistance to social containment, 131–2
social intimacy, immersive, 129
social relations, and atmosphere, 50
solidarity, with animals, 43
Sons and Daughters for Identity and Justice Against Forgetting (H.I.J.O.S.), 79
soundscapes
　in *Armando y Genoveva*, 83, 89–90
　in *Perriférico*, 34, 35, 38, 39, 41, 44
Southworth, Michael F., 35
space
　auditory space, 40–1
　and emotional interconnectedness, 121, 122
　'in-betweenness,' 84
　liminal space, 105
　paradoxical space, 127
　peripheral space, 126–7
　and place, 15–16, 44
　primitive space, 114
　'third space,' 84
spatial juxtaposition, in *El actor principal*, 127–8
specters
　artists' metaphorical use of, 104–5
　as 'conceptual metaphors,' 106–7
　Derrida's notion of, 110
spectrality
　in *Cuadros en la oscuridad*, 104–7, 109–10, 119
　Jameson's interpretation of, 110
spectropolitics, in *Cuadros en la oscuridad*, 110, 111
Spinoza, Baruch, 72
Spivak, Gayatri, 11
strangeness
　in *El actor principal*, 135
　atmosphere of, 49–50
street children, 20, 113
　in *Ángeles*, 146–63
subjectivity
　'active subjectivity,' 10
　marginalized subjectivities, 7–14
　multidimensional subjectivities in *Ángeles*, 154, 157
subversiveness, in *El premio*, 72–4
suffering, 61, 147
suicide
　in *Ángeles*, 147, 149, 158, 159
　of reappropriated adults and family members, 79–81

surprise
  in *Marilina*, 47, 48, 52
  in *Música de ambulancia*, 47, 55
Swedzky, Javier, 53
'synaesthetic realism,' 15

'tactile epistemologies,' 155; see also haptic . . .; touch
Tan, Ed S., 77
Tarkovsky, Andrey, 134
Telemann, Georg Philipp, 38
terminal illness, in *Música de ambulancia*, 55–63
theft, in *Ángeles*, 160–1
'third space,' 84
togetherness, evanescent, 133, 142
Tompkins, Cynthia, 86
totalitarianism, internalization of, 107
touch
  in *El actor principal*, 133, 134, 138, 140
  in *Ángeles*, 155–6
  in *Armando y Genoveva*, 86–7, 88, 91–3
  inter-embodiment, 122–3
  and listening, 93, 94
  in *Marilina*, 51
  and memory, 93
  in *Música de ambulancia*, 61
  reconceptualization of, 51
  and skin, 155, 156
  see also haptic . . .; 'tactile epistemologies'
toxicity, in *Ángeles*, 156–7
traffic noise, musical analogy, 38
transgressiveness
  of children, 113
  of smells, 57
trust, in *El actor principal*, 139
Tuan, Yi-Fu, 44

the unsaid/unspeakable, rendering of, in *El actor principal*, 136, 141–2
urban settings
  multisensory dimensions, 36–7, 38, 51–2
  and 'ocular-centricity,' 38
  soundscape in *Periférico*, 34, 35, 38, 39
  see also city

video clips, city as, 40
videogame-playing, in *Música de ambulancia*, 56
Viola, Bill, 42
violence
  in *Ángeles*, 157, 158, 159, 160, 161
  gender-based violence, 140–1
  political violence, 67, 71, 78–9, 90
  towards animals, 33
the visual, cultural hegemony of, 14
voice-over narration, 5, 6
  in *Armando y Genoveva*, 85, 86, 89, 97
  in autobiographical documentaries, 89
  and photographic images, 88–9
vomiting, in *Música de ambulancia*, 56–7

war atrocities, remembrance of in *El actor principal*, 130
Warner, Marina, 113
Williams, Raymond, 66

women filmmakers, 7, 14–15
Wong, Cindy, 126

Zedillo, Ernesto, 39

EU representative:
Easy Access System Europe
Mustamäe tee 50, 10621 Tallinn, Estonia
Gpsr.requests@easproject.com

www.ingramcontent.com/pod-product-compliance
Lightning Source LLC
Chambersburg PA
CBHW071415160426
43195CB00013B/1703